SOUTH-WESTERN
CENGAGE Learning·

BCOM5
Carol Lehman, Debbie DuFrene, Robyn Walker

Senior Vice President, LRS/Acquisitions &
   Solutions Planning: Jack W. Calhoun

Editorial Director, Business & Economics:
   Erin Joyner

Publisher: Mike Schenk

Acquisitions Editor: Jason Fremder

Managing Development Editor:
   Joanne Dauksewicz

Editorial Assistant: Megan Fischer

Brand Manager: Kristen Hurd

Content Project Manager: Darrell E. Frye

Media Editor: John Rich

Manufacturing Planner: Ron Montgomery

Production Service: Integra Software Services

Sr. Art Director: Stacy Jenkins Shirley

Internal and Cover Designer: Craig Ramsdell

Cover Image: ©Thomas Barwick/
   Getty Images

Rights Acquisitions Specialist:
   Deanna Ettinger

ExamView® is a registered trademark of Instruction Corp. Windows is a
registered trademark of the Microsoft Corporation used herein under license.
Macintosh and Power Macintosh are registered trademarks of Apple
Computer, Inc. used herein under license.
© 2008 Cengage Learning. All Rights Reserved.

Cengage Learning WebTutor™ is a trademark of Cengage Learning.

Library of Congress Control Number: 2012953887

Student Edition package ISBN-13: 978-1-285-09424-3
Student Edition package ISBN-10: 1-285-09424-7

Student Edition ISBN-13: 978-1-285-09480-9
Student Edition ISBN-10: 1-285-09480-8

South-Western
5191 Natorp Boulevard
Mason, OH 45040
USA

Cengage Learning is a leading provider of customized learning
solutions with office locations around the globe, including Singapore,
the United Kingdom, Australia, Mexico, Brazil, and Japan. Locate your
local office at: **www.cengage.com/global**

Cengage Learning products are represented in Canada by Nelson Education, Ltd.

For your course and learning solutions, visit **www.cengage.com**

Purchase any of our products at your local college store or at our preferred
online store **www.cengagebrain.com**

Printed in the United States of America
1 2 3 4 5 6 7 16 15 14 13

Communication Foundations 2

1 Establishing a Framework for Business Communication 2

2 Focusing on Interpersonal and Group Communication 20

Communication Analysis 36

3 Planning Spoken and Written Messages 36

4 Preparing Written Messages 50

Communication through Voice, Electronic, and Written Messages 72

5 Communicating Electronically 72

6 Delivering Good- and Neutral-News Messages 88

7 Delivering Bad-News Messages 108

8 Delivering Persuasive Messages 128

Communication Through Reports and Business Presentations 148

9 Understanding the Report Process and Research Methods 148

10 Managing Data and Using Graphics 168

11 Organizing and Preparing Reports and Proposals 182

12 Designing and Delivering Business Presentations 206

Communication for Employment 228

13 Preparing Résumés and Application Messages 228

14 Interviewing for a Job and Preparing Employment Messages 258

Grammar and Usage Appendix 274

References 290

Index 293

PART 1
Communication Foundations 2

1 Establishing a Framework for Business Communication 2

1-1 Value of Communication 3

1-2 The Communication Process 3

1-3 Communicating Within Organizations 4

1-3a Communication Flow in Organizations 4

1-3b Levels of Communication 8

1-4 Contextual Forces Influencing Business Communication 9

1-4a Legal and Ethical Constraints 9

1-4b Diversity Challenges 12

1-4c Changing Technology 15

1-4d Team Environment 16

2 Focusing on Interpersonal and Group Communication 20

2-1 Behavioral Theories That Impact Communication 21

2-1a Recognizing Human Needs 21

2-1b Stroking 21

2-1c Exploring the Johari Window 22

2-1b Contrasting Management Styles 22

2-2 Nonverbal Communication 23

2-2a Metacommunication 23

2-2b Kinesic Messages 24

2-2c Understanding Nonverbal Messages 24

2-3 Listening as a Communication Skill 25

2-3a Listening for a Specific Purpose 26

2-3b Bad Listening Habits 26

2-4 Group Communication 27

2-4a Increasing Focus on Groups 27

2-4b Characteristics of Effective Groups 29

2-4c Group Roles 29

2-4d From Groups to Teams 30

2-5 Meeting Management 32

2-5a Face-to-Face Meetings 32

2-5b Electronic Meetings 32

2-5c Suggestions for Effective Meetings 33

PART 2
Communication Analysis 36

3 Planning Spoken and Written Messages 36

3-1 Step 1: Consider the Applicable Contextual Forces 37

3-1a Organizational Culture 37

3-1b Dimensions of Context 39

3-2 Step 2: Determine the Purpose and Select an Appropriate Channel and Medium 40

3-2a Selecting the Channel and Medium 40

3-3 Step 3: Envision the Audience 42

3-4 Step 4: Adapt the Message to the Audience's needs and concerns 44

3-4a Focus on the Audience's Point of View 45

3-4b Communicate Ethically and Responsibly 45

3-5 Step 5: Organize the Message 47

3-5a Outline to Benefit the Sender and the Audience 47

3-5b Sequence Ideas to Achieve Desired Goals 47

4 Preparing Written Messages 50

4-1 Step 6: Prepare the First Draft 51

4-1a Craft Powerful Sentences 51

4-1b Develop Coherent Paragraphs 53

4-2 Revise and Proofread 56

4-2a Cultivate a Frame of Mind for Effective Revising and Proofreading 56

4-2b Apply Visual Enhancements to Improve Readability 57

4-2c Improve Readability 58

4-3 Step 7: Revise for Style and Tone 60

4-4 Proofreading for Mechanical Correctness 67

© Stockbyte/Getty Images

© iStockphoto.com/drflet

PART 3
Communication through Voice, Electronic, and Written Messages 72

5 Communicating Electronically 72

5-1 Electronic Mail Communication 73
- **5-1a** Advantages of Email 73
- **5-1b** Guidelines for Preparing Email Messages 73
- **5-1c** Effective Use of Email 74
- **5-1d** Instant and Text Messaging 76
- **5-1e** Text Messaging 77
- **5-1f** Electronic Messages and the Law 79

5-2 Web Page Communication and Social Media 80
- **5-2a** Writing for a Web Site 80
- **5-2b** Social Media 81

5-3 Voice and Wireless Communication 83
- **5-3a** Voice Mail Communication 83
- **5-3b** Cell Phone Communication 83
- **5-3c** Wireless Communication and the Future 84

5-4 Appropriate Use of Technology 85
- **5-4a** Determine the Purpose of the Message 85
- **5-4b** Determine Whether the Information Is Personal or Confidential 85
- **5-4c** Decide Whether Positive Human Relations Are Sacrificed 85

6 Delivering Good- and Neutral-News Messages 88

6-1 Deductive Organizational Pattern 89

6-2 Good-News Messages 90
- **6-2a** Positive News 90
- **6-2b** Thank-You and Appreciation Messages 90

6-3 Routine Claims 94
- **6-3a** Claim Message 94
- **6-3b** Favorable Response to a Claim Message 94

6-4 Routine Requests 97
- **6-4a** Requests for Information 97
- **6-4b** Favorable Response to a Routine Request 98
- **6-4c** Positive Response to a Favor Request 99
- **6-4d** Form Messages for Routine Responses 99

6-5 Routine Messages about Orders and Credit 101
- **6-5a** Acknowledging Customer Orders 101
- **6-5b** Providing Credit Information 101
- **6-5c** Extending Credit 102

6-6 Procedural Messages 104

7 Delivering Bad-News Messages 108

7-1 Choosing an Appropriate Channel and Organizational Pattern 109
- **7-1a** Channel Choice and Commitment to Tact 109
- **7-1b** Use of the Inductive Approach to Build Goodwill 109
- **7-1c** Exceptions to the Inductive Approach 111

7-2 Developing a Bad-News Message 111
- **7-2a** Writing the Introductory Paragraph 111
- **7-2b** Presenting the Facts, Analysis, and Reasons 112
- **7-2c** Writing the Bad-News Statement 113
- **7-2d** Offering a Counterproposal or "Silver Lining" Idea 114
- **7-2e** Closing Positively 115

7-3 Refusing a Request 115

7-4 Denying a Claim 116

7-5 Denying Credit 120

7-6 Delivering Constructive Criticism 122

7-7 Communicating Negative Organizational News 123
- **7-7a** Breaking Bad News 124
- **7-7b** Responding to Crisis Situations 126

8 Delivering Persuasive Messages 128

8-1 Persuasion Strategies 129
- **8-1a** Plan Before You Write 129
- **8-1b** Use the Inductive Approach 130
- **8-1c** Apply Sound Writing Principles 130

8-2 Sales Messages 131
- **8-2a** Gain Attention 132
- **8-2b** Focus on a Central Selling Feature 132
- **8-2c** Use an Original Approach 133
- **8-2d** Generate Interest by Introducing the Product, Service, or Idea 133
- **8-2e** Create Desire by Providing Convincing Evidence 134
- **8-2f** Motivate Action 137

© iStockphoto.com/Valerie Loiseleux

© iStockphoto.com/Hamza Türkkol

© iStockphoto.com/Michal Rozanski

© iStockphoto.com/Pali Rao

8-3 Persuasive Requests 140
 8-3a Making a Claim 141
 8-3b Asking a Favor 141
 8-3c Requesting Information 143
 8-3d Persuading Within an Organization 143

PART 4
Communication Through Reports and Business Presentations 148

9 Understanding the Report Process and Research Methods 148

9-1 Characteristics of Reports 149
 9-1a Types of Reports 149
 9-1b Proposals 151

9-2 Basis for Reports: The Problem-Solving Process 151
 9-2a Recognizing and Defining the Problem 151

9-3 Selecting a Method of Gathering Information 153
 9-3a Secondary Research 153
 9-3b Primary Research 156

9-4 Collecting and Organizing the Data 157
 9-4a Collecting Secondary Data 157
 9-4b Collecting Data through Surveys 159
 9-4c Avoiding Data-Gathering Errors 161
 9-4d Documenting Sources of Information 161

9-5 Arriving at an Answer 164
 9-5a Analyzing the Data 164
 9-5b Interpreting the Data 165

10 Managing Data and Using Graphics 168

10-1 Communicating Quantitative Information 169

10-2 Using Graphics 170
 10-2a Effective and Ethical Use of Graphics 170

10-3 Types of Graphic Aids 171
 10-3a Tables 172
 10-3b Bar Charts 172
 10-3c Line Charts 175
 10-3d Pie Charts 175
 10-3e Maps 177
 10-3f Flowcharts 177
 10-3g Other Graphics 178

10-4 Including Graphics in Text 179
 10-4a Positioning Graphics in Text 179

11 Organizing and Preparing Reports and Proposals 182

11-1 Parts of a Formal Report 183
 11-1a Preliminary Parts of a Report 183
 11-1b Report Text 186
 11-1c Report Addenda 186

11-2 Organization of Formal Reports 187
 11-2a Writing Convincing and Effective Reports 187

11-3 Choosing a Writing Style for Formal Reports 190
 11-3a Enhancing Credibility 191

11-4 Short Reports 192
 11-4a Memorandum, Email, and Letter Reports 192
 11-4b Form Reports 192

11-5 Proposals 199
 11-5a Proposal Structure 200
 11-5b Proposal Preparation 202

12 Designing and Delivering Business Presentations 206

12-1 Planning an Effective Business Presentation 207
 12-1a Identify Your Purpose 207
 12-1b Know Your Audience 207

12-2 Organizing the Content 208
 12-2a Introduction 208
 12-2b Body 210
 12-2c Closing 211

12-3 Designing Compelling Presentation Visuals 211
 12-3a Types of Presentation Visuals 211
 12-3b Design of Presentation Visuals 211
 12-3c Design Tips for Audience Handouts and Notes Pages 214

12-4 Refining Your Delivery 214
 12-4a Delivery Method 214
 12-4b Vocal Qualities 216
 12-4c Delivery Style 218

12-5 Adapting to Alternate Delivery Situations 221
 12-5a Culturally Diverse Audiences 221
 12-5b Team Presentations 223
 12-5c Distance Presentations 224

© iStockphoto.com/Talaj

© First Light/Alamy

© iStockphoto.com/Jon Schulte

© iStockphoto.com/Albert Smirnov

Résumé appearance is critical.

PART 5
Communication for Employment 228

13 Preparing Résumés and Application Messages 228

13-1 Preparing for the Job Search 229
  13-1a Gathering Essential Information 229
  13-1b Identifying Potential Career Opportunities 229

13-2 Planning a Targeted Résumé 233
  13-2a Standard Parts of a Résumé 233
  13-2b Types of Résumés 238

13-3 Preparing Résumés for Print and Electronic Delivery 239
  13-3a Preparing a Print (Designed) Résumé 239
  13-3b Preparing Electronic Résumé Submissions 240

13-4 Supplementing a Résumé 246
  13-4a Professional Portfolios 246
  13-4b Employment Videos 248

13-5 Composing Application Messages 249
  13-5a Persuasive Organization 251
  13-5b General Writing Guidelines 253
  13-5c Finishing Touches 254

14 Interviewing for a Job and Preparing Employment Messages 258

14-1 Understanding Types of Employment Interviews 259
  14-1a Structured Interviews 259
  14-1b Unstructured Interviews 259
  14-1c Stress Interviews 260
  14-1d Series Interviews 260
  14-1e Virtual Interviews 260

14-2 Preparing for an Interview 261
  14-2a Research the Company 261
  14-2b Study Yourself 262
  14-2c Plan Your Appearance 262
  14-2d Plan Your Time and Materials 262
  14-2e Practice 262

14-3 Conducting a Successful Interview 263
  14-3a The Opening Formalities 263
  14-3b The Information Exchange 264
  14-3c The Closing 267

14-4 Preparing Other Employment Messages 267
  14-4a Application Forms 267
  14-4b Follow-Up Messages 268
  14-4c Thank-You Messages 268
  14-4d Job-Acceptance Messages 270
  14-4e Job-Refusal Messages 270
  14-4f Resignation Messages 270
  14-4g Recommendation Requests 272

Grammar and Usage Appendix 274
References 290
Index 293

© jitloac/Shutterstock

© iStockphoto.com/Andrew Rich

Establishing a Framework for Business Communication

OBJECTIVES

1-1 Define communication and describe the value of communication in business.

1-2 Explain the communication process model and the ultimate objective of the communication process.

1-3 Discuss how information flows in an organization.

1-4 Explain how legal and ethical constraints, diversity challenges, changing technology, and team environment act as contextual forces that influence the process of business communication.

1-1 Value of Communication

We communicate to satisfy needs in both our work and private lives. Each of us wants to be heard, appreciated, and wanted. We also want to accomplish tasks and achieve goals. Generally people communicate for three basic purposes: to inform, to persuade, and to entertain. However, in the professional workplace some of these purposes have greater importance. Informing and persuading are common purposes of communication in the workplace; entertainment less so. In addition, establishing and maintaining our credibility and positive relationships with others are also important purposes in an organizational setting.

What is communication? Communication is the process of exchanging and interpreting information and meaning between or among individuals through a system of symbols, signs, and behavior. In ideal situations, the goal is to reach mutual understanding. Studies indicate that managers typically spend 60 to 80 percent of their time involved in communication. In your career activities, you will communicate in a wide variety of ways, including

- attending meetings and listening and contributing to decision making and problem solving;
- writing various types of messages to inform and persuade others about your ideas and the services and products your organization provides;
- presenting information and persuasive messages to large and small groups in face-to-face and virtual environments;
- explaining and clarifying management procedures and work assignments;
- coordinating the work of various employees, departments, and other work groups;
- evaluating and counseling employees;
- promoting the company's products/services and image using a variety of channels in various contexts.

1-2 The Communication Process

Effective business communication is essential to success in today's work environments. Recent surveys of executives document that abilities in writing and speaking are major determinants of career success in many fields.[1] Although essential to personal and professional success, effective business communication does not occur automatically. Your own experiences likely have taught you that a message is not interpreted correctly just because you transmitted it. An effective communicator anticipates possible breakdowns in the communication process—the unlimited ways the message can be misunderstood. This mind-set provides the concentration to plan and design the initial message effectively and to be prepared to intervene at the appropriate time to ensure that the message received is on target.

Consider the transactional process model of communication presented in Figure 1-1. These seemingly simple steps actually represent a very complex process.

A number of communication process models exist. The transactional model is useful, though, because it illustrates the complexity of the communication process and reveals some of the challenges to effective communication that might emerge in a communication encounter.

BCOM

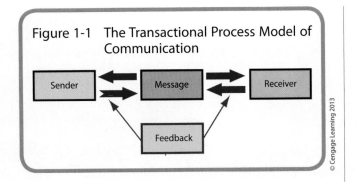

Figure 1-1 The Transactional Process Model of Communication

Sender → Message → Receiver

Feedback

© Cengage Learning 2013

interferences
also called *barriers*; numerous factors that hinder the communication process

organizational communication
the movement of information within the company structure

According to the transactional process model, two parties involved in a communication encounter are potentially both communicating at the same time, particularly if the encounter is face to face. That's because in face-to-face communication situations, parties to the encounter are continuously interpreting each other's nonverbal signals. Some scholars say more than 90 percent of the information in a face-to-face encounter may be sent nonverbally. But even in a cell-phone conversation, silences and tone of voice may be interpreted in various ways. Even a written message may provide information about the writer that he or she did not intend to convey.

In an ideal communication situation, one party would be able to **encode** his or her message in such a way that the receiving party would understand it exactly as intended. However, this goal can be challenging for a variety of reasons, or what are called **interferences** or *barriers* to effective communication. For example,

- differences in educational level, experience, culture, and other characteristics of the sender and the receiver increase the complexity of encoding and decoding a message;
- physical interferences in the channel, including a noisy environment, interruptions, and uncomfortable surroundings, can occur;
- mental distractions, such as being preoccupied with other matters and developing a response, rather than listening, create barriers to understanding.

Because of these barriers and because both parties to a communication encounter may be sending information both orally and nonverbally simultaneously, it can be very challenging to ensure that the information is received as intended. For this reason, it is particularly important to check for understanding rather than assume that it has taken place, particularly when communicating important messages or to audiences that are less familiar to us.

You can surely compile a list of other barriers that affect your ability to communicate with friends, instructors, coworkers, supervisors, and others. By being aware of them, you can concentrate on removing these interferences.

1-3 Communicating within Organizations

To be successful, organizations must create an environment that energizes and encourages employees to accomplish tasks by promoting genuine openness and effective communication. **Organizational communication** is concerned with the movement of information within the company structure. Regardless of your career or level within an organization, your ability to communicate will affect not only the success of the organization but also your personal success and advancement within that organization.

1-3a Communication Flow in Organizations

Communication occurs in a variety of ways within an organization. Some communication flows are planned and structured; others are not. Some communication flows can be formally depicted, whereas some defy description.

What nonverbal signals are being shown in this photo?

Peter Bernik/Shutterstock.com

Formal and Informal Communication Networks

Communication within an organization involves both formal and informal networks.

- **Formal communication network.** This channel is typified by the formal organization chart, which is created by management to define individual and group relationships and to specify lines of responsibility. Essentially, the formal system is dictated by the managerial, technical, cultural, and structural environment of the organization. Within this system, people are required to behave and to communicate in certain ways simply to get work done.

- **Informal communication network.** This network, which is commonly called "the grapevine," continuously develops as people interact within the formal system to accommodate their social and psychological needs. Because the informal network undergoes continual changes and does not parallel the organizational chart, it cannot be depicted accurately by any graphic means.

When employees rely almost entirely on the formal communication system as a guide to behavior, the system might be identified as a *bureaucracy*. Procedures manuals, job descriptions, organization charts, and other written materials dictate the required behavior. Communication channels are followed strictly, and red tape is abundant. Procedures are generally followed exactly; terms such as *rules* and *policies* serve as sufficient reasons for actions. Even the most formal organizations, however, cannot function long before an informal communication system emerges. As people operate within the organized system, they interact on a person-to-person basis and create an environment conducive to meeting their personal emotions, prejudices, likes, and dislikes.

In a workplace, employees are generally expected to satisfy a formal system of arriving at work on time, fulfilling their job duties, working well with others, and addressing their supervisor's requests. However, some employees may not openly accept these expectations and may arrive at work late and spend an undue amount of time "around the water cooler." If these informal practices become more widely spread, the purposes of the group may move from a focus on completing tasks to that of socializing with others. Obviously, the informal system benefits people because it meets their needs, but it also may affect the overall communication of the group in important ways.

The Informal Communication Network

As people talk casually during breaks, text one another, or chat online, the focus usually shifts from topic to topic. One of the usual topics is work—job, company, supervisor, fellow employees. Even though the formal system includes definite communication channels, the grapevine tends to develop and operate within all organizations. Consider these points related to the accuracy and value of grapevine communication:

- As a communication network, the grapevine has a reputation for being speedy but inaccurate. In the absence of alarms, the grapevine might be the most effective way to let occupants know that the building is on fire. It certainly beats sending an email.

- Although the grapevine often is thought of as a channel for inaccurate communication, in reality it is no more or less accurate than other channels. Even formal communication can become inaccurate and filtered as it passes from level to level in the organizational hierarchy.

- The inaccuracy of the grapevine has more to do with the message input than with the output. For example, the grapevine is noted as a carrier of rumors, primarily because it carries informal messages. If the input is a rumor, and nothing more, the output obviously will be inaccurate. But the output might be an accurate description of the original rumor.

- In a business office, news about promotions, personnel changes, company policy changes, and annual salary adjustments often is communicated through the grapevine long before being conveyed through formal channels. The process works similarly in colleges, where information about choice instructors typically is not officially published but is known by students through the grapevine. How best to prepare for examinations, instructor attitudes on attendance and homework, and even faculty personnel changes are messages that travel over the grapevine.

- A misconception about the grapevine is that the message passes from person to person until it finally reaches a person who can't pass it on—the end of

the line. Actually, the grapevine works as a network channel. Typically, one person tells two or three others, who each tell two or three others, who each tell two or three others, and so on. Thus, the message might spread to a huge number of people in a short time, especially now that the grapevine has gone hi-tech and social networking sites have become "gossip central."

- The grapevine has no single, consistent source. Messages might originate anywhere and follow various routes.

Due at least in part to widespread downsizing and corporate scandals during the last few years, employees in many organizations are demanding that they be better informed. Some companies have implemented new formal ways, such as newsletters and intranets, as well as informal ways, including blogs and Twitter, for sharing information with their internal constituents. Company openness with employees about management decisions and financial issues means conveying more information through the formal system rather than risking its miscommunication through informal channels. The software company SAS has been on the list of the 100 Best Companies to Work For for 14 years. Its perks include on-site healthcare, high quality childcare, summer camp for kids, car cleaning, a beauty salon, and more. Says one manager: "People stay at SAS in large part because they are happy … I would argue that people don't leave SAS because they feel regarded—seen, attended to and cared for.

downward communication
a type of communication that flows from supervisor to employee, from policy makers to operating personnel, or from top to bottom on the organization chart

I have stayed for that reason, and love what I do for that reason."[2]

An informal communication network will emerge from even the most carefully designed formal system. Managers who ignore this fact are attempting to manage blindfolded. Instead of denying or condemning the grapevine, the effective manager will learn to *use* the informal communication network. The grapevine, for instance, can be useful in counteracting rumors and false information.

Directions of Communication Flow

The direction in which communication flows in an organization can be downward, upward, or horizontal, as shown in Figure 1-2. Because these three terms are used frequently in communication discussions, they deserve clarification. Although the concept of flow seems simple, direction has meaning for those participating in the organizational communication process.

Downward Communication

Downward communication flows from supervisor to employee, from policy makers to operating personnel, or from top to bottom on the organization chart. A simple policy statement from the top of the organization might grow into a formal plan for operation at lower levels. Teaching people how to perform their specific tasks is an element of downward communication. Another element is orientation to a company's rules, practices, procedures, history, and goals. Employees learn about the quality of their job performance through downward communication.

Downward communication normally involves both written and spoken methods and makes use of the following assumptions:

Downward Communication

- People at high levels in the organization usually have greater knowledge of the organization's mission and goals than do people at lower levels.

- Both spoken and written messages tend to become larger as they move downward through organizational levels. This expansion results from attempts to prevent distortion and is more noticeable in written messages.

- Spoken messages are subject to greater changes in meaning than are written messages.

OBJECTIVES

2-1 Explain how behavioral theories about human needs, trust and disclosure, and motivation relate to business communication.

2-2 Describe the role of nonverbal messages in communication.

2-3 Identify aspects of effective listening.

2-4 Identify factors affecting group and team communication.

2-5 Discuss aspects of effective meeting management.

2-1 Behavioral Theories That Impact Communication

Interpersonal intelligence pertains to the ability to read, empathize, and understand others.[1] People with interpersonal intelligence are good with people and thrive in social interaction. Rather than being a quality that some are born with and others are not, interpersonal intelligence can be improved by broadening your understanding of human behavior and motivation and practicing certain behaviors when in interpersonal situations. Knowledge from the fields of sociology and psychology is helpful to understanding human needs and providing you with valuable insights about how to achieve effective communication in the workplace.

2-1a Recognizing Human Needs

Psychologist Abraham Maslow developed the concept of a hierarchy of needs through which people progress. In our society, most people have reasonably satisfied their two lower-level needs: (1) physiological needs (food and basic provision) and (2) security and safety needs (shelter and protection from the elements and physical danger). Beyond these two basic need levels, people progress to satisfy the three upper-level needs: (3) social needs for love, acceptance, and belonging; (4) ego or esteem needs to be heard, appreciated, and wanted; and (5) self-actualizing needs, including the need to achieve one's fullest potential through professional, philanthropic, political, educational, and artistic channels.

As people satisfy needs at one level, they move on to the next. The levels that have been satisfied still are present, but their importance diminishes. Effective communicators are able to identify and appeal to need levels in various individuals or groups. Advertising is designed to appeal to need levels. Luxury car and dream vacation ads appeal to ego needs, teeth whitening and anti-aging product messages appeal to social needs, and identity theft, health and fitness, and environmentally friendly commercials appeal to security and safety needs. Efforts to help employees satisfy their needs are essential, since a satisfied worker is generally more productive than a dissatisfied one. In communication activities, a sender's message is more likely to appeal to the receiver if the receiver's need is accurately identified.

2-1b Stroking

People engage in communication with others in the hope that the outcome might lead to mutual trust, mutual pleasure, and psychological well-being. The communication exchange is a means of sharing information about things, ideas, tasks, and selves.

Each communication interaction, whether casual or formal, provides an emotional **stroke** that can have either a positive or a negative effect on your feelings about yourself and others. Getting a pat on the back from the supervisor, receiving a congratulatory phone call or text message, and being listened to by another person are examples of everyday positive strokes. Negative strokes might include receiving a hurtful comment, being avoided or left out of conversation, and receiving a reprimand

interpersonal intelligence
the ability to read, empathize, and understand others

stroke
emotional response one gets in a communication interaction that has either a positive or negative effect on feelings about oneself and others

Log onto www.cengagebrain.com for additional resources including flashcards, games, self-quizzing for chapter review, grammar exercises, and more.

BCOM

from a superior. By paying attention to the importance of strokes, managers can greatly improve communication and people's feelings about their work.

2-1c Exploring the Johari Window

As relationships develop, the people involved continue to learn about each other and themselves, as shown by the Johari Window in Figure 2-1. Area I, the free or open area, represents what we know about ourselves and what others know about us. Area II, the blind area, designates those things others know about us but that we don't know about ourselves; for example, you are the only person who can't see your physical self as it really is. Things we know about ourselves but that others don't know about us occupy the hidden or secret area III. Area IV includes the unknown: things we don't know about ourselves and others don't know about us, such as our ability to handle emergency situations if we've never been faced with them.

Each of the window areas can vary in size according to the degree to which we learn about ourselves and are willing to disclose things about ourselves to others. Reciprocal sharing occurs when people develop *trust* in each other. When a confidant demonstrates that he or she can be trusted, trust is reinforced and leads to an expansion of the open area of the Johari Window. Usually we are willing to tell people about various things that aren't truly personal. But we share personal thoughts, ambitions, and inner feelings only with selected others—those whom we have learned to trust. The relationships existing between supervisor and employee, doctor and patient, and lawyer and client are those of trust, but only in specific areas. In more intimate relationships with significant others, siblings, and parents, deeper, personal feelings are entrusted to each other.

The idea that trust and openness lead to better communication between two people also applies to groups. Managers engaged in *organizational development* (OD) are concerned with developing successful organizations by building effective small groups. They believe small group effectiveness evolves mostly from a high level of mutual trust among group members. The aim of OD is to open emotional as well as task-oriented

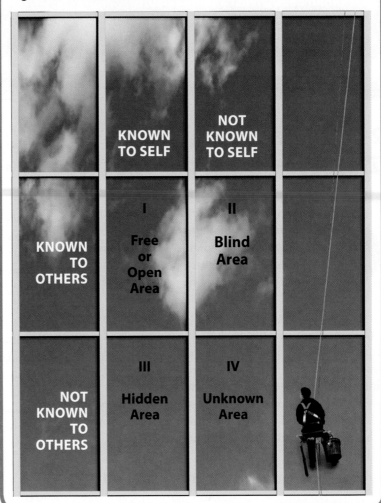

Figure 2-1   The Johari Window

	KNOWN TO SELF	NOT KNOWN TO SELF
KNOWN TO OTHERS	I Free or Open Area	II Blind Area
NOT KNOWN TO OTHERS	III Hidden Area	IV Unknown Area

communication. To accomplish this aim, groups often become involved in encounter sessions designed to enlarge the open areas of the Johari Window.[2]

2-1d Contrasting Management Styles

Douglas McGregor, a management theorist, attempted to distinguish between the older, traditional view that workers are concerned only about satisfying lower-level needs and the more contemporary view that productivity can be enhanced by assisting workers in satisfying higher-level needs. Under the older view, management exercised strong control, emphasized the job to the exclusion of concern for the individual, and sought to motivate solely through external incentives—a job and a paycheck. McGregor labeled this management style Theory X. Under the contemporary style, Theory Y, management strives to balance control and individual freedom. By treating the individual as a mature person, management lessens the need for external motivation; treated as adults, people will act as adults.

The situational leadership model developed by Paul Hersey and Kenneth Blanchard does not prescribe a single leadership style, but advocates that what is appropriate in each case depends on the follower (subordinate) and the task to be performed. **Directive behavior** is characterized by the leader's giving detailed rules and instructions and monitoring closely that they are followed. The leader decides what is to be done and how. In contrast, **supportive behavior** is characterized by the leader's listening, communicating, recognizing, and encouraging. Different degrees of directive and supportive behavior can be desirable, given the situation.[3] Combining the ideas of Maslow and McGregor with those of Hersey and Blanchard leads to the conclusion that "the right job for the person" is a better philosophy than "the right person for the job."

The **Total Quality Management** movement focuses on creating a more responsible role for the worker in an organization. In a Total Quality Management environment, decision-making power is distributed to the people closest to the problem, who usually have the best information sources and solutions. Each employee, from the president to the custodian, is expected to solve problems, participate in team-building efforts, and expand the scope of his or her role in the organization. The goal of employee empowerment is to build a work environment in which all employees take pride in their work accomplishments and begin motivating themselves from within rather than through traditional extrinsic incentives.[4] Managers of many companies understand that empowering employees to initiate continuous improvements is critical for survival. Only companies producing quality products and services will survive in today's world market.

Leadership studies have taken a new turn in recent years with the emergence of the social constructionist view of leadership. A social constructionist view sees leadership differently than the psychological approach of the management discipline. A social constructionist view sees leadership as a co-constructed reality that emerges from the interaction of social actors. What this means is that certain leadership behaviors are acceptable to group members while others are not. Because of this, a person may position him or herself as a leader, but others may not perceive these communication behaviors as corresponding with their perception of a leader.

From this perspective, the leader of a group may not be the formally appointed manager or in certain situations, as discussed in Chapter 1, leadership may be distributed among team members. The value of this approach to leadership is its focus on the importance of communication practices in creating leadership.

2-2 Nonverbal Communication

Managers use verbal and nonverbal messages to communicate ideas to employees. *Verbal* means "through the use of words," either written or spoken. *Nonverbal* means "without the use of words." Although major attention in communication study is given to verbal messages, studies show that nonverbal elements can account for more than 90 percent of the total meaning of a message.[5] Nonverbal communication includes *metacommunication* and *kinesic messages*.

2-2a Metacommunication

A **metacommunication** is a message that, although *not* expressed in words, accompanies a message that *is* expressed in words. For example, "Don't be late for work" communicates caution; yet the sentence might imply (but not express in words) such additional ideas as "You are frequently late, and I'm warning you," or "I doubt your dependability." "Your solution is perfect" might also convey a metacommunication such as "You are efficient," or "I certainly like your work." Whether you are speaking or writing, you can be confident that those who receive your messages will be sensitive to the messages expressed in words and to the accompanying messages that are present but not expressed in words.

directive behavior
characterized by leaders who give detailed rules and instructions and monitor closely that they are followed

supportive behavior
characterized by leaders who listen, communicate, recognize, and encourage their followers

Total Quality Management
focuses on creating a more responsible role for the worker in an organization by distributing decision-making power to the people closest to the problem, empowering employees to initiate continuous improvements

metacommunication
a nonverbal message that, although not expressed in words, accompanies a message that is expressed in words

2-2b Kinesic Messages

People constantly send meaning through kinesic communication, an idea expressed through nonverbal behavior. In other words, receivers gain additional meaning from what they see and hear—the visual and the vocal:

- **Visual kinesic communication**—gestures, winks, smiles, frowns, sighs, attire, grooming, and all kinds of body movements.
- **Vocal kinesic communication**—intonation, projection, and resonance of the voice.

Following are some examples of kinesic messages and the meanings they can convey.

Action	Possible Kinesic Message
A wink or light chuckle follows a statement.	**"Don't believe what I just said."**
A manager is habitually late for staff meetings and with email replies.	**"My time is more important than yours. You can wait for me." Alternately, the action might be ordinary for a manager not born in the United States.**
A group leader sits at a position other than at the head of the table.	**"I want to demonstrate my equality with other members."**
An employee wears clothing that reveals tattoos, which violates the company's dress code.	**"Rules are for other people; I can do what I want." Alternately, "I do not understand the expectations."**
A job applicant submits a résumé containing errors.	**"My language skills are deficient." Alternately, "I didn't care to do my best."**

2-2c Understanding Nonverbal Messages

Metacommunications and kinesic messages have characteristics that all communicators should take into account.

- **Nonverbal messages cannot be avoided.** Both written and spoken words convey ideas in addition to the ideas contained in the words used. All actions—and even the lack of action—have meaning to those who observe them.

- **Nonverbal messages can have different meanings for different people.** If a team member smiles after making a statement, one member might conclude that the speaker was

trying to be funny; another might conclude that the speaker was pleased about having made such a great contribution; another might see the smile as indicating friendliness.

- **Nonverbal messages vary between and within cultures.** Not only do nonverbal messages have different meanings from culture to culture, but men and women from the same culture typically exhibit different body language. As a rule, U.S. men make less body contact with other men than do women with women. Acceptable male body language might include a handshake or a pat on the back, while women are afforded more flexibility in making body contact with each other.

- **Nonverbal messages can be intentional or unintentional.** "You are right about that" can be intended to mean "I agree with you" or "You are right on *this* issue, but you have been wrong on all others discussed."

- **Nonverbal messages can contradict the accompanying verbal message and affect whether your message is understood or believed.** The adage "actions speak louder than words" reveals much about how people perceive messages. Picture a person who says, "I'm happy to be here," but looks at the floor, talks in a weak and halting voice, and clasps his hands timidly in front of his body. Because his verbal and nonverbal messages are contradictory, his audience might not trust his words. Similarly, consider the negative effect of a sloppy personal appearance by a job candidate.

- **Nonverbal messages can receive more attention than verbal messages.** If a supervisor repeatedly glances at his cell phone for text messages or rhythmically taps a pen while making a statement, the words might not register in the employee's mind. An error in basic grammar might receive more attention than the idea that is being transmitted.

- **Nonverbal messages provide clues about the sender's background and motives.** For example, excessive use of big words might suggest that a person reads widely or has an above-average education; it might also

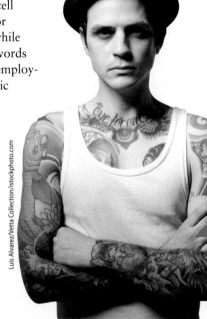

Luis Alvarez/Vetta Collection/istockphoto.com

visual kinesic communication
gestures, winks, smiles, frowns, sighs, attire, grooming, and all kinds of body movements

vocal kinesic communication
intonation, projection, and resonance of the voice

suggest a need for social recognition or insecurity about his or her social background.

- **Nonverbal messages are influenced by the circumstances surrounding the communication.** Assume that two men, Ganesh and Jacob, are friends at work. When they are together on the job, Ganesh sometimes puts his hand on Jacob's shoulder. To Jacob, the act could mean nothing more than "We are close friends." But suppose Ganesh is a member of a committee that subsequently denies a promotion for Jacob. Afterward, the same act could mean "We are still friends," but it could also cause resentment. Because of the circumstances, the same act could now mean something such as "Watch the hand that pats; it can also stab."

- **Nonverbal messages can be beneficial or harmful.** Words or actions can be accompanied by nonverbal messages that help or hurt the sender's purpose. Metacommunications and kinesic communications can convey something such as "I am efficient in my business and considerate of others," or they can convey the opposite. They cannot be eliminated, but you can make them work for you instead of against you.

2-3 Listening as a Communication Skill

Despite the fact that many professionals believe incorrectly that business communication is about presentation and not interaction, most managers spend a major part of their day listening and speaking with others. Listening to supervisors, employees, customers, and colleagues commonly consumes more of business employees' time than reading, writing, and speaking combined. Listening is an interpersonal skill as critical as the skill of speaking. According to Peter Nulty, a former board member of *Fortune* magazine and a blogger for Wells Fargo Daily Advantage, "Of all the skills of leadership, listening is the most valuable—and one of the least understood. Most captains of industry only listen sometimes, and they remain ordinary leaders. But a few, the great ones, never stop listening. That's how they get word before anyone else of unseen problems and opportunities."[6]

Listening depends on your abilities to receive and decode both verbal and nonverbal messages. The best-devised

EFFECTIVE LISTENING HABITS PAY OFF IN SEVERAL WAYS:

- ☑ Good listeners are liked by others because they satisfy the basic human needs of being heard and being wanted.
- ☑ People who listen well are able to separate fact from fiction, cope effectively with false persuasion, and avoid having others use them for personal gain.
- ☑ Effective listening leads to sensitivity and tolerance toward key individuals who are critical to the organization's success, such as employees, customers, and suppliers.
- ☑ Effective listeners are engaged and constantly learning—gaining knowledge and skills that lead to increased creativity, job performance, advancement, and satisfaction.
- ☑ Job satisfaction increases when people know what is going on, when they are heard, and when they participate in the mutual trust that develops from good communication.

messages and sophisticated communication systems will not work unless people on the receiving end of spoken messages actually listen. Senders of spoken messages must assume their receivers can and will listen, just as senders of written messages must assume their receivers can and will read.

Comstock Images/Photos.com

2-3a Listening for a Specific Purpose

Individuals satisfy a variety of purposes through listening: (1) interacting socially, (2) receiving information, (3) solving problems, and (4) sharing feelings with others. Each activity may call for a different style of listening or for a combination of styles.

- **Casual listening**. Listening for pleasure, recreation, amusement, and relaxation is casual listening. Some people listen to music all day long for relaxation and to mask unwanted sounds during daily routines, work periods, and daily commutes. Aspects of casual listening are as follows:
  - It provides relaxing breaks from more serious tasks and supports our emotional health.
  - It illustrates that people are selective listeners. You listen to what you want to hear. In a crowded room in which everyone seems to be talking, you can block out all the noise and engage in the conversation you are having with someone.
  - It doesn't require much emotional or physical effort.
- **Listening for information**. Listening for information involves the search for data or material. In a lecture class, for example, the instructor usually has a strategy for guiding the class to desired goals. The instructor will probably stress several major points and use supporting evidence to prove or to reinforce them. When engaged in this type of listening, you could become so focused on recording every detail that you take copious notes with no organization. When listening for information:
  - Use an outlining process to help you capture main ideas and supporting subpoints in a logical way.
  - Watch the speaker as you listen to him or her, since most speakers exhibit a set of mannerisms composed of gestures and vocal inflections to indicate the degree of importance or seriousness that they attach to portions of their presentations.
- **Intensive listening**. When you listen to obtain information, solve problems, or persuade or dissuade (as in arguments), you are engaged in intensive listening. Intensive listening involves greater use of your analytical ability to proceed through problem-solving steps. When listening intensively:

- Become a good summarizer.
- Trace the development of the discussion and then move from there to your own analysis.
- **Empathetic listening**. *Empathy* occurs when a person attempts to share another's feelings or emotions. Counselors attempt to use empathetic listening in dealing with their clients, and good friends listen empathetically to each other. Empathy is a valuable trait developed by people skilled in interpersonal relations. When you take the time to listen to another, the courtesy is usually returned. When listening empathetically:

  - Avoid preoccupation with your own problems. Talking too much and giving strong nonverbal signals of disinterest destroy others' desire to talk.
  - Remember that total empathy can never be achieved simply because no two people are exactly alike. The more similar our experiences, however, the better the opportunity to put ourselves in the other person's shoes. Listening with empathy involves some genuine tact along with other good listening habits.

You might have to combine listening intensively and listening empathetically in some situations. Performance appraisal interviews, disciplinary conferences, and other sensitive discussions between supervisors and employees require listening intensively for accurate understanding of the message and listening for feelings, preconceived points of view, and background.

2-3b Bad Listening Habits

Most of us have developed bad listening habits in one or more of the following areas:

- **Faking attention.** Have you ever been introduced to someone only to realize 30 seconds later that you missed the name? We can look directly at a person, nod, smile, and *pretend* to be listening.
- **Allowing disruptions.** We welcome disruptions of almost any sort when we are engaged in somewhat difficult listening. The next time someone enters your classroom or meeting room, notice how almost everyone in the room turns away from the speaker and the topic to observe the latecomer.
- **Overlistening.** When we attempt to record many details in writing or in memory we can *overlisten* and miss the speaker's major points.
- **Stereotyping.** We make spontaneous judgments about others based on such issues as appearances, mannerisms, dress, and speech delivery. If a speaker doesn't meet our standards in these areas, we simply turn off our listening and assume the speaker can't have much to say.

casual listening
listening for pleasure, recreation, amusement, and relaxation

listening for information
listening that involves the search for data or material

intensive listening
listening to obtain information, solve problems, or persuade or dissuade

empathetic listening
listening to others in an attempt to share their feelings or emotions

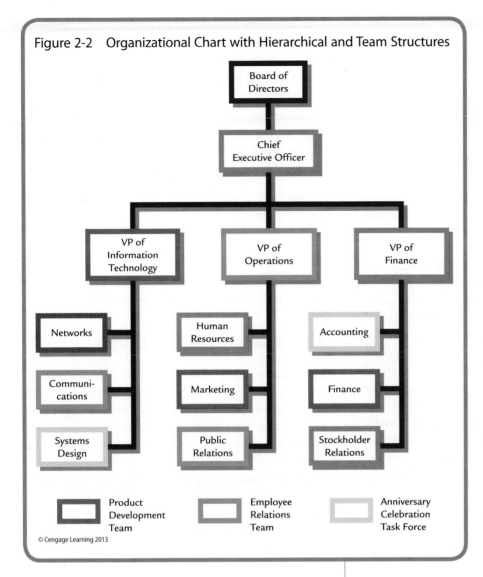

Figure 2-2 Organizational Chart with Hierarchical and Team Structures

- Product Development Team
- Employee Relations Team
- Anniversary Celebration Task Force

© Cengage Learning 2013

- **Cooperation.** They have a shared sense of purpose, mutual gain, and teamwork.
- **Communication.** They know that information must flow smoothly between top management and workers. Team members are willing to face confrontation and unpleasantness when necessary.
- **Contribution.** All members share their different backgrounds, skills, and abilities with the team.

Teams have existed for hundreds of years throughout many countries and cultures. Teams are more flexible than larger organizational groupings because they can be assembled, deployed, refocused, and disbanded more quickly, usually in ways that enhance rather than

product development team
usually cross functional in nature; a group of employees who concentrates on innovation and the development cycle of new products

forming
stage one of team development in which team members become acquainted with each other and the assigned task

storming
stage two of team development in which team members deal with conflicting personalities, goals, and ideas

norming
stage three of team development in which team members develop strategies and activities that promote goal achievement

performing
stage four of team development in which team members reach the optimal performance level

For a variety of reasons, teams are often unable to advance through all four stages of development. Even long-term teams might never reach the optimal performing stage, settling instead for the acceptable performance of the norming stage.

Research into what makes workplace teams effective indicates that training is beneficial for participants in such areas as problem solving, goal setting, conflict resolution, risk taking, active listening, and recognizing the interests and achievements of others. Participants need to be able to satisfy one another's basic needs for belonging, personal recognition, and support. Team members at the performing stage of team development exhibit the following behaviors[9]:

- **Commitment.** They are focused on the mission, values, goals, and expectations of the team and the organization.

disrupt more permanent structures and processes. Organizational changes are often necessary, however, since support must be in place for performance evaluation, recognition, communication, and training systems. Strategies for bringing about needed change might include arranging site visits to similar organizations that already have teams, bringing in a successful team to speak to the organization, and bringing in consultants to discuss the team development process.

2-5 Meeting Management

Meetings are essential for communication in organizations. They present opportunities to acquire and disseminate valuable information, develop skills, and make favorable impressions on colleagues, supervisors, and subordinates. U.S. businesses spend more money on conducting meetings than do businesses in any other country in the world, and they also spend more time in meetings than do people of other countries.[10] International meetings are imperative for solid business reasons but are facing greater planning scrutiny because of tightening travel budgets and a recovering global economy.

Workers frequently have negative attitudes toward meetings because they are perceived as a waste of time. Studies support this opinion, revealing that as much as one-third of the time spent in meetings is unproductive. Negative attitudes toward meetings can be changed when meetings are conducted properly, giving attention to correct procedures and behavior. Successful meetings don't just happen; rather, they occur by design. Careful planning and attention to specific guidelines can help ensure the success of your meetings, whether they are conducted in a face-to-face format or electronically.

2-5a Face-to-Face Meetings

Face-to-face meetings continue to be the most-used meeting format in most organizations. They offer distinct advantages and are appropriate in the following situations[11]:

Jacob Wackerhausen/Photos.com

☑ When you need the richest nonverbal cues, including body, voice, proximity, and touch.

☑ When the issues are especially sensitive.

☑ When the participants don't know one another.

☑ When establishing group rapport and relationships is crucial.

☑ When the participants can be in the same place at the same time.

Face-to-face meetings can be enhanced with the use of various media tools such as flipcharts, handouts, and electronic slide decks. While face-to-face meetings provide a rich nonverbal context and direct human contact, they also have certain limitations. In addition to the obvious logistical issues of schedules and distance, face-to-face meetings may be dominated by overly vocal, quick-to-speak, and high-status members.

2-5b Electronic Meetings

Electronic meetings allow companies to reduce travel budgets, save professional time, and minimize the environmental impact caused by travel. A variety of technologies is available to facilitate electronic meetings. Participants may communicate with one another through telephones, computers, or video broadcast equipment using groupware or meeting management software applications. Electronic meetings offer certain advantages. They facilitate geographically dispersed groups because they provide the choice of meeting at different places/same time, different places/different times, same place/same time, or same place/different times. Electronic meetings also speed up meeting follow-up activities because decisions and action items can be recorded electronically.

Electronic meetings also have certain limitations[12]:

- They cannot replace face-to-face contact, especially when group efforts are just beginning and when groups are trying to build group values, trust, and emotional ties.

- They can make it harder to reach consensus, because more ideas are generated and because it might be harder to interpret the strength of other members' commitment to their proposals.

- The success of same-time meetings is dependent on all participants having excellent keyboarding skills to engage in rapid-fire, in-depth discussion. This limitation might be overcome as the use of voice input systems becomes more prevalent.

Figure 2-3 **SAMPLE :-)** Formal Generic Agenda for Meetings

Agenda for [name of group] Meeting
Prepared on [date agenda created]
By [name of author of agenda]

Attendees: [those invited to attend, often in alphabetical order]
Date and time of meeting:
Location of meeting:
Subject: [major issues to be discussed or purpose of meeting]
Agenda items:

1. Call to order
2. Routine business [procedural or administrative matters]   (10–15 minutes)
   a. Approval of agenda for this meeting
   b. Reading and approval of minutes of last meeting
   c. Committee reports
3. Old business [unfinished matters from previous meeting]   (15–20 minutes)
   a. Discussion of issue(s) carried over from previous meeting
   b. Issue(s) arising from decision(s) made at previous meeting
4. New business   (20–25 minutes)
   a. Most important issue
   b. Next most important issue
   c. Other issues in decreasing order of importance
   d. Business from the floor not included on the agenda
      [only as time permits; otherwise, these issues should be
      addressed in the next meeting]
5. Adjournment

© Cengage Learning 2014

Meetings of one 16-person department cost one company $1.6 million a year in lost productivity.[13]

2-5c Suggestions for Effective Meetings

Whether you engage in face-to-face or electronic meetings, observing the following guidelines can help to ensure that your meetings are productive:

- **Limit meeting length and frequency.** Any meeting held for longer than an hour or more frequently than once a month should be scrutinized. Ask yourself whether the meeting is necessary. Perhaps the purpose can be achieved in another way, such as email, instant messaging, or telephone.

- **Make satisfactory arrangements.** Select a date and time convenient for the majority of expected participants. For face-to-face meetings, plan the meeting site with consideration for appropriate seating for attendees, media equipment, temperature and lighting, and necessary supplies. For electronic meetings, check hardware and software and connectivity components.

- **Distribute the agenda well in advance.** The **agenda** is a meeting outline that includes important information: date, beginning and ending times, place, topics to be discussed, and responsibilities of those

agenda
a meeting outline that includes important information (e.g., date, beginning and ending times, place, topics to be discussed, and responsibilities of those involved)

brainstorming
the generation of many ideas from among team members

consensus
represents the collective opinion of the group, or the informal rule that all team members can live with at least 70 percent of what is agreed upon

involved. Having the agenda prior to the meeting allows participants to know what is expected of them. A sample agenda template is provided in Figure 2-3.

- **Encourage participation.** While it is certainly easier for one person to make decisions, the quality of the decision making is often improved by involving the team. Rational decision making may begin with **brainstorming**, the generation of many ideas from among team members. Brainstormed ideas can then be discussed and ranked, followed by some form of voting.

- **Maintain order.** An organized democratic process ensures that the will of the majority prevails, the minority is heard, and group goals are achieved as expeditiously as possible. Proper parliamentary procedure may be followed in formal meetings, as outlined in sources such as *Robert's Rules of Order* and *Jones' Parliamentary Procedure at a Glance*. For less

formal meetings, the use of parliamentary procedure may not be necessary to ensure effective contribution by attendees.

- **Manage conflict.** In an autocratic organization, conflict might be avoided because employees are conditioned to be submissive. Such an environment, however, leads to smoldering resentment. On the other hand, conflict is a normal part of any team effort and can lead to creative discussion and superior outcomes. Maintaining focus on issues and not personalities helps ensure that conflict is productive rather than destructive.

- **Seek consensus.** While unanimous agreement on decisions is an optimal outcome, total agreement cannot always be achieved. **Consensus** represents the collective opinion of the group, or the informal rule that all team members can live with at least 70 percent of what is agreed upon.

- **Prepare thorough minutes.** Minutes provide a concise record of meeting actions, ensure the tracking and follow-up of issues from previous meetings, and assist in the implementation of previously reached decisions.

Face-to-face meetings continue to be a frequently used format in most organizations.

Meetings are an important management tool and are useful for idea exchange. They also provide opportunities for you, as a meeting participant, to communicate impressions of power and status. Knowing how to present yourself and your ideas and exhibiting knowledge about correct meeting management will assist you in your career advancement.

STUDY TOOLS

CHAPTER 2

Located at back of the textbook

❑ **Rip out Chapter Review Card**

Located at www.cengagebrain.com

❑ **Review Key Terms Flashcards (Print or Online)**

❑ **Download Audio Summaries for on-the-go review**

❑ **Complete Practice Quizzes to prepare for tests**

❑ **Play "Beat the Clock" to master concepts**

❑ **Complete the Crossword Puzzle to review key terms**

❑ **Watch the video about McDonaldson, a fictitious but all-too-realistic ad agency, whose employees struggle with contemporary business communication issues**

Planning Spoken and Written Messages

3-1 Consider contextual forces that may affect whether, how, to whom, and when a message is sent.

3-2 Identify the purpose of the message and the appropriate channel and medium.

3-3 Develop clear perceptions of the audience to enhance the impact and persuasiveness of the message, improve goodwill, and establish and maintain the credibility of the communicator.

3-4 Apply tactics for adapting messages to the audience, including those for communicating ethically and responsibly.

3-5 Recognize the importance of organization when planning the first draft.

In a report titled "Writing: A Ticket to Work…or a Ticket Out," the National Commission on Writing reported that two-thirds of salaried employees in large companies have some writing responsibilities, and getting hired and promoted in many industries requires strong writing abilities. While writing is important in most managerial-level jobs, the Commission also concluded that one-third of employees in corporate America write poorly. Knowing that effective communication is tied to the corporate bottom line and many employees can't write well, businesses are investing $3.1 billion annually to train employees to write.[1] Remedies are needed to prevent confusion, waste, errors, lost productivity, and a damaged corporate image—all caused by employees, customers, and clients muddling their way through unreadable messages.

As a capable communicator, you can immediately add value to your organization and set yourself apart from your peers who are struggling to articulate ideas in writing and in presentations. Communication that commands attention and can be understood easily is essential for survival during the information explosion we are experiencing today. On the job, you will be expected to process volumes of available information and shape useful messages that respond to the needs of customers or clients, coworkers and supervisors, and other key business partners. Additionally, increased use of electronic communication (email, texts, instant messages, blogs, videoconferences, etc.) will require you to be technologically savvy and capable of adapting the rules of good communication to the demands of emerging technology.

How can you learn to plan and prepare powerful business messages? The systematic analysis process as outlined in Figure 3-1 will help you develop messages that save you and your organization valuable time and resources and portray you as a capable, energetic professional. A thorough analysis of the audience and your specific communication assignment will empower you to create a first draft efficiently and to revise and proofread your message for accuracy, conciseness, and appropriate tone.

3-1 Step 1: Consider the Applicable Contextual Forces

Chapter 1 discussed four contextual forces that may affect whether, how, to whom, and when a message is sent. These were legal and ethical constraints, diversity challenges, changing technology, and team environment. In addition to these four forces, communication patterns within an organization are a contextual force that should also be considered when planning a message. The organizational culture as well as the four dimensions of context may influence how, whether, and when a message is sent. These two issues are discussed in the sections that follow.

3-1a Organizational Culture

Organizational culture is "a pattern of shared basic assumptions that the group learned as it solved its problems of external adaptation and internal integration and which has worked well enough to be taught to new members as the correct way to perceive, think, and feel in relation to these problems" (Schein, 1992, p. 12).

BCOM

Figure 3-1 Process for Planning and Preparing Spoken and Written Messages

STEP 1	**STEP 2**	**STEP 3**	**STEP 4**	**STEP 5**	**STEP* 6**
Consider the applicable contextual forces	Determine the purpose and select an appropriate channel and medium	Envision the audience	Adapt the message to the audience's needs and concerns	Organize the message	Prepare the first draft

*You will focus on the planning process (Steps 1–5) in this chapter; you will learn to prepare the message in Chapter 4 (Step 6).

"**COMMUNICATION THAT COMMANDS ATTENTION AND CAN BE UNDERSTOOD EASILY IS ESSENTIAL FOR SURVIVAL DURING THE INFORMATION EXPLOSION WE ARE EXPERIENCING TODAY.**"

Boreham and Morgan (2004) note that "Schein makes the crucial claim that an organization's culture determines what it can and cannot do, and that the extent of individual members' socialization into that culture determines what they can and cannot do" (p. 309). This is true of actions and behaviors as well as communicative practices and behaviors.

In other words, organizational culture affects the type, amount, and quality of communication within an organization. The culture of a business provides part of the *context* for interpreting the meaning of everyday organizational life, as well as determining what are considered appropriate messages and the proper or expected ways to convey them.

For example, Zappos, an online retailer, has created a good deal of its reputation through its message about its unique corporate culture: Its number one core value is to "deliver WOW through service" to its customers. The use of "WOW" is just one clue to Zappos' unique culture. Other values include "create fun and a little weirdness," "do more with less," "build open and honest relationships," and "be humble." Compare these values with the type of culture that you might find in an investment banking firm in which competition, individualism, and the drive for profits and bonuses would likely be key elements and it should be easy to see how culture might affect how communication occurs and what is expected and accepted within an organization in terms of behaviors.

Research suggests that there are seven primary characteristics that, when taken as a whole, capture the essence of an organization's culture (O'Reilly et al., 1991; Chatman & Jehn, 1994).[2] These are

1. **Innovation and risk taking**, or the degree to which employees are encouraged to innovate and take risks

2. **Attention to detail**, or the degree to which employees are expected to exhibit precision, analytical skills, and attention to detail

3. **Outcome orientation**, or the degree to which management focuses on results or outcomes rather than on the techniques and processes used to achieve these outcomes

4. **People orientation**, or the degree to which management decisions consider the effect of outcomes on people within the organization

5. **Team orientation**, or the degree to which work activities are organized around teams rather than individuals

6. **Aggressiveness**, or the degree to which people are aggressive and competitive rather than easygoing

7. **Stability**, or the degree to which organizational activities emphasize maintaining the status quo rather than focusing on change

organizational culture
a pattern of shared basic assumptions that the group learned as it solved its problems of external adaptation and internal integration and which has worked well enough to be taught to new members as the correct way to perceive, think, and feel in relation to these problems

how your *perception* affects your ability to accurately or completely interpret an optical illusion.

Perception of reality is also limited by previous experiences and our attitudes toward the sender of the message. We support ideas that are in line with our own and decide whether to focus on the positive or the negative of a situation. We may simply refuse to hear a message that doesn't fit into our view of the world.

Much of the confusion in communication is caused by differences in the sender's and receiver's perceptions. For example, a manager's brief email requesting a status report on a task may come across as curt to the employees. Perceptions vary between individuals with similar backgrounds, and even more so when people from different cultures, generations, and genders communicate.

Overcoming perceptual barriers is difficult but essential if you are to craft messages that meet the needs and concerns of your audience. To help you envision the audience, first focus on relevant information you know about the receiver. The more familiar you are with the receiver, the easier this task will be. When communicating with an individual, you immediately recall a clear picture of the receiver—his or her physical appearance, background (education, occupation, religion, culture), values, opinions, preferences, and so on. Most importantly, your knowledge of the receiver's reaction in similar, previous experiences will aid you in anticipating how this receiver is likely to react in the current situation. Consider the following audience characteristics:

- **Age.** A message answering an elementary-school student's request for information from your company would not be worded the same as a message answering a similar request from an adult.

- **Economic level.** A solicitation for a business donation for a charity project written to a small business owner would likely differ from one written to a representative of a major corporation.

- **Educational/occupational background.** The technical jargon and acronyms used in a financial proposal sent to bank loan officers may be inappropriate in a proposal sent to a group of private investors.

- **Needs and concerns of the audience.** Just as successful sales personnel begin by identifying the needs of the prospective buyer, an effective manager attempts to understand the receiver's frame of reference as a basis for organizing the message and developing the content.

- **Culture.** The vast cultural differences between people (e.g., language, expressions, customs, values, and religion) increase the complexity of the communication process. An email containing typical American expressions (e.g., "The frustration should cool down soon" and "the competition is backed to the wall") would likely confuse a manager from a different culture. Differences in values influence communication styles and message patterns. For example, Japanese readers value the beauty and flow of words and prefer an indirect writing approach, unlike Americans who prefer clarity and conciseness.[4]

- **Rapport.** A sensitive message prepared for a long-time client may differ significantly from a message prepared for a newly acquired client. Emails discussing expectations for completing an assignment may be briefer and more direct when sent to an employee with whom you share a strong business relationship built on mutual trust. The rapport created by previous dealings with the recipient aids understanding in a current situation.

- **Expectations.** Because accountants, lawyers, and other professionals are expected to meet high standards, a message from one of them containing errors in grammar or spelling would likely cause a receiver to question the credibility of the source.

You may find that envisioning an audience you know well is often such a conscious action that you may not even recognize that you are doing it. On the other hand, envisioning those you do not know well requires additional effort. In these cases, simply assume an

R. Gino Santa Maria/Shutterstock

It can be difficult to see the world as others do.

empathetic attitude toward the receiver to assist you in identifying his or her frame of reference (knowledge, feelings, and emotions). In other words, project mentally how you believe you would feel or react in a similar situation and use that information to communicate understanding back to the person.

Consider the use (or lack) of empathy in the following workplace examples:

SAMPLE MESSAGE

Example 1: A U.S. manager's instructions to a new employee from an Asian culture:

I don't think we are even in the ballpark here in terms of the cost estimate. If we can't get these numbers down, we will be out of the game in terms of what the competition might offer. We want to come up with a proposal that will knock this out of the park! Do you understand?

Example 2: An excerpt from a message sent to M. Bobby Christiansen, who happens to be female:

Mr. Christensen

The video-on-demand system that you expressed interest in is now available as an option in our minivans. Our sales manager would be happy to provide a demonstration at your convenience. Please stop by on your next maintenance visit.

PROBLEM ANALYSIS

- *The use of expressions peculiar to U.S. environment confuse and intimidate.*

- *Open-ended question at the end disregards importance of saving face to a person of Asian culture. Cultural influences may prevent employee from asking questions that might indicate lack of understanding.*

- *Misspelling receiver's name, misinterpreting gender, and showing disrespect for receiver.*

- *Omission of contact information reduces writer's credibility and shows lack of genuine concern for sender's needs.*

- *Overlooking mechanical errors implies incompetence or carelessness.*

Taking the time and effort to obtain a strong mental picture of your audience through firsthand knowledge or your empathetic attitude *before* you write will enhance your message in the following ways:

1. **Establishes rapport and credibility needed to build long-lasting personal and business relationships.** Your receivers will appreciate your attempt to connect and understand their feelings. A likely outcome is mutual trust, which can greatly improve communication and people's feelings about you, your ideas, and themselves (as shown in the discussion of the Johari Window in Chapter 2).

2. **Permits you to address the audience's needs and concerns.** Such knowledge allows you to select relevant content and to communicate in a suitable style.

3. **Simplifies the task of organizing your message.** From your knowledge of yourself and from your experiences with others, you can reasonably predict receivers' reactions to various types of messages. To illustrate, ask yourself these questions:

   - Would I react favorably to a message saying my request is being granted or that a new client is genuinely pleased with a job I'd just completed?

   - Would I experience a feeling of disappointment when I learn that my request has been refused or that my promised pay raise is being postponed?

   - Would I need compelling arguments to convince me to purchase a new product or support a new company policy?

Now, reread the questions as though you were the message recipient. Because you know *your* answers, you can predict *others'* answers with some degree of accuracy. Such predictions are possible because of commonality in human behavior.

Your commitment to identifying the needs and concerns of your audience before you communicate is invaluable in today's workplace. Organizations must focus on providing quality customer service and developing work environments supportive of talented, diverse workers. Alienating valuable customers and talented employees as a result of poor audience analysis is not an option in today's competitive environment.

3-4 Step 4: Adapt the Message to the Audience's Needs and Concerns

After you have envisioned your audience, you are ready to adapt your message to fit the specific needs of your audience. Adaptations include focusing on the audience's point of view; communicating ethically and responsibly; building and protecting goodwill; using simple, contemporary language; writing concisely; and projecting a positive, tactful tone.

3-4a Focus on the Audience's Point of View

Ideas are more interesting and appealing if they are expressed from the audience's viewpoint. Developing a "you attitude" rather than a "me attitude" involves thinking in terms of the other person's interests and trying to see a problem from the other's point of view. A letter, memo, email, or phone call reflecting a "you attitude" sends a direct signal of sincere concern for the receiver's needs and interest.

The use of the word *you* (appropriately used) conveys to receivers a feeling that messages are specifically for them. However, if the first-person pronoun *I* is used frequently, especially as the subject, the sender may impress others as being self-centered—always talking about self. Compare the following examples of sender-centered and receiver-centered statements:

"I"- or Sender-Centered	"You"- or Receiver-Centered
I want to let you know what a great job you have done as leader of the sales team.	Congratulations on landing the Tritek account!
We will be changing the reporting deadline for sales soon.	You will find below the new schedule for the reporting of sales figures.

Compliments (words of deserved praise) are another effective way of increasing an audience's receptiveness to ideas that follow. Give sincere compliments judiciously as they can do more harm than good if paid at the wrong time, in the wrong setting, in the presence of the wrong people, or for the wrong reasons. Likewise, avoid flattery (words of undeserved praise). Although the recipient may accept your flattery as a sincere compliment, it is more likely that the recipient will interpret your undeserved praise as an attempt to seek to gain favor or special attention. Suspicion of your motive makes effective communication less likely.

3-4b Communicate Ethically and Responsibly

The familiar directive "with power comes responsibility" applies to your use of communication skills. Because business communication affects the lives of many, you must accept responsibility for using it to uphold your own personal values and your company's standards of ethical conduct. Before speaking or writing, use the following guidelines to help you communicate ethically and responsibly.

HOW TO CULTIVATE A "YOU ATTITUDE"

To cultivate a "you attitude," concentrate on the following questions:

- Does the message address the receiver's major needs and concerns?
- Would the receiver feel this message is receiver-centered? Is the receiver kept clearly in the picture?
- Will the receiver perceive the ideas to be fair, logical, and ethical?
- Are ideas expressed clearly and concisely (to avoid lost time, money, and possible embarrassment caused when messages are misunderstood)?
- Does the message promote positive business relationships—even when the message is negative? For example, are *please, thank you,* and other courtesies used when appropriate? Are ideas stated tactfully and positively and in a manner that preserves the receiver's self-worth and cultivates future business?
- Is the message sent promptly and through the preferred channel to indicate courtesy?
- Does the message reflect the high standards of a business professional: accurate and appealing document design, quality printing, and absence of misspellings and grammatical errors?

kaarsten/Shutterstock

- **Is the information stated as truthfully, honestly, and fairly as possible?** Good communicators recognize that ensuring a free flow of essential information is in the interest of the public and the organization. Merck, the manufacturer of the prescription pain reliever Vioxx, was sued by thousands of patients and patients' families for withholding information about known heart risks associated with taking the drug.[5] Similarly, failure to report the nature of his investment practices led to the arrest of the accountant of Bernard Madoff, the man who admittedly cheated thousands of investors out of billions of dollars in an illegal scheme. The SEC has accused Madoff's accountant, David Friehling, of lying to the American Institute of Certified Public Accountants rather than subject his audit work to peer review.[6] Your honor, honesty, and credibility will build strong, long-lasting relationships and lead to the long-term success of your company. Sending complete, accurate, and timely information regardless of whether it supports your interests will help you build credibility.
- **Does the message embellish or exaggerate the facts?** Legal guidelines related to advertising provide clear guidance for avoiding *fraud*, the misrepresentation of products or services; however, overzealous

sales representatives or imaginative writers can use language skillfully to create less-than-accurate perceptions in the minds of receivers. Businesses have learned the hard way that overstating the capabilities of a product or service (promising more than can be delivered) is not good for business in the long run. Researchers are at times tempted to overstate their findings to ensure continued funding or greater publicity. Eric T. Peohlman, a medical researcher, acknowledged that while at the University of Vermont he fabricated data in 17 applications for federal grants to make his work seem more promising. Under a plea agreement, he was barred for life from receiving federal funding and had to pay back $180,000, as well as asking scientific journals to retract and correct 10 articles he had authored.[7]

While surveys indicate many job seekers believe companies expect résumé padding, companies repeatedly report that this perception is not true. Marilee Jones, dean of admissions at Massachusetts Institute of Technology, and David Edmonson, the former CEO of Radio Shack, resigned high-profile jobs for misstating their academic records. George O'Leary stepped down five days after been named head football coach at Notre Dame, admitting he lied about receiving a master's degree and playing college football.[8]

Skill in communicating persuasively will be important throughout your profession. The techniques you will read about in this text, such as those related to writing a winning résumé and application message, will be helpful as you begin your career; however, these techniques should *not* be used if your motive is to exploit the receiver.

- **Are the ideas expressed clearly and understandably?** If a message is to be seen as honest, you must be reasonably confident that the receiver can understand it. Ethical communicators select words that convey the exact meaning intended and that are within the reader's vocabulary.

- **Is your viewpoint supported with objective facts?** Are facts accurately documented to allow the reader to judge the credibility of the source and to give credit where credit is due? Can opinions be clearly distinguished from facts? Have you evaluated honestly any real or perceived conflict of interest that could prevent you from preparing an unbiased message?

- **Are ideas stated with tact and consideration that preserves the receiver's self-worth?** The metaphor "An arrow, once it is shot, cannot be recalled" describes

libel
written defamatory remarks

slander
spoken defamatory remarks

the irrevocable damage caused by cruel or unkind words.[9] Ego-destroying criticism, excessive anger, sarcasm, hurtful nicknames, betrayed secrets, rumors, and malicious gossip pose serious ethical problems in the workplace because they can ruin reputations, humiliate, and damage a person's self-worth. Serious legal issues arise when negative statements are false, constituting defamation. Written defamatory remarks are referred to as **libel**, and similar spoken remarks are referred to as **slander**. If you choose to make negative statements about a person, be sure the facts in question are supported. Additionally, you'll hone your abilities to convey negative information and to handle sensitive situations in a constructive, timely manner rather than ignoring them until they are out of control. For considerate, fair, and civilized use of words, follow this simple rule: Communicate with and about others with the same kindness and fairness that you wish others to use when communicating with and about you.

- **Are graphics carefully designed to avoid distorting facts and relationships?** Communicating ethically involves reporting data as clearly and accurately as possible. Misleading graphics result either from the developers' deliberate attempt to confuse the audience or from their lack of expertise in constructing ethical graphics.

Communication's Golden Rule: Communicate with and about others with the same kindness and fairness that you wish others to use when communicating with and about you.

© iStockphoto.com/Anton Vakhlachev

OBJECTIVES

4-1 Apply techniques for developing effective sentences and unified and coherent paragraphs.

4-2 Prepare visually appealing documents that grab the audience's attention and increase comprehension.

4-3 Identify factors affecting readability and revise messages to improve readability.

4-4 Revise and proofread a message for content, organization, style, and tone; mechanics; and format and layout.

In Chapter 3, you learned about the importance of following a systematic process to develop business messages. The applications in Chapter 3 guided you in developing a clear, logical plan for your message that focuses on the needs of the receiver (Steps 1–5). Effectively capturing your ideas for various business communication situations involves skillful use of language and careful attention to accuracy and readability issues—the remaining two steps in this important process are shown in Figure 4-1.

4-1 Step 6: Prepare the First Draft

Once you have determined whether the message should be presented deductively (main idea first) or inductively (explanation and details first) and have planned the logical sequence of minor points, you are ready to begin composing the message.

Normally, writing rapidly (with intent to rewrite certain portions, if necessary) is better than slow, deliberate writing (with intent to avoid any need for rewriting portions). The latter approach can be frustrating and can reduce the quality of the finished work. Time is wasted in thinking of one way to express an idea, discarding it either before or after it is written, waiting for new inspiration, and rereading preceding sentences.

Concentrating on getting your ideas down as quickly as you can is an efficient approach to writing. During this process, remember that you are preparing a draft and not the final copy. If you are composing at the computer, you can quickly and easily revise your draft throughout the composition process. This seamless approach to writing allows you to continue to improve your working draft until the moment you are ready to submit the final copy. Numerous electronic writing tools are available, and technology will continue to unfold to enhance the writing process.

4-1a Craft Powerful Sentences

Well-developed sentences help the receiver understand the message clearly and react favorably to the writer or speaker. In this section, you will learn about predominant use of active voice and emphasis of important points, which affect the clarity and human relations of your message.

Rely on Active Voice

Business communicators normally use active voice more heavily than passive voice because active voice conveys ideas more vividly. In sentences in which the subject is the *doer* of action, the verbs are called *active*. In sentences in which the subject is the *receiver* of action, the verbs are called *passive*. Review the differences in the impact of **passive voice** and **active voice**:

Passive Voice	Active Voice
<u>Press releases are sent</u> to national media outlets on a daily basis from our corporate communication office.	<u>Our corporate communication office sends</u> press releases to national media outlets on a daily basis.

The active sentence invites the receiver to see the communication office as actively engaged with the media, while the passive sentence draws attention to the press releases. Using active voice makes the subject the actor, which

passive voice
when the subject of a sentence is the receiver of an action

active voice
when the subject of a sentence is the doer of an action

Figure 4-1 Process for Planning and Preparing Spoken and Written Messages

STEP 1	STEP 2	STEP 3	STEP 4	STEP 5	STEP* 6	STEP* 7
Consider the applicable contextual forces	Determine the purpose and select an appropriate channel and medium	Envision the audience	Adapt the message to the audience's needs and concerns	Organize the message	Prepare the first draft	Revise and proofread for accuracy and desired impact

*You focused on the planning process (Steps 1–5) in Chapter 3; you will learn to prepare the message (Steps 6-7) in this chapter.

makes the idea easier to understand. Sentences written using passive voice give receivers a less distinct picture. In the passive sentence, the receiver becomes aware that something was done to the press releases, but it does not reveal who did it.

Even when a passive sentence contains additional words to reveal the doer, the imagery is less distinct than it would be if the sentence were active: *Press releases created by the corporate communications staff are sent daily to national media outlets.* "Press releases" gets the most attention because it is the subject. The sentence seems to let a receiver know the *result* of action before revealing the doer; therefore, the sentence is less emphatic.

Although active voice conveys ideas more vividly, passive voice is useful for the following purposes:

- Concealing the doer. ("The reports have been compiled.")
- Placing more emphasis on *what* was done and who or what it was *done to* than on who *did* it. ("The reports have been compiled by our sales representatives.")
- Subordinating an unpleasant thought or avoiding finger-pointing. ("The Accounting Department has not been notified of this delay" rather than "You have not notified the Accounting Department of this delay.")

Emphasize Important Ideas

A landscape artist wants some features in a picture to stand out boldly and others to get little attention. A musician sounds some notes loudly and others softly. Likewise, a writer or speaker wants some ideas to be *emphasized* and others to be *de-emphasized*. Normally, pleasant and important ideas should be emphasized; unpleasant and insignificant ideas should be

Natthapol Vanasrivilai/istockphoto.com

de-emphasized. Emphasis techniques include sentence structure, repetition, words that label, position, and space and format.

Sentence Structure For emphasis, place an idea in a simple sentence. The simple sentence in the following example has one independent clause. Because no other idea competes with it for attention, this idea is emphasized.

Simple Sentence Is More Emphatic	Compound Sentence Is Less Emphatic
Larry works with customers daily.	Larry works with customers daily, but he would prefer focusing on administrative duties.

For emphasis, place an idea in an independent clause; for de-emphasis, place an idea in a dependent clause. In the following compound sentence, the idea of taking a job is in an independent clause. Because an independent clause makes sense if the rest of the sentence is omitted, an independent clause is more emphatic than a dependent clause. In the complex sentence, the idea of taking a job is in a dependent clause. By itself, the clause would not make complete sense. Compared with the independent clause that follows ("Nicole really preferred …"), the idea in the dependent clause is de-emphasized.

Compound Sentence Is More Emphatic	Complex Sentence Is Less Emphatic
Larry works with customers daily, but he would prefer focusing on administrative duties.	**Although he works with customers on a daily basis, Larry would prefer focusing on administrative duties.**

Repetition

To emphasize a word, let it appear more than once in a sentence. For example, a clever advertisement by OfficeMax used the word *stuff* repeatedly to describe generically several types of office-supply needs ranging from paper clips to color copies, and then ended succinctly with "OfficeMax … for your office stuff." Likewise, in the following example, "reception" receives more emphasis when the word is repeated.

Less Emphatic	More Emphatic
Her promotion was well received because of …	**Her promotion was well received; this reception is attributed to …**

Words that Label

For emphasis or de-emphasis, use words that label ideas as significant or insignificant. Note the labeling words used in the following examples to emphasize or de-emphasize an idea:

> *But most important of all …*
> *A less significant aspect was …*

Position

To emphasize a word or an idea, position it first or last in a sentence, clause, paragraph, or presentation. Note the additional emphasis placed on the words *positive reception* and *disappointment* in the examples in the right column because these words appear as the *first* or the *last* words in their clauses.

Less Emphatic	More Emphatic
Her hard work contributed to the <u>positive reception</u> for her promotion; otherwise, <u>disappointment</u> may have been the result.	**A <u>positive reception</u> resulted from her hard work; <u>disappointment</u> may have resulted without it.**
Her promotion was <u>well received</u> because of her hard work; without that, <u>disappointment</u> may have been the result.	**Her promotion <u>was well received</u>; without her hard work, it may have been a <u>disappointment</u>.**

In paragraphs, the first and last words are in particularly emphatic positions. An idea that deserves emphasis can be placed in either position, but an idea that does not deserve emphasis can be placed in the middle of a long paragraph. The word *I*, which is frequently overused in messages, is especially noticeable if it appears as the first word. *I* is more noticeable if it appears as the first word in *every* paragraph. Avoid using the word *However* as the first word in a paragraph if the preceding paragraph is neutral or positive. These words imply that the next idea will be negative. Unless the purpose is to place emphasis on negatives, such words as *denied*, *rejected*, and *disappointed* should not appear as the last words in a paragraph.

Likewise, the central idea of a written or spoken report appears in the introduction (the beginning) and the conclusion (the end). Good transition sentences synthesize ideas at the end of each major division.

Space and Format

The various divisions of a report or spoken presentation are not expected to be of equal length, but an extraordinary amount of space devoted to a topic attaches special significance to that topic. Similarly, a topic that receives an especially small amount of space is de-emphasized. The manner in which information is physically arranged affects the emphasis it receives and consequently the overall impact of the message.

4-1b Develop Coherent Paragraphs

Well-constructed sentences are combined into paragraphs that discuss a portion of the topic being discussed. To write effective paragraphs, you must learn to (a) develop deductive or inductive paragraphs consistently, (b) link ideas to achieve coherence, (c) keep paragraphs unified, and (d) vary sentence and paragraph length.

Position the Topic Sentence Appropriately

Typically, paragraphs contain one sentence that identifies the portion of the topic being discussed and presents the central idea. That sentence is commonly called a **topic sentence**. For example, consider operating instructions prepared for company-owned GPS navigation systems. The overall topic is how to get satisfactory performance from the device. One portion of that topic is setup; another portion (paragraph) discusses operation; and so forth. Within each paragraph, one sentence serves a special function. Sentences that list the steps can appear as one paragraph, perhaps with steps numbered as follows:

To set up the system, take the following steps:

1. *Connect …*
2. *Go to menu settings to …*

In this illustration, the paragraphs are **deductive**; that is, the topic sentence *precedes* details. When topic sentences *follow* details, the paragraphs are **inductive**. As discussed previously, the receiver's likely reaction to the main idea (pleased, displeased, interested, not interested) aids in selecting the appropriate sequence.

When the subject matter is complicated and the details are numerous, paragraphs sometimes begin with a main idea, follow with details, and end with a summarizing sentence. But the main idea might not be in the first sentence; the idea could need a preliminary statement. Receivers appreciate consistency in the placement of topic sentences. Once they catch on to the writer or speaker's pattern, they know where to look for main ideas.

These suggestions seldom apply to the first and last sentences of letters, memos, and email messages. Such sentences frequently appear as single-sentence paragraphs. But for reports and long paragraphs of letters, strive for paragraphs that are consistently deductive or inductive. Regardless of which is selected, topic sentences are clearly linked with details that precede or follow.

topic sentence
a sentence that identifies the portion of the topic being discussed and presents the central idea of the paragraph

deductive paragraph
a paragraph in which the topic sentence precedes the details

inductive paragraph
a paragraph in which the topic sentence follows the details

coherence
cohesion, so that each sentence in some way is linked to the preceding sentences

Link Ideas to Achieve Coherence

Careful writers use coherence techniques to keep receivers from experiencing abrupt changes in thought. Although the word **coherence** is used sometimes to mean "clarity" or "understandability," it is used throughout this text to mean "cohesion." If writing or speaking is coherent, the sentences stick together; each sentence is in some way linked to the preceding sentences. Avoid abrupt changes in thought, and link each sentence to a preceding sentence.

The following techniques for linking sentences are common:

1. **Repeat a word that was used in the preceding sentence.** The second sentence in the following example is an obvious continuation of the idea presented in the preceding sentence.

   … to take responsibility for the decision. This responsibility can be shared …

2. **Use a pronoun that represents a noun used in the preceding sentence.** Because "it" means "responsibility," the second sentence below is linked directly with the first.

   … to take this responsibility. It can be shared …

3. **Use connecting words.** Examples include *however, therefore, yet, nevertheless, consequently, also,* and *in addition.* "However" implies "We're continuing with the same topic, just moving into a different phase." Remember, though, that good techniques can be overused. Unnecessary connectors are space consuming and distracting. Usually they can be spotted (and crossed out) in proofreading.

   … to take this responsibility. However, few are willing to …

Just as sentences within a paragraph must link, paragraphs within a document must also link. Unless a writer or speaker is careful, the move from one major topic to the next will seem abrupt. A good transition sentence can bridge the gap between the two topics by summing up the preceding topic and leading a receiver to expect the next topic:

Cost factors, then, seemed prohibitive until efficiency factors were investigated.

This sentence could serve as a transition between the "Cost" and "Efficiency" division headings. Because a transition sentence comes at the end of one segment and before the next, it emphasizes the central idea of the preceding segment and confirms the relationship of the two segments. While transition sentences are helpful if properly used, they can be overused. For most

Communicating Electronically

OBJECTIVES

5-1 Discuss the effective use of email, instant messaging, and text messaging in business communication.

5-2 Explain principles for writing effectively for the Web.

5-3 Discuss the effective use of voice and wireless technologies in business communication.

5-4 Consider legal and ethical implications associated with the use of communication technology.

5-1 Electronic Mail Communication

As you read in Chapter 1, the continuous evolution of technology has expanded communication options. Email, instant messaging, Web communications, and voice and wireless technologies are important tools for accomplishing company goals. In fact, email has overtaken the telephone in terms of the most common workplace communication tool.[1] The ability to use email communications effectively is essential to success in virtually every career.

5-1a Advantages of Email

Electronic mail, or email, offers numerous advantages. Its ready availability, convenience, and ease of use have resulted in its skyrocketing popularity. The advantages of email are numerous:

- **It facilitates the fast, convenient flow of information among users at various locations and time zones.** Mail service is often too slow for communicating timely information, and the telephone system is inconvenient and costly when communicating with people located in several locations and time zones. For these reasons, email is especially effective when sending a single message to several recipients and when needing to communicate 24 hours a day, 365 days a year.

Log onto www.cengagebrain.com for additional resources including flashcards, games, self-quizzing for chapter review, grammar exercises, and more.

- **It increases efficiency.** Email reduces "telephone tag" and unnecessary telephone interruptions caused when delivering messages that are unlikely to require a verbal response.

- **It reduces costs.** Sending email messages represents a substantial savings to companies in long-distance telephone costs and postal mail-outs.

- **It reduces paper waste.** Often an electronic message can be read and immediately discarded without the need for a printed copy.

5-1b Guidelines for Preparing Email Messages

Following these guidelines will enable you to use email efficiently and effectively when communicating with both valued coworkers and outside parties:

- **Send to single or multiple addressees.** The same message can be sent to one or many recipients simultaneously. Sending an email message to multiple recipients routinely involves keying the email address of each recipient into a distribution list and selecting the distribution list as the recipient.

- **Provide a useful subject line.** A descriptive subject line assists the receiver's understanding of the message and is helpful for future reference to it. Additionally, a well-written subject line in an email message will help the receiver sort through an overloaded mailbox and read messages in priority order. When writing a subject line, think of the five Ws—Who, What, When, Where, and Why—to give you some clues for wording. For instance, "Budget Committee Meeting on Thursday" is a more meaningful subject line than "Meeting."

- **Restate the subject in the body of the message.** The body of the message should be a complete thought and should not rely on the subject line for elaboration. A good opening sentence might be a repetition of most of the subject line. Even if the reader skipped the subject line, the message would still be clear, logical, and complete.

- **Focus on a single topic directed toward the receiver's needs.** An email message is generally limited to one

BCOM

netiquette
the buzzword for proper
behavior on the Internet

idea rather than addressing several issues. If you address more than one topic in a single email message, chances are the recipient will forget to respond to all points discussed. Discussing one topic allows you to write a descriptive subject line, and the receiver can file the single subject message in a separate mailbox if desired. If you must send a lengthy email, preview the topics to be covered in the introduction and then divide the message into logical sections for easy comprehension.

- **Sequence your ideas based on anticipated reader reaction.** As you learned previously, ideas should be organized deductively when a message contains good news or neutral information; inductive organization is recommended when the message contains bad news or is intended to persuade. Email messages should be organized according to the sequence of ideas—for example, time order, order of importance, or geography. As a general rule, present the information in the order it is likely to be needed. For example, describe the nature and purpose of an upcoming meeting before giving the specifics (date, place, time).

- **Make careful use of jargon, technical words, and shortened terms.** The use of jargon and technical terms is more common in email messages than in business letters. Such shortcuts save time with audiences who will understand the intent. In practicing empathy, however, consider whether the receiver will likely understand the terms used.

- **Use graphic highlighting to add emphasis.** Enumerated or bulleted lists, tables, graphs, pictures, or other images can be either integrated into the content of the email or attached as supporting material.

- **Revise your email before sending.** Even the average email requires at least one pass to ensure that the intended message is clear, concise, and error-free. The number of passes increases depending on the number of people receiving the email and the complexity of

---

TO RECAP—EMAIL ADVANTAGES

- ☑ Allows communication 24 hours a day, 365 days a year.
- ☑ Reduces telephone interruptions by delivering messages that are unlikely to require a verbal response.
- ☑ Saves companies the costs of long-distance telephone bills and postal mail-outs.
- ☑ Reduces the need to print messages.

---

the message. Revising for brevity and conciseness is a primary goal for messages that are often read on the run and on mobile devices. Keep to one screen, eliminate redundancies, and tighten wording. Avoid off-topic material that detracts from the email's single subject, as well as clever or amusing statements that are funny only to the writer.[2] Direct, concise messages sometimes sound impersonal and curt if not revised for goodwill. Question whether a phone call would be more appropriate for the message; a businesslike, yet conversational tone might sound less aggressive or demanding. Revise emails to achieve a similar tone.[3] Use the email spell check and then proofread onscreen for content and grammatical errors.

5-1c Effective Use of Email

The email message in Figure 5-1 illustrates guidelines for using professional email. The sender begins his email message reminding the recipient of this week's budget meeting. The paragraphs that follow include timely information about the meeting and a forward-looking close.

While email offers various advantages in speed and convenience, problems arise when it is managed inappropriately. Learning fundamental **netiquette**, the buzzword for proper behavior on the Internet, will assure your online success. The following guidelines will assist you in using email effectively:

- **Check mail promptly.** Generally, a response to email is expected within 24 hours. Ignoring messages from coworkers can erode efforts to create an open, honest, and cooperative work environment. On the other hand, responding every second could indicate that you are paying more attention to your email than your job.

- **Do not contribute to email overload.** To avoid clogging the system with unnecessary messages, follow these simple guidelines:

  - Be certain individuals need a copy of the email, and forward an email from another person only with the original writer's permission.

  - Never address an email requesting general action to more than one person if you want to receive an individual response. Sharing responsibility will lead to no one taking responsibility.

  - Avoid sending formatted documents. Messages with varying fonts, special print features (e.g., bold, italics, etc.), and images take longer to download, require more storage space, and could be unreadable on some computers. In addition, enhancing routine email messages does not support the goals of competitive organizations, and

Figure 5-1 GOOD :-) Good Example of an Email Message

New Message

To: Frederick James
From: Lori Wadsworth
Subject: Budget Committee meeting on Thursday

Budget committee agenda.docx

Hi Fred,

Please remember that this month's budget committee meeting will be held this Thursday beginning at 10 a.m. in the first-floor conference room. You will find the agenda for the meeting attached to this message.

As discussed in last month's meeting, we will discuss ways to cut departmental expenses by 5 percent next fiscal year. Please bring your budget information for fiscal year 2012 to the meeting for reference purposes.

I look forward to discussing your recommendations for next year.

Regards,

Lori Wadsworth, Operations

- Provides subject line that is meaningful to reader and writer.

- Includes salutation and closing to personalize message.

- Conveys short, concise message limited to one idea and one screen.

---

employees and clients or customers might resent such frivolous use of time.

- Edit the original message when you reply to email if the entire body of the original message is not needed for context. Instead, you can cut and paste pertinent sections within a reply that you believe will help the recipient understand your reply. You can also key brief comments in all caps below the original section.

- Follow company policy for personal use of email. Obtain a private email account if you are job hunting or sending many private messages to friends and relatives.

- **Use email selectively.** Send short, direct messages for routine matters that need not be handled immediately (scheduling meetings, giving your supervisor quick updates, or addressing other uncomplicated issues).

- **Do not send messages when you are angry.** Email containing sensitive, highly emotional messages could be easily misinterpreted because of the absence

of nonverbal communication (facial expressions, voice tone, and body language). Sending a *flame*, the online term used to describe a heated, sarcastic, sometimes abusive message or posting, might prompt a receiver to send a retaliatory response. Email messages written in anger and filled with emotion and sarcasm could result in embarrassment or even end up as evidence in litigation. Because of the potential damage to relationships and legal liability, read email messages carefully before sending them. Unless a response is urgent, store a heated message for an hour until you have cooled off and thought about the issue clearly and rationally. When you *must* respond immediately, you might acknowledge that your response is emotional and has not been thoroughly considered. Give this warning by using words such as "I need to vent my frustration for a few paragraphs" or "flame on—I'm writing in anger."[4]

- **Exercise caution against email viruses and hoaxes.** An ounce of prevention can avert the problems caused by deadly *viruses* that destroy data files or annoying messages that simply waste your time while they are executing. Install an *antivirus software program* that will scan your hard drive each time you start the computer or access external devices, and keep backups of important files. Be suspicious of email messages that contain attachments if they are from people you don't know. Email text is usually safe to open, but the attachment could contain an executable file that can affect your computer's operations. **Social networking sites** such as Facebook and MySpace are also common sources of viruses and spyware.

Additionally, be wary of *computer hoaxes*—email messages that incite panic, typically related to risks of computer viruses or deadly threats, and urge you to forward them to as many people as possible. Forwarding a hoax can be embarrassing and causes inefficiency by overloading email boxes and flooding computer security personnel with inquiries from alarmed recipients of your message. Investigate the possible hoax by visiting Web sites such as the following that post virus alerts and hoax information and provide tips for identifying a potential hoax:

- Urban legends: www.urbanlegends.com

- Snopes: www.snopes.com

- Truth or Fiction: www.truthorfiction.com

If a bogus message is forwarded to you, reply to the person politely that the message is a hoax. This

action allows you to help stop the spread of the malicious message and will educate one more person about the evils of hoaxes.

- **Develop an effective system for handling email.** Some simple organization will allow you to make better use of your email capability:

  - Set up separate accounts for receiving messages that require your direct attention.

  - Keep your email inbox clean by reading an email and taking action immediately. Delete messages you are not using and those not likely to be considered relevant for legal purposes.

  - Move saved messages into a limited number of email folders for quick retrieval. The email search feature is also useful for identifying saved messages quickly. If you receive many messages, consider setting up your account to sort and prioritize messages, send form letters as replies to messages received with a particular subject line, automatically forward specified email, and sound an alarm when you receive a message from a particular person.

5-1d Instant and Text Messaging

Business use of **instant messaging** has experienced phenomenal growth. Analysts estimate that in 90 percent of companies, some employees use IM, whether to close a sale, collaborate with a colleague, or just trade pleasantries with a colleague.[5] This real-time email technology allows the sender to know when someone is available to respond immediately.

The best known IM programs are free and require no special hardware and little training. With some programs, users can exchange graphics and audio and video

Alberto Zornetta/Shutterstock.com

USE THE TOOLS.

• Rip out the Review Cards in the back of your book to study.
Or Visit CourseMate for:
• Full, interactive eBook (search, highlight, take notes)
• Review Flashcards (Print or Online) to master key terms
• Test yourself with Auto-Graded Quizzes
• Bring concepts to life with Games, Videos,
  and Animations!

Go to CourseMate for BCOM5 to begin using these tools.
Access at **www.cengagebrain.com**.

Complete the Speak Up
survey in CourseMate at
www.cengagebrain.com

f Follow us at
www.facebook.com/4ltrpress

Delivering Good- and Neutral-News Messages

OBJECTIVES

6-1 Describe the deductive outline for good and neutral news and its adaptations for specific situations and for international audiences.

6-2 Prepare messages that convey good news, including thank-you and appreciation messages.

6-3 Write messages presenting routine claims and requests and favorable responses to them.

6-4 Write messages acknowledging customer orders, providing credit information, and extending credit.

6-5 Prepare procedural messages that ensure clear and consistent application.

6-1 Deductive Organizational Pattern

You read in Chapter 4 that you can organize business messages either *deductively* or *inductively* depending on your prediction of the receiver's reaction to your main idea. Learning to organize business messages according to the appropriate outline will improve your chances of preparing a document that elicits the response or action you desire.

In this chapter, you will learn to compose messages that convey ideas that a receiver likely will find either *pleasing* or *neutral*. Messages that convey pleasant information are referred to as **good-news messages**. Messages that are of interest to the receiver but are not likely to generate an emotional reaction are referred to as **neutral-news messages**. The strategies discussed for structuring good-news and neutral-news messages generally can be applied to North American audiences. Because message expectations and social conventions differ from culture to culture, the effective writer will adapt as necessary when writing for various audiences. People in organizations use a number of channels to communicate with internal and external audiences. When sending a message that is positive or neutral, you have numerous choices, as shown in Figure 6-1 below. Depending on the message, recipient, and constraints of time and location, the best channel might be spoken or electronic. In addition to the electronic and verbal tools presented in Chapter 5 (email, instant messaging, Web communications, and phone), companies also use written documents such as memorandums and letters to communicate information.

The principles for preparing memorandums (commonly referred to as *memos*) are similar to those you've already applied when composing email messages, as both are channels for sharing information of a somewhat informal nature. Memos provide a tangible means of sharing information with people inside an organization. Letters are more formal, because they are used to convey information to external audiences such as customers, clients, business partners, or suppliers. Regardless of whether the audience is an internal or external one, communication should be carefully structured to achieve the desired purpose.

Good-news or neutral-news messages follow a **deductive** or **direct sequence**—the message begins with the main idea. To present good news and neutral information deductively, begin with the major idea, followed by supporting details as depicted in Figure 6-1. In both outlines, the third point (closing thought) might be omitted without seriously impairing effectiveness; however, including it unifies the message and avoids abruptness.

The deductive pattern has several advantages:

- The first sentence is easy to write. After it is written, the details follow easily.

- The first sentence gets the attention it deserves in this emphatic position.

- Encountering good news in the first sentence puts receivers in a pleasant frame of mind, and they are receptive to the details that follow.

- The arrangement might save receivers some time. Once they understand the important idea, they can move rapidly through the supporting details.

good-news messages
messages that convey pleasant information

neutral-news messages
messages that are of interest to the reader but are not likely to generate an emotional reaction

deductive (or direct) sequence
when the message begins with the main idea followed by supporting details

Figure 6-1   Direct Outline Used in Good- and Neutral-News Messages Sent in Written, Electronic, or Spoken Form

Thank you

Letter
Memo
Written

Email
Instant message
Website
Blog
Text message
Electronic

In person
Telephone
Voice mail
Spoken

OPENING: ✓

States the pleasant or main idea

BODY: ✓

Provides details and explanation

CLOSING: ✓

Reminds receiver of the good news or main idea, and includes a future-oriented closing thought

© iStockphoto.com/Hamza Türkkol/© iStockphoto.com/Michal Rozanski/© iStockphoto.com/LajosRepasi

As you study sample deductive messages in this chapter, note the *poor example* notations that clearly mark the examples of ineffective writing. Detailed comments highlight important writing strategies that have been applied or violated. While gaining experience in developing effective messages, you will also learn to recognize standard business formats. Fully formatted messages are shown as printed documents (letters on company letterhead or paper memos) or as electronic formats (email messages or online input screens).

6-2 Good-News Messages

essages delivering good news are organized using a direct approach as illustrated in Figure 6-1. For illustration, you'll study examples of messages that convey positive news as well as thank-you and appreciation messages that generate goodwill.

6-2a Positive News

The memo sent to all employees in Figure 6-2 begins directly with the main idea: the approval of a flextime work schedule policy. The discussion that follows includes a brief review of the policy and ends positively by encouraging employees to seek additional information from the company Web site or contact the writer.

6-2b Thank-You and Appreciation Messages

Empathetic managers take advantage of occasions to write goodwill messages that build strong, lasting relationships with employees, clients, customers, and various other groups. People are usually not reluctant to

Figure 6-2 **GOOD** 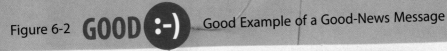 Good Example of a Good-News Message

INTEROFFICE MEMORANDUM

TO: All Employees
FROM: Geno Lombardo, Human Resources Manager   GL
DATE: May 15, 2013
SUBJECT: Flex-timePolicy Takes Effect January 1

A flex-time policy has been approved for ProGames, Inc. effective January 1. Flextime is a term used to define an alternate work schedule by which an employee may work within specific limits dictated by the needs of the job and is subject to management review and approval.

Individual departments may use a flextime work schedule subject to the following conditions:

- The normal work week shall continue as either a 5 day, 37.5 hour, work week for Headquarters employees or a 5 day, 40 hour, work week for Operations employees.

- Each Department Head will ensure coverage during its "core hours" of operation. The department Director/Manager has the discretion to determine staffing coverage to meet the operating requirements of the department.

- Department Heads will be responsible for resolving intradepartmental schedule conflicts and assuring that proper coverage is maintained.

- A departments Director/Manager may, at his/her sole discretion, implement, continue, or discontinue flextime work schedules. At the sole discretion of the Director/Manager, an employee may be re-assigned to work core hours at any time.

- Computation of Vacation/Earned/Overtime/Sick Leave: The accrual and usage of these benefits is the same for employees working flextime as for those working a standard schedule.

Please visit the HR Web site for the complete flextime policy and illustrations of possible work schedules. If you have questions as you begin making changes to your work schedule, please call me at ext. 59.

Format Pointers

Uses template with standard memo headings for efficient production.

Includes writer's initials after printed name and title.

- **Starts with main idea—announcement of new policy.**

- **Provides clear explanation to ensure policy is understood. Formats as bullet list for quick, easy reference to specific. details.**

- **Encourages readers to ask questions or view additional information on company intranet.**

To Express Thanks for a Gift

Thank you for the box of chocolates in recognition of your gratitude for my help with the Rupert product presentation. I was happy to contribute to such an innovative sales program, one that I hope will be recognized as a model for future presentations. Please stop by my office for a chocolate to celebrate your success!

Ewa Walicka/Shutterstock.com

say, "Thank you," "What a great performance," "You have certainly helped me," and so on. Despite good intentions, however, often people don't get around to sending thank-you and appreciation messages. Because of their rarity, written appreciation messages are especially meaningful—even treasured.

Thank-You Messages

After receiving a gift, being a guest, attending an interview, or benefiting in various other ways, a thoughtful person will take the time to send a written thank-you message. A simple handwritten or electronically sent note is sufficient for some social situations. However, when written from a professional office to respond to a business situation, the message might be printed on company letterhead. Your message should be written deductively and reflect your sincere feelings of gratitude. The thank-you messages shown above (1) identify the circumstances for which the writer is

To Extend Thanks for Hospitality

Thank you for opening your home for our department barbecue. Your beautiful garden and inviting pool made the event one of our best summer parties yet. I enjoyed meeting your lovely family and especially wanted to thank your husband for grilling all those delicious burgers and brats. Thanks again for your generosity in sharing your home and family with your colleagues.

grateful and (2) provide specific reasons the action is appreciated.

Appreciation Messages

You will write appreciation messages to recognize, reward, and encourage the receiver; however, you will also gain happiness from commending a deserving person. Such positive thinking can be a favorable influence on your own attitude and performance. In appropriate situations, you might wish to address an appreciation message to an individual's supervisor and send a copy of the document to the individual to share the positive comments. In any case, an appreciation message should be sent to commend deserving people and not for possible self-gain.

For full potential value, follow these guidelines for appreciation messages:

- **Send in a timely manner.** Sending an appreciation message within a few days of the circumstance will emphasize your genuineness. The receiver might question the sincerity of appreciation messages that are sent long overdue.

- **Avoid exaggerated language that is hardly believable.** You might believe the exaggerated statements to be true, but the recipient might find them unbelievable and insincere. Strong language with unsupported statements raises questions about your motive for the message.

- **Make specific comments about outstanding qualities or performance.** Compared to Figure 6-3, the following message might lack the impact of one that contains more detail and is written with more care. Although the sender cared enough to say thank you, the message could have been given to any speaker, even if the sender had slept through the entire seminar. Similarly, a note merely closed with "sincerely" does not necessarily make the ideas seem sincere. Including specific remarks about understanding and applying the speaker's main points makes the message meaningful and sincere.

Original: Your seminar on working in virtual teams was very much appreciated. You are an excellent speaker and provided many useful ideas. Thank you.

Improved: This past week, our team met to begin applying the principles you discussed last week in your "Working in Virtual Teams" seminar.

One of the most important takeaways from the class was the emphasis you placed on creating and communicating clear procedures for work processes. Based upon your suggestions, our team created a draft of these guidelines during our first meeting. Thank you for the suggestions that have put my colleagues and me on the path to becoming a more effective virtual team.

6-4 Routine Requests

Like claims, requests are divided into two groups: **routine requests** and **persuasive requests**. Persuasive requests, which are discussed in Chapter 8, assume that action will be taken after persuasive arguments are presented. Routine requests and favorable responses to them follow the deductive sequence.

Victor Correia/Shutterstock.com

6-4a Requests for Information

Requests for information about people, prices, products, and services are common. Because these requests from customers and clients are door openers for future business, businesses accept them optimistically. At the same time, they arrive at an opinion about the sender based on the quality of the message. Follow the points in the deductive outline for preparing effective requests you are confident will be fulfilled.

The message in Figure 6-8 does not follow the deductive outline that is appropriate for a routine request. The request is too vague and the sales manager receiving the message is not provided with enough useful information.

Note that the revision in Figure 6-9 starts with a direct request for specific information. Then as much detail as necessary is presented to enable the receiver to answer specifically. The revision ends confidently with appreciation for the action requested. The email message is short, but because it conveys enough information and has a tone of politeness, it is effective.

> **routine requests**
> messages that assume that a request will be granted quickly and willingly, without persuasion
>
> **persuasive requests**
> messages that assume that a requested action will be taken after persuasive arguments are presented

---

Figure 6-8 **BAD :-(** Poor Example of a Routine Request

Subject: Need information

I have been searching for a relaxing location for my organization's national conference to be held in late May of next year. From looking at your Web site, it appears that Virginia Beach meets almost all our criteria. However, I am uncertain as to whether your hotel can accommodate our needs.

We expect that we may have as many as 700 attendees and perhaps half may need hotel accommodations. In addition, we expect as many as 200 travel and travel-related companies to purchase booths to showcase their products and services. Does your hotel have facilities to meet these needs?

I look forward to receiving your reply as quickly as possible.

- *The subject line could be more informational.*
- *The introduction could more clearly state the purpose of the message.*
- *The writer's needs could be stated more clearly and systematically.*
- *The generic close fails to build goodwill or a sense of urgency.*

Figure 6-9 **GOOD** :-) Good Example of a Routine Request

New Message

To: Deann Summers <dsummers@vbresort.com>

From: Larry Taylor <ltaylor@ncpa.org>

Subject: Information Needed for Planning Large Convention in Virginia Beach

Ms. Summers,

The helpful information on your Web site describing the panoramic views of the ocean and unique shopping and restaurant possibilities offered on Palisades Avenue suggests that Virginia Beach could be an ideal location for our three-day annual consumer products convention. To assist us in selecting the site for this event scheduled for late May 2013, please provide the following information:

- Does your hotel contain a conference center with space for 200 sales booths and three smaller rooms for concurrent sales presentations and press announcements?

- Can the conference hotel provide a block of 350 rooms, preferably at conference rate? If not, are there other suitable hotels nearby?

- Does the hotel have the capacity to feed 700 attendees during the three-day event at its in-house cafes and restaurants? If not, could you please provide a list of other nearby establishments that might meet the needs of attendees for breakfast, lunch, and dinner?

- Could your concierge staff provide a list of attractions and other venues that attendees might visit during the conference dates?

The information you provide could likely confirm our expectation that the Virginia Beach Resort can meet our conference needs. At that point you will be contacted to assist us in making necessary reservations. Should you wish to talk to me directly, please call (307) 213-6770.

Thanks,

Larry Taylor, Executive Director
National Consumer Products Association
307-213-6770, Fax: 307-213-6775
token@nta.org

States request clearly.

Asks specific questions with necessary explanation; uses list for emphasis.

Expresses appreciation and alludes to benefits for quick action.

Opens door for personal dialogue by providing telephone number.

Format Pointers
Provides salutation appropriate for company.

Includes a complete signature block below writer's name for complete reference.

6-4b Favorable Response to a Routine Request

The message in Figure 6-10 on page 99 responds favorably but with little enthusiasm to an online request for detailed information related to conference accommodations at a Pacific Coast hotel. With a little planning and consideration for the executive planning a major event, the message in Figure 6-11 on page 100 could have been written just as quickly. Note the specific answers

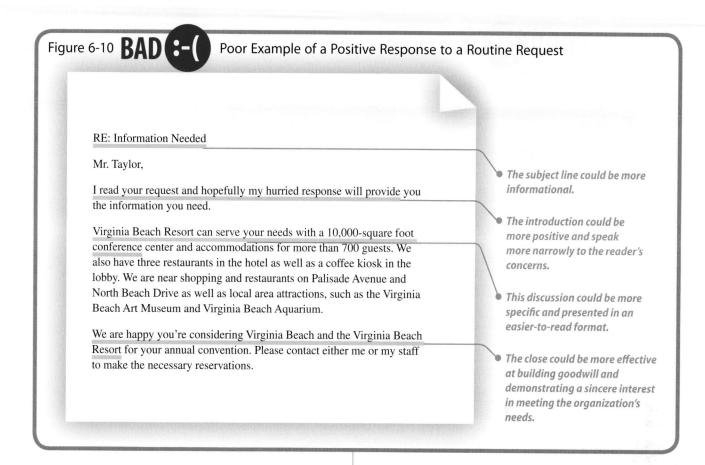

Figure 6-10 **BAD :-(** Poor Example of a Positive Response to a Routine Request

RE: Information Needed

Mr. Taylor,

I read your request and hopefully my hurried response will provide you the information you need.

Virginia Beach Resort can serve your needs with a 10,000-square foot conference center and accommodations for more than 700 guests. We also have three restaurants in the hotel as well as a coffee kiosk in the lobby. We are near shopping and restaurants on Palisade Avenue and North Beach Drive as well as local area attractions, such as the Virginia Beach Art Museum and Virginia Beach Aquarium.

We are happy you're considering Virginia Beach and the Virginia Beach Resort for your annual convention. Please contact either me or my staff to make the necessary reservations.

The subject line could be more informational.

The introduction could be more positive and speak more narrowly to the reader's concerns.

This discussion could be more specific and presented in an easier-to-read format.

The close could be more effective at building goodwill and demonstrating a sincere interest in meeting the organization's needs.

to the manager's questions prepared in the convenient Q&A format and the helpful, sincere tone.

6-4c Positive Response to a Favor Request

Occasionally, as a business professional, you will be asked for special favors. You might receive invitations to speak at various civic or education events, spearhead fund-raising and other service projects, or offer your expertise in other ways. If you say "Yes," you might as well say it enthusiastically. Sending an unplanned, stereotyped acceptance suggests that the contribution will be similar.

If you find yourself responding to invitations frequently, you can draft a form message that you'll revise for each invitation you receive. Go to www.cengagebrain.com to view a TV production manager's gracious acceptance of an invitation to emcee an awards program for a civic group. This well-written acceptance illustrates how form messages can be effectively individualized to enable businesses to communicate quickly and efficiently.

6-4d Form Messages for Routine Responses

Form messages are a fast and efficient way of transmitting frequently recurring messages to which receiver reaction is likely favorable or neutral. Inputting the customer's name, address, and other variables (information that differs for each receiver) personalizes each message to meet the needs of its receiver. Companies might use form paragraphs that have been saved as template documents. When composing a document, select the appropriate paragraph according to your receiver's request. After assembling the selected files on the computer screen, input the particular information for the situation (e.g., name and address) and print a copy of the personalized message on letterhead to send to the receiver.

Form letters have earned a negative connotation because of their tendency to be impersonal. Many people simply refuse to read such letters for that reason. Personalizing a form letter can circumvent this problem.

Figure 6-11 **GOOD** :-) Good Example of a Positive Response to a Routine Request

---

New Message

To: Larry Taylor <ltaylor@ncpa.org>

From: Deann Summers <dsummers@vbresort.com>

Subject: Assistance for Planning Exciting Convention in Virginia Beach

---

Mr. Taylor,

Virginia Beach and the Virginia Beach Resort are the ideal location for the National Consumer Products Association's annual convention. My staff and I can assist you with all your lodging, conference, and entertainment reservations.

Q: Does your hotel contain a conference center with space for 200 sales booths and three smaller rooms for sales presentations/press announcements?

A: Virginia Beach Resorts' Conference Center can easily meet your needs. We have a 10,000-square-foot conference space as well as 10 smaller meeting rooms.

Q: Can the hotel provide a block of 350 rooms at conference rate?

A: Yes, the Virginia Beach Resorts has 700 boutique-style rooms that are available for conferences of 200 people or more at a 15 percent rate reduction.

Q: Does the hotel have the capacity to feed 700 attendees during the three-day event at its in-house cafes and restaurants?

A: Virginia Beach Resort provides a unique dining experience in its three restaurants: The Car-hop Diner, the Keys Grill, and the Blue Crab Bistro. A coffee bar is conveniently located in our lobby. Just outside our door on Palisade Avenue, more than a dozen restaurants are within easy walking distance.

Q: Could your concierge staff provide a list of attractions and other venues that attendees might visit during the conference?

A: Virginia Beach Resort is within walking distance of the Virginia Beach Museum of Art that houses the world's largest collection of folk art. Nearby is Virginia Beach Aquarium with more than 3,000 species of marine animals. A short bus or taxi ride takes visitors to world-class shopping and restaurants on North Beach Drive. Of course, other attractions include the beach and various water sports, such as surfing, kayaking, and paddle-boarding.

Please call my direct line (509) 569-6768 for more advice on organizing an exciting event on the shores of the beautiful Atlantic Ocean.

Thanks,

Deann Summers, Sales Manager
Virginia Beach Resort

Revises subject line after clicking "reply" to communicate enthusiasm for providing exceptional personalized service.

Shows sincere interest in request and person.

Highlights specific answers to recipient's questions using an articulate, concise writing style.

Encourages direct call and provides more useful information that communicates genuine interest in person and event.

Format Pointer
Uses Q&A format to enhance readability of response to series of detailed questions.

Delivering Bad-News Messages

To accomplish this goal, begin with a well-written first paragraph that transitions the receiver smoothly into the reasons section. Then, develop the reasons section following these guidelines:

- **Provide a smooth transition from the opening paragraph to the explanation.** The buffer should help set the stage for a logical movement into the discussion of the reasons.

- **Include a concise discussion of one or more reasons that are logical to the receiver.** Read the section aloud to identify flaws in logic or the need for additional explanation.

- **Show receiver benefit and/or consideration.** Emphasize how the receiver will benefit from the decision. Avoid insincere, empty statements such as "To improve our service to you, …"

- **Avoid using "company policy" as the reason.** Disclose the reason behind the policy, which likely will include benefits to the receiver. For example, a customer is more likely to understand and accept a 15 percent restocking fee if the policy is not presented as the "reason" for the refusal.

The principles for developing the reasons section are illustrated in Figure 7-2, a letter written by an event-planning firm refusing a planning engagement.

7-2c Writing the Bad-News Statement

A paragraph that presents the reasoning behind a refusal at least partially conveys the refusal before it is stated directly or indirectly. Yet one sentence needs to convey (directly or by implication) the conclusion to which the preceding details have been leading. A refusal (bad news) needs to be clear; however, you can subordinate the refusal so that the reasons get the deserved emphasis. The following techniques will help you achieve this goal.

- **Position the bad-news statement strategically.** Using the inductive outline positions the bad-news statement in a less important position—sandwiched between an opening buffer statement and a positive closing. Additionally, the refusal statement should be included in the same paragraph as the reasons, since placing it in a paragraph by itself would give too much emphasis to the bad news. When the preceding explanation is tactful and relevant, resentment over the bad news is minimized. Positioning the bad-news statement in the dependent clause of a complex sentence will also cushion the bad news. This technique places the bad news in a less visible,

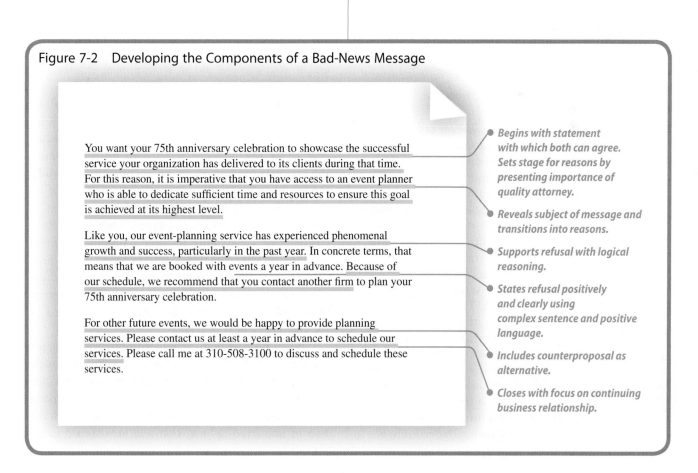

Figure 7-2   Developing the Components of a Bad-News Message

You want your 75th anniversary celebration to showcase the successful service your organization has delivered to its clients during that time. For this reason, it is imperative that you have access to an event planner who is able to dedicate sufficient time and resources to ensure this goal is achieved at its highest level.

Begins with statement with which both can agree. Sets stage for reasons by presenting importance of quality attorney.

Like you, our event-planning service has experienced phenomenal growth and success, particularly in the past year. In concrete terms, that means that we are booked with events a year in advance. Because of our schedule, we recommend that you contact another firm to plan your 75th anniversary celebration.

Reveals subject of message and transitions into reasons.

Supports refusal with logical reasoning.

States refusal positively and clearly using complex sentence and positive language.

For other future events, we would be happy to provide planning services. Please contact us at least a year in advance to schedule our services. Please call me at 310-508-3100 to discuss and schedule these services.

Includes counterproposal as alternative.

Closes with focus on continuing business relationship.

less emphatic position. In the sentence, *"Although the company's current financial condition prevents us from providing raises this year, we hope to make up for the freeze when conditions improve,"* the emphasis is directed toward a promise of raises at another time.

- **Use passive voice, general terms, and abstract nouns.** Review the *emphasis techniques* that you studied in Chapter 3 as you consider methods for presenting bad news with human relations in mind.

- **Use positive language to accentuate the positive.** Simply focus on the good instead of the bad, the pleasant instead of the unpleasant, or what can be done instead of what cannot be done. Compared with a negative idea presented in negative terms, a negative idea presented in positive terms is more likely to be accepted. When you are tempted to use the following terms, search instead for words or ideas that sound more positive:

Words that Evoke Negative Feelings

complaint incompetent misled regrettable error inexcusable mistake unfortunate failure lied neglect wrong

Words that Evoke Positive Feelings

accurate concise enthusiasm productive approval durable generous recommendation assist energetic gratitude respect

- **Imply the refusal when the receiver can understand the message without a definite statement of the bad news.** By *implying* the "No" answer, the response has the following positive characteristics: (1) it uses positive language, (2) it conveys reasons or at least a positive attitude, and (3) it seems more respectful. For example, during the noon hour one employee says to another, "Will you go with me to see this afternoon's baseball game?" "No, I won't" communicates a negative response, but it seems unnecessarily direct and harsh. The same message (invitation is rejected) can be clearly stated in an *indirect* way (by implication) by saying "I must get my work done," or even, "I'm a football fan." Note the positive tone of the following implied refusals:

counterproposal

in a bad-news message, an alternative to the action requested that follows the negative news and can assist in preserving future relationships with the receiver

Implied Refusal	Underlying Message
I wish I could.	- Other responsibilities prohibit, but recipient would like to accept.
Had you selected our newest calling plan, you could have reduced your monthly rates by 10 percent or more.	- States a condition under which answer would have been "Yes" instead of "No." Note use of subjunctive words "had" and "could."
By accepting the new terms, Southern Wood Products would have doubled its energy costs.	- States the obviously unacceptable results of complying with request.

7-2d Offering a Counterproposal or "Silver Lining" Idea

Following negative news with an alternative action, referred to as a **counterproposal**, will assist in preserving a relationship with the receiver. Because it states what you *can* do, including a counterproposal might eliminate the need to state the refusal directly. The counterproposal can follow a refusal stated in a tactful, sensitive manner. When global Internet services and media company AOL was faced with laying off 2,000 workers, the silver lining offered was a generous severance package and aid in transitioning to other job opportunities.[1]

While the counterproposal might represent a tangible benefit, at times it is more intangible in nature. For instance, in a letter that informs a job applicant that he or she was not selected to fill the position, the counterproposal might be an offer to reconsider the applicant's résumé when other appropriate positions become available. Any counterproposal must, of course, be reasonable. For instance, when informing a customer of an inability to meet a promised delivery deadline, an unreasonable counterproposal would be to offer the merchandise at no charge. A reasonable counterproposal might be to include some additional items at no charge or to offer a discount certificate good on the customer's next order.

When no reasonable counterproposal is apparent, the sender might be able to offer a silver lining thought that turns the discussion back into the positive direction. For instance, a statement to tenants announcing an increase in rent might be followed by a description of improved lighting that will be installed in the

Offering a counterproposal or "silver lining" idea can assist in preserving a relationship with the receiver of bad news.

Fotokkden/Shutterstock

parking lot of the apartment complex. When offering a counterproposal or silver lining statement, care must be taken to ensure that the idea does not seem superficial or minimize the recipient's situation.

7-2e Closing Positively

After presenting valid reasons and a tactful refusal followed with a counterproposal or silver lining statement, a closing paragraph should demonstrate empathy without further reference to the bad news. A pleasant closing paragraph should close with an empathetic tone and achieve the following goals:

- **De-emphasize the unpleasant part of the message.** End on a positive note that takes the emphasis away from the bad news previously presented. A statement of refusal (or bad news) in the last sentence or paragraph would place too much emphasis on it. Preferably, *reasons* (instead of bad news) should remain uppermost in the receiver's mind. Placing bad news last would make the ending seem cold and abrupt.

When no reasonable counterproposal is apparent, the sender might be able to offer a silver lining thought that turns the discussion back into the positive direction.

- **Add a unifying quality to the message.** Make your final sentence an *appropriate* closing that brings a unifying quality to the whole message. Repetition of a word or reference to some positive idea that appears early in the message serves this purpose well.

Avoid restatement of the refusal or direct reference to it. This paragraph is usually shorter than the preceding explanatory paragraphs, often one or two sentences.

- **Include a positive, forward-looking idea.** This idea might include a reference to some pleasant aspect of the preceding discussion or a future aspect of the business relationship, resale or sales promotion, or an offer to help in some way. Consider the following closures that apply these suggestions:

Reference to some pleasant aspect of the preceding discussion:
"Your decision to refinance your mortgage last year was a wise choice." Home mortgage and other provisions had been mentioned in the early part of a letter to a client who was refused a double-indemnity settlement.

Use of resale or sales promotional material:
"Selecting our new hybrid Breeze with its 50-miles-per-gallon fuel usage was a wise decision with today's gas prices." A reminder that the hybrid has superior gas mileage will assist in regaining goodwill after a customer's request for free repair has been refused.

An expression of willingness to assist in some other way:
Specifically, you might offer an alternative solution to the receiver's problem or useful information that could not be presented logically with the bad news. *"Our representative will show you some samples during next week's sales call."* The samples are being proposed as a possible solution to the receiver's problem.

Note the closing paragraph in Figure 7-2 is a positive, forward-looking statement that includes sales promotion of other services the accounting firm can offer.

7-3 Refusing a Request

It's a good idea to use the inductive approach (reasons before refusal) for refusing requests for a favor, an action, or even a donation. Present clear, understandable reasons in a way that minimizes the receiver's disappointment.

You can examine a company's refusal to provide an executive to speak in a communication class in Figure 7-3. This *response* to prior correspondence uses the same principles of sequence and style that are

Avoid Including the Following Types of Statements in the Closing Paragraph:

- **Trite statements that might seem shallow and superficial.** The well-worn statement, "Thank you for your interest," is often used thoughtlessly. It might seem shallow and superficial. "When we can be of further help, please do not hesitate to call or write" is also well worn and negative. *Further help* might seem especially inappropriate to someone who has just read a denial.
- **Statements that could undermine the validity of your refusal.** The statement "We trust this explanation is satisfactory" or "We hope you will understand our position" could be taken as a confession of doubt about the validity of the decision. Use of *position* seems to heighten controversy; positions are expected to be defended. Saying "We are sorry to disappoint you" risks a negative reply: "If it made you feel so bad, why did you do it?" It can also be interpreted as an apology for the action taken. If a decision merits an apology, its validity might be questionable.
- **Statements that encourage future controversy.** Statements such as "If you have questions, please do not hesitate to let us know" could also be perceived as doubt and possibly communicate a willingness to change the decision. If the decision is firm, including this type of closing could result in your having to communicate the negative message a second time.

Study the Techniques Used to Cushion This Bad-News Statement:

Although Richardson Contracting was selected as the building contractor, expertise with environmentally friendly construction techniques was considered a plus for S and S Builders.

- States what was done rather than what was not done.
- Includes a positive idea ("expertise with environmentally friendly construction techniques") to accentuate a positive aspect and cushion the bad news.
- Uses passive voice ("Richardson Contracting was selected") to depersonalize the message.
- Places the bad news in the dependent clause of a complex sentence ("although Richardson Contracting was selected"). The positive idea in the independent clause ("expertise with environmentally friendly construction techniques") will receive more attention.

recommended for messages that *initiate* communication about unpleasant topics. The same principles apply whether the communication is a spoken message, letter, memo, or email message.

Companies have learned that building employee relationships is just as important as developing customer goodwill. Refusing employees' requests requires sensitivity and complete, honest explanations, qualities not included in the bad email in Figure 7-4. The manager's hasty and vague response to a valued employee's request to create an employee game room uses a direct, blunt approach. In the revision illustrated in Figure 7-5,

the manager takes the time to prepare a response that reflects detailed explanation supporting the refusal and genuine respect for the employee.

7-4 Denying a Claim

ompanies face a challenging task of refusing claims from customers while maintaining goodwill and building customer loyalty. Claim refusals are necessary when a

116   Part 3: Communication through Voice, Electronic, and Written Messages

Figure 7-7 **GOOD** :-) Good Example of a Claim Denial

NEWPORT LEISURE INDUSTRIES

860 MONMOUTH STREET
NEWPORT, KY 41071-6218

TELEPHONE: 800-555-6000
FAX: 800-555-0583

March 14, 2013

Linda Turner
Extreme Sports
1905 Southhaven Street
Taos, NM 87501-7313

Dear Ms. Turner:

Restocking of Returned Merchandise

The FairWeather hiking boots you stocked this past season are skillfully constructed and made from the most durable materials available. Maintaining a wide selection of quality outdoor footwear is an excellent strategy for developing customer loyalty and maximizing your sales.

Our refund policies provide you the opportunity to keep a fully stocked inventory at the lowest possible cost. You receive full refunds for merchandise returned within 10 days of receipt. For unsold merchandise returned after the primary selling season, a modest 15 percent restocking fee is charged to cover our costs of holding this merchandise until next season. The credit applied to your account for $2,069.75 covers merchandise you returned at the end of February.

While relaxing from another great winter sports season, take a look at our new FairWeather footwear and other items available in the enclosed catalog for the 2013 winter season. You can save 10 percent by ordering products before August 1.

Sincerely,

Gary Ford

Gary Ford
Credit Manager

Enclosure: Catalog

Legal and ethical consideration avoids corrective language that might insult, belittle, or offend.

Uses subject line that identifies subject without revealing refusal.

Uses resale to cushion bad news and lead into explanation.

Presents clear explanation of reasons behind policy with emphasis on ways reader benefits.

Implies refusal by stating amount credited to account.

Shifts emphasis away from refusal by presenting silver lining sales promotion for next season's merchandise.

Specifies enclosure to emphasize importance of exact items.

Why Explain Credit Denial?

☑ Writers can show fairness of the decision.

☑ Receivers are entitled to the truth.

☑ Receivers can learn to adjust bad habits.

Both writers and readers benefit from the explanation of the reasons behind the denial. For writers, the explanation helps to establish fair-mindedness; it shows that the decision was not arbitrary. For receivers, the explanation not only presents the truth to which they are entitled, it also has guidance value. From it they learn to adjust habits and, as a result, qualify for credit purchases later.

Remygerega/Dreamstime LLC

the credit denial letter and invite the applicant to call or come in to discuss the reasons. Alternately, they might suggest that the receiver obtain further information from the credit reporting agency whose name, address, and telephone number are provided.

7-6 Delivering Constructive Criticism

A person who has had a bad experience as a result of another person's conduct might be reluctant to write or speak about that experience. However, because one person took the time to communicate, many could benefit. Although not always easy or pleasant, communicating about negatives can be thought of as a social responsibility. For example, a person who returns from a long stay at a major hotel might, upon returning home, write a letter or email message to the management commending certain employees. If the stay had not been pleasant and weaknesses in hotel operation had been detected, a tactful message pointing out the negatives would probably be appreciated. Future guests could benefit from the effort of that one person.

Before communicating about the problem, an individual should recognize the following risks: being stereotyped as a complainer, being associated with negative thoughts and perceived in negative terms, and appearing to challenge management's decisions concerning hotel operations. Yet such risks might be worth taking because of the benefits:

- The communicator gets a feeling of having exercised a responsibility.
- Management learns of changes that need to be made.
- The hotel staff about whom the message is written modifies techniques and is thus more successful.
- Other guests will have more enjoyable stays in the hotel.

In the decision to communicate about negatives, the primary consideration is intent. If the intent is to hurt or to get even, the message should not be sent. Including false information would be *unethical* and *illegal*. To avoid litigation charges and to respond ethically, include only specific facts you can verify and avoid evaluative words that present opinions about the person's

Because of the legal implications involved in denying credit, legal counsel should review your credit denial messages to ensure that they comply with laws related to fair credit practices. For example, the Equal Credit Opportunity Act (ECOA) requires that the credit applicant be notified of the credit decision within 30 calendar days following application. Applicants who are denied credit must be informed of the reasons for the refusal. If the decision was based on information obtained from a consumer reporting agency (as opposed to financial statements or other information provided by the applicant), the credit denial must include the name, address, and telephone number of the agency. It must also remind applicants that the **Fair Credit Reporting Act** provides them the right to know the nature of the information in their credit file. In addition, credit denials must include a standard statement that the ECOA prohibits creditors from discriminating against credit applicants on the basis of a number of protected characteristics (race, color, religion, national origin, sex, marital status, and age).

To avoid litigation, some companies choose to omit the explanation from

Fair Credit Reporting Act
federal law that provides consumers the right to know the nature of the information in their credit file and gives them other protections when they apply for and are denied credit

Figure 7-8 **BAD :-(** Poor Example of a Constructive Criticism

Sarah Frank, a temporary administrative assistant your firm sent to us, is not working out well. She is constantly accepting cellphone calls, even while clients are waiting for help in our lobby. The constant distraction of her phone conversations, sometimes highly personal, has resulted in several complaints from important clients. Sarah has asked clients to wait up to 20 minutes while she finishes personal phone calls.

Although extensive knowledge of administrative duties is important, Sarah's lack of respect for others far outweighs her professional experience. I seriously hope Sarah is able to take steps to correct the situation.

A more positive or neutral introduction would help to better maintain goodwill.

This information should be placed in a second paragraph that describes specific behaviors to maintain neutrality.

The close would better maintain goodwill if it were more positive in tone and content.

character or ability. For example, instead of presenting facts, the message in Figure 7-8 judges the staff member sent to perform administrative assistant duties at a client's office. Overall, the message is short, general, and negative. By comparison, the revision in Figure 7-9 has positive intent, is factual, uses positive language, and leaves judgment to the recipient.

7-7 Communicating Negative Organizational News

Being able to initiate messages that convey bad news is as important as responding "No" to messages from customers/clients and others outside the company. Employees and the public are seeking, and expecting, *honest* answers from management about situations adversely affecting the company—slumping profits, massive layoffs, bankruptcy, a variety of major changes in the organization, and negative publicity that affects the overall health of the business and retirement plans, to name a few.

Managers who can communicate negative information in a sensitive, honest, and timely way can calm fears and doubts and build positive employee and public relations. Effective managers recognize that employee morale, as well as public goodwill, is fragile—easily damaged and difficult to repair. If handled well, these bad-news messages related to the organization can be opportunities to treat employees, customers, and the general public with respect, thus building unity and trust.

Strong internal communication is a key to involving employees in corporate strategies and building an important sense of community. Transparency can have a positive effect on an organization's culture. According to a recent workplace survey, open, honest communication between corporate leaders and employees can lead to a more productive and ethical workplace. According to Deloitte Chairman Sharon Allen, motivating communication patterns are "increasingly critical to retaining talent and preserving the health of today's organizations."[2]

Obviously, business and competitive reasons prevent a company from always being completely transparent with its staff, but every attempt should be made to do so when possible. The best companies use a variety of communication tools that promote an open exchange of honest, candid communication and welcome input from employees. Newsletters, email updates, town hall or focus meetings, videoconferencing, phone calls, and

Figure 7-9 **GOOD :-)** Good Example of a Constructive Criticism

Office Systems Incorporated
2500 lincoln Green Road/Austin,
TX 78710-2500 / Phone: 512-555-9000 / Fax: 512-555-6573.

March 24, 2013

Charles Smythe
Smythe and Associates
3504 Elm Street
Chicago, IL 50340

Dear Mr. Smythe:

Your firm has served our temporary personnel needs for nearly 10 years with excellent results. Sarah Frank, a temporary administrative assistant we acquired from your firm, has done an excellent job of scheduling client appointments and following up with phone calls.

While working at the front desk, Sarah's attention is constantly diverted from waiting on clients by her receipt of personal cellphone calls. The constant distraction from these calls—sometimes highly intimate in nature—has caused some of our clients to complain that she is preoccupied with non-business matters.

More specifically, several important clients said that they had waited up to 20 minutes while Sarah completed personal phone calls in their presence. Sarah is obviously quite good at some aspects of her job; her expertise in managing administrative duties explains why she is represented by your firm. Please convey my concerns to Sarah confidentially so that the rest of her time in our office will go smoothly for her and for us.

Sincerely,

Dena Singleton
Human Resources Manager

- Introduces discussion of audit work underway.

- *Conveys fair-mindedness and establishes credibility by acknowledging good as well as bad points.*

- *Presents verifiable statements without labeling them in negative, judgmental terms.*

- *Ends on pleasant note that seeks to add credibility to preceding negatives.*

Legal and Ethical Considerations
- *Conveys positive intent to help— not to hurt or get even.*

- *Avoids potential litigation charges by including specific, verifiable facts and avoiding evaluative, judgmental statements.*

- *Uses "confidential" as safeguard; information is intended for professional use only, not designed to hurt or to be thought of as gossip.*

Format Pointer
- *Uses letter channel rather than email to communicate a sensitive message.*

---

discussion boards drive home relevant messages and allow employees to pose questions to management. This quality two-way communication involves employees in corporate strategies; employees who are aware of company goals and potential problems feel connected and accountable. Informed employees are also better prepared for bad news when it must be shared.

7-7a Breaking Bad News

Assuming this long-term commitment to keep employees informed, the following suggestions provide guidance in breaking bad news to employees and the public[3]:

- **Convey the bad news as soon as possible.** Timeliness will minimize damage caused by rumors and will give employees the concern and respect they deserve. Nestlé Purina and others in the pet food industry acted early and effectively to recall potentially deadly pet food tainted with wheat gluten from China and to assure pet owners that steps were in place to ensure healthy ingredients would be used in the future.[4]

- **Give a complete, rational explanation of the problem.** Be candid about what is happening, why, and its effect on employees, customers, and the public. Provide enough detail to establish your credibility and provide context so your audience can

OBJECTIVES

8-1 Develop effective outlines and appeals for messages that persuade.

8-2 Write effective sales messages.

8-3 Write effective persuasive requests (making a claim or asking for a favor or information) and persuasion within an organization.

8-1 Persuasion Strategies

Business people regularly seek to persuade others. **Persuasion** is the ability to influence others to accept your point of view. It is not an attempt to trap someone into taking action favorable to the communicator. Instead, it is an honest, organized presentation of information on which a person can choose to act. Professionals in all fields benefit from well-prepared communications that persuade others to accept their ideas or buy their products, services, or ideas.

How do you learn to persuade others through spoken and written communication? Have you ever made a persuasive request, written employment documents or an essay for college entry or a scholarship, or given a campaign speech? If so, you already have experience with this type of communication. While the persuasive concepts discussed in this chapter are directed primarily at written communication, they can also be applied in many spoken communication situations.

For persuasion to be effective, you must understand your product, service, or idea; know your audience; anticipate the arguments that might come from the audience; and have a rational and logical response to those arguments. Remember, persuasion need not be a hard sell; it can simply be a way of getting a client or your supervisor to say yes. Although much of this chapter concentrates on selling products and services, similar principles apply to selling an idea, your organization, and your own abilities.

Log onto www.cengagebrain.com for additional resources including flashcards, games, self-quizzing for chapter review, grammar exercises, and more.

8-1a Plan Before You Write

Success in writing is directly related to success in preliminary thinking. If the right questions have been asked and answered, the composing will be easier and the message will be more persuasive. Specifically, you need information about (1) your product, service, or idea; (2) your audience; and (3) the desired action.

Know the Product, Service, or Idea

You cannot be satisfied with knowing the product, service, or idea in a general way; you need details. Get your information by (1) reading available literature; (2) using the product and watching others use it; (3) comparing the product, service, or idea with others; (4) conducting tests and experiments; and (5) soliciting reports from users.

Before you write, you need concrete answers to such questions as these:

- What will the product, service, or idea do for the receiver(s)?

  "What is the major difference?"
  "What is the cost to the receiver?"
  "What will it do for the receiver?"
  "What are its superior features?"
  "Who is the competition?"

- What are its superior features (e.g., design and workmanship or receiver benefit)?

- How is the product or service different from its competition? How is the proposed idea superior to other viable alternatives?

- What is the cost to the receiver?

Similar questions must be answered about other viable alternatives or competing products. Of particular importance is the question, "What is the

kai zhang/alubalish/iStockphoto.com

persuasion
the ability of a sender to influence others to accept his or her point of view

major difference?" People are inclined to choose an item (or alternative) that has some distinct advantage. For example, some people might choose a particular car model because of its style and available options; still others might choose the model because of its safety record.

Know the Receiver

Who are the people to whom the persuasive message is directed? What are their wants and needs? Is a persuasive message to be written and addressed to an individual or to a group? If it is addressed to a group, what characteristics do the members have in common? What are their common goals, their occupational levels, and their educational status? To what extent have their needs and wants been satisfied? How might cultural differences affect your message?

Recall the discussion of Maslow's need hierarchy in Chapter 2. Some people might respond favorably to appeals to physiological, security, and safety needs (to save time and money, to be comfortable, to be healthy, or to avoid danger). People with such needs would be impressed with a discussion of the benefits of convenience, durability, efficiency, or serviceability. Others might respond favorably to appeals to their social, ego, and self-actualizing needs (to be loved, entertained, remembered, popular, praised, appreciated, or respected). Consider the varying appeals used in a memo to employees and to supervisors seeking support of teleworking. The memo to employees would appeal to the need for greater flexibility and reduced stress. Appeals directed at supervisors would focus on increased productivity and morale, reduced costs for office space, and compliance with the Clean Air Act, a federal law requiring companies to reduce air pollution and traffic congestion.

Identify the Desired Action

What do you want the receiver to do? Complete an online order and make a payment? Receive a demonstration version for trial? Return a card requesting a representative to call? Email for more information? Approve a request? Accept a significant change in service, style, and procedures? Whatever the desired action, you need to have a clear definition of it before composing your message.

8-1b Use the Inductive Approach

More than 100 years ago, Sherwin Cody summarized the persuasive process into four basic steps called **AIDA**.[1] The steps have been varied somewhat and have had different labels, but the fundamentals remain relatively unchanged. The persuasive approach illustrated in Figure 8-1 is inductive. The main idea, which is the request for action, appears in the *last* paragraph after presenting the details—convincing reasons for the receiver to comply with the request.

Each step is essential, but the steps do not necessarily require equal amounts of space. Good persuasive messages do not require separate sentences and paragraphs for each phase of the outline. The message *could* gain the receiver's attention and interest in the same sentence, and creating desire *could* require many paragraphs.

8-1c Apply Sound Writing Principles

The principles of unity, coherence, and emphasis are just as important in persuasive messages as in other messages. In addition, the following principles seem to be especially helpful in preparing persuasive messages:

- **Keep paragraphs short.** The spaces between paragraphs show the dividing place between ideas, improve appearance, and provide convenient resting places for the eyes. Hold the first and last paragraph to three or fewer lines; a one-line paragraph (even a very short line) is acceptable. You can even use paragraphs less than one sentence long by putting four or five words on the first line and completing the sentence in a new paragraph. Be careful to include key attention-getting words that either introduce the product, service, or idea or lead to its introduction.

- **Use concrete nouns and active verbs.** Concrete nouns and active verbs help receivers see the product, service, or idea and its benefits more vividly than do abstract nouns and passive verbs.

- **Use specific language.** General words won't mean much unless they are well supported with specifics. Specific language is space consuming (saying that something is "great" requires fewer words than telling what makes it so); therefore, persuasive messages are usually longer than other messages. Still, persuasive messages need to be concise; they should say what needs to be said without wasting words.

- **Let receivers have the spotlight.** If receivers are made the subject of some of the sentences, if they can visualize themselves with the product in their hands, or if they

Figure 8-1 Inductive Outline Used in Persuasive Messages Sent in Written, Electronic, or Spoken Form

Written
- Letter
- Memo

Electronic
- Email
- Instant message
- Website
- Blog
- Text message

Spoken
- In person
- Telephone
- Voice mail

A ATTENTION: Get the receiver's attention

I INTEREST: Introduce the product, service, or idea and arouse interest in it

D DESIRE: Create desire by presenting convincing evidence of the value of the product, service, or idea

A ACTION: Encourage action

© iStockphoto.com/Hamza Türkkol / © iStockphoto.com/Michal Rozanski / © iStockphoto.com/LajosRepasi

can get the feel of using it for enjoyment or to solve problems, the chances of creating a desire are increased.

- **Stress a central selling point or appeal.** A thorough analysis ordinarily will reveal some feature that is unique or some benefit that is not provided by other viable alternatives—the **central selling point**. This point of difference can be developed into a theme that is woven throughout the entire message. Or, instead of using a point of difference as a central selling point, a writer could choose to stress a major satisfaction to be gained from using the item or doing as asked. A central selling point (*theme*) should be introduced early and reinforced throughout the remainder of the message.

8-2 Sales Messages

The four-point persuasive outline is appropriate for an *unsolicited sales message*—a letter, memo, or email message written to someone who has not requested it.

A *solicited sales message* has been requested by a potential buyer or supporter; that is, the message is prepared to answer this interested person's questions.

A person requesting sales information has given some attention to the product, service, or idea already; therefore, an attention-getting sentence is hardly essential. However, such a sentence is needed when the receiver is not known to have expressed an interest previously. The very

Velychko/Shutterstock.com

central selling point
the primary appeal on which a persuasive message focuses

first sentence, then, is deliberately designed to make a receiver put aside other thoughts and concentrate on the rest of the message.

8-2a Gain Attention

Various techniques have been successful in convincing receivers to consider an unsolicited sales message. Regardless of the technique used, the attention-getter should achieve several important objectives: introduce a relationship, focus on a central selling feature, and use an original approach.

Some Commonly Used Attention-Getting Devices Include:

→ **A personal experience:** When a doctor gives you instructions, how often have you thought, "I wish you had time to explain" or "I wish I knew more about medical matters"?

→ **A solution to a problem (outstanding feature/benefit):** Imagine creating a customized multimedia presentation that. . . .

→ **A startling announcement:** More teens die as a result of suicide each month than die in auto accidents in the same time period.

→ **A what-if opening:** What if I told you there is a savings plan that will enable you to retire three years earlier?

→ **A question:** Why should you invest in a company that has lost money for six straight years?

→ **A story:** Here's a typical day in the life of a manager who uses an iPad.

→ **A proverb or quote from a famous person:** Vince Lombardi, one of the most successful coaches in the history of football, once said, "If winning isn't everything, why do they keep score?" At Winning Edge, we specialize in making you the winner you were born to be.

→ **A split sentence:** Sandy beaches, turquoise water, and warm breezes … it's all awaiting you on your Mesa cruise.

→ **An analogy:** Like a good neighbor, State Farm is there.

Other attention-getters include a gift, an offer, a bargain, or a comment on an enclosed product sample.

Introduce a Relationship Between the Receiver and the Product, Service, or Idea

Remaining sentences grow naturally from this beginning sentence. If receivers do not see the relationship between the first sentence and the sales appeal, they could react negatively to the whole message—they might think they have been tricked into reading it. For example, consider the following poor attention-getter:

 Would you like to be the chief executive officer of one of America's largest companies? As CEO of Graham Enterprises, you can launch new products, invest in third world countries, or arrange billion dollar buyouts. Graham Enterprises is one of several companies at your command in the new computer software game developed by Creative Diversions Software.

The beginning sentence of the preceding ineffective example is emphatic because it is a short question. However, it suggests the message will be about obtaining a top management position, which it is not. All three sentences combined suggest high pressure. The computer software game has relevant virtues, and one of them could have been emphasized by placing it in the first sentence.

8-2b Focus on a Central Selling Feature

Almost every product, service, or idea will in some respects be superior to its competition. If not, such factors as favorable price, fast delivery, or superior service can be used as the primary appeal. This central selling point must be emphasized, and one of the most effective ways to emphasize a point is by position in the message. An outstanding feature mentioned in the middle of a message might go unnoticed, but it will stand out if mentioned in the first sentence. Note how the following opening sentence introduces the central selling feature and leads naturally into the sentences that follow:

 One of Soviet Georgia's senior citizens thought Dannon was an excellent yogurt. She ought to know. She's been eating yogurt for 137 years.

Dannon Yogurt is a part of a healthy nutrition plan that can add years to your life, too. It's high in important nutrients including calcium, protein, vitamin B12, potassium, phosphorus, and riboflavin, as well as being a great way to reduce fat and calories from your meals.

to create a desire to take action and providing a logical argument to overcome any anticipated resistance.

8-3a Making a Claim

Claim messages are often routine because the basis for the claim is a guarantee or some other assurance that an adjustment will be made without need of persuasion. However, when an immediate remedy is doubtful, persuasion is necessary. In a typical large business, customer service representatives handle claims.

Often, any reasonable claim will be adjusted to the customer's satisfaction. Therefore, venting strong displeasure in the claim message will likely alienate the claims adjuster—the one person whose cooperation is needed. Remember, adjusters might have had little or nothing to do with the manufacture and sale of the product or direct delivery of the service. They did not create the need for the claim.

Companies should welcome claims. Only a small percentage of claims are from unethical individuals; the great bulk is from people who believe they have a legitimate complaint. Research indicates that only 4 percent of customers complain, so for every complaint received, many more customers have been satisfied. Complaints help companies identify problem areas and correct them. Another advantage that companies derive from the claim process is that when complaints are handled appropriately, complainers can become very loyal customers.[5] Thus, the way a complaint is handled determines, to a large extent, the goodwill toward the company.

Like sales messages, persuasive claims should use an inductive sequence. Unlike routine claim messages, persuasive claims do not begin by asking for an adjustment.

The poor example shown in Figure 8-5 could be improved by (1) writing inductively (to reduce the chance of a negative reaction in the first sentence), and (2) stressing an appeal throughout the message (to emphasize an incentive for taking favorable action). In a persuasive claim, an appeal serves the same purpose that a central selling feature does in a sales message. Both serve as a theme; both remind the receiver of a benefit gained from doing as asked. Note the application of these techniques in the revision in Figure 8-6 below

Knowledge of effective claim writing should never be used as a means of taking advantage of someone. Hiding an unjustifiable claim under a cloak of untrue statements is difficult and strictly unethical. Adjusters typically are fair-minded people who will give the benefit of the doubt, but they will not satisfy an unhappy customer simply to avoid a problem.

8-3b Asking a Favor

Occasionally, everyone has to ask someone else for a special favor—action for which there is little reward, time, or inclination. For example, suppose a professional association wants to host its annual fund-raiser dinner at an exclusive country club. The program chair of the association must write the club's general manager requesting permission to use the facility. Will a deductive message be successful?

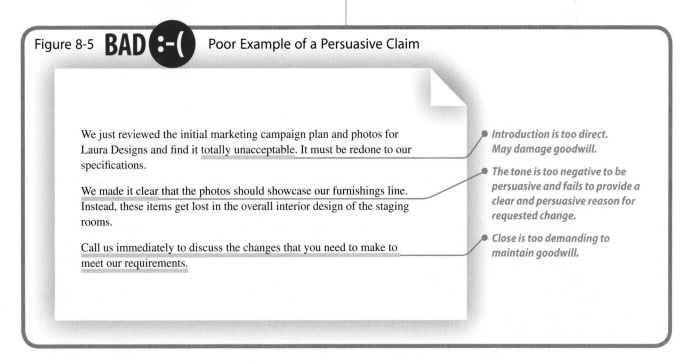

Figure 8-5 **BAD 8-(** Poor Example of a Persuasive Claim

We just reviewed the initial marketing campaign plan and photos for Laura Designs and find it totally unacceptable. It must be redone to our specifications.

We made it clear that the photos should showcase our furnishings line. Instead, these items get lost in the overall interior design of the staging rooms.

Call us immediately to discuss the changes that you need to make to meet our requirements.

Introduction is too direct. May damage goodwill.

The tone is too negative to be persuasive and fails to provide a clear and persuasive reason for requested change.

Close is too demanding to maintain goodwill.

Figure 8-6 **GOOD :-)** Good Example of a Persuasive Claim

Streetware Inc.
2304 42th Street, Hoboken, NJ 12001, 203-662-4400

August 26, 2013

Denise Walker
Advertising Director
Alpha Marketing Inc.
234 27th Avenue
New York, NY 03201

Dear Denise:

When Laura Designs negotiated with your firm to produce our first social media marketing campaign, we were impressed with your previous track record of success. Especially impressive was your marketing campaign for Metropolitan Fabrics, with its obvious appeal to upscale, urban consumers, our target market.

In our meeting with your creative team, we focused on the techniques used in the Metropolitan Fabrics' campaign and specifically asked to see images of upscale homes furnished with items from our product line. After viewing the initial plan and sample photographs for the campaign, we were disappointed with the staging of our products in the photographs. Although the photographs were of beautifully designed interiors, our products did not stand out in the overall design.

With Alpha's reputation for creative marketing campaigns, we are confident that the photographs can be reshot to meet our expectations. We are happy to meet with you again if you would like more specific suggestions regarding changes. Please call me at 203-662-4434 if a meeting would be helpful in this regard.

Sincerely,

Billy Lewis

Billy Lewis
Marketing Manager

- Seeks attention by giving sincere compliment that reveals subject of message.

- Continues central appeal—commitment to creative production—while providing needed details.

- Presents reasoning that leads to request and subtle reminder of central appeal.

- Connects specific request with firm's commitment to develop a creative production.

Legal and Ethical Consideration
- Uses letter rather than less formal email format to add formality to contractual agreement.

When a deductive approach is used in a persuasive situation, chances of getting cooperation are minimal. For example, what might be a probable reaction to the following beginning sentence? *Please send me, without charge, your $450 interactive video training game on workplace safety.*

If the first sentence gets a negative reaction, a decision to refuse might be made instantly. Having thought "No," the receiver might not read the rest of the message or might hold stubbornly to that decision in spite of a well-written persuasive argument that follows the opening sentence. Note that the letter in Figure 8-7 below asks the favor before presenting any benefit for doing so. The letter illustrated in Figure 8-8 uses an inductive approach and applies the principles discussed earlier. As this message shows, if the preceding paragraphs adequately emphasize a receiver's reward for complying, the final paragraph need not shout loudly for action.

Figure 8-7 **BAD** :-(Poor Example of a Persuasive Request (Asking a Favor)

There are no spa care products available in your store. We live in a beach community where many people have backyard spas. Have you considered stocking spa care products, along with the pool products you already carry?

You've probably already considered this, but I would be very interested in having this option when shopping at your store.

Does not use an inductive approach to set a more positive tone. Fails to provide clear reasons to comply with the request.

Close does little to build goodwill or encourage compliance.

8-3c Requesting Information

Requests for information are common in business. Information for research reports frequently is obtained by questionnaire, and the reliability of results is strongly influenced by the percentage of return. If a message inviting respondents to complete a questionnaire is written carelessly, the number of responses might be insufficient.

The most serious weakness is asking for action too quickly and providing no incentive for action. Sometimes the reward for taking action is small and indirect, but the message needs to make these benefits evident.

8-3d Persuading Within an Organization

The majority of memos are of a routine nature and essential for the day-to-day operation of the business; for example, giving instructions for performing work assignments, scheduling meetings, providing project progress reports, and so on. In many organizations, such matters are handled through the use of email rather than paper memos. These routine messages, as well as messages conveying good news, are written deductively. However, some circumstances require that a supervisor write a persuasive message that motivates employees to accept a change in their jobs that might have a negative effect on the employees or generate resistance (e.g., a job transfer, change in work procedures, software upgrade).

For example, imagine that Pub on the Green restaurant was faced with the challenge of communicating to its employees a significant change in service and style, which included new uniforms. Rather than coercing or demanding that employees accept the change, a letter from the president could emphasize reasons the changes were being made (benefits to guests, the company, and the employees) and the employee's important role in implementing the changes. Using a lighthearted, entertaining approach, the message could include (a) a visual model of the fresh, crisp, and professional look the company expected with the uniform change and (b) helpful information on ways to achieve this look. The following excerpt shows how a "you" orientation and "style flashes" could be interwoven into the letter:

- *Make sure your hair is neatly tied back. Messy hair is a problem for Guests—they don't want it getting it into their food. You might even get a better tip.*

Özgür Donmaz/iStockphoto.com

Figure 8-8 **GOOD :-)** Good Example of a Persuasive Request (Asking a Favor)

November 22, 2012

Georgia Bacall
Owner and Manager
Bayside Hardware
345 Center Avenue
Daytona, FL 04006

Dear Ms. Bacall:

As a regular customer of Bayside Hardware, I have appreciated your efforts to meet the needs of residents of the local community. The recent addition of a gardening center was welcomed by many who otherwise would need to drive to neighboring Sand Harbor to buy bedding and vegetable plants.

Another helpful change would be to add spa care products to your existing pool care area. As you probably know, many homeowners in the community own spas and no other store in the community provides spa care products. Being able to purchase these products at your store would provide convenience to spa owners and additional visits to your store.

By enhancing your product offerings, you build a reputation as the local supplier for all items needed by the homeowner, increasing store traffic, customer loyalty, and sales.

Sincerely,

Lila Turnbill

Lila Turnbill

Begins with sincere compliment that sets stage for request that follows.

Explains rationale for request with discussion of benefits to store and its customers.

Connects specific action to rewards for taking action.

- *Don't wear a lot of bling. Guests may think you don't need as large a tip.*

- *Remember to smile. Your smile is the first sign to Guests that their Pub on the Green experience will be a memorable one. Your smile tells Guests, "I'm glad you came!" But don't just take our word for it. A recent Bay College study found that smiling reflects an awareness of other people and their needs. That's probably why a "winning smile" is so charming!*

The detailed language leaves no doubt in an employee's mind as to what management considers clean, crisp, and professional. However, by continually emphasizing the benefits employees gain from the change, management garners support for the high standards being imposed.

Similarly, employees must often make persuasive requests of their supervisors. For example, they might recommend a change in procedure, acquisition of equipment

OBJECTIVES

9-1 Identify the characteristics of a report and the various classifications of business reports.

9-2 Apply steps in the problem-solving process and methods for solving a problem.

9-3 Use appropriate printed, electronic, and primary sources of information.

9-4 Demonstrate appropriate methods of collecting, organizing, and referencing information.

9-5 Explain techniques for the logical analysis and interpretation of data.

9-1 Characteristics of Reports

"Hi, Theo. This is Karen in the legal department. Do you know whether the contract for the new building addition will be ready today? Management wants me to review it so we can move on it by next week."

"Hi, Karen. Yes, the contractor signed it Tuesday. I will have Larry run it up to your office right now. It's pretty much boiler plate, though, so it shouldn't take long to review."

This brief exchange illustrates a simple reporting task. A question has been posed; the answer given (along with supporting information) satisfies the reporting requirement. Although Theo might never have studied report preparation, he did an excellent job; so Karen in turn can report to her supervisor. Theo's spoken report is a simple illustration of the four main characteristics of reports:

- **Reports typically travel upward in an organization because they usually are requested by a higher authority.** In most cases, people would not generate reports unless requested to do so.

- **Reports are logically organized.** In Theo's case, he answered Karen's question first and then supported the answer with evidence to justify it. Through your study of message organization, you learned the difference between deductive and inductive organization. Theo's report was deductively organized. If Theo had given the supporting evidence first and followed that

with the answer that he would meet the deadline, the organization of his reply would have been inductive and would still have been logical.

- **Reports are objective.** Because reports contribute to decision making and problem solving, they should be as objective as possible; when nonobjective (subjective) material is included, the report writer should make that known.

- **Reports are generally prepared for a limited audience.** This characteristic is particularly true of reports traveling within an organization and means that reports, like letters, memos, and emails, should be prepared with the receivers' needs in mind.

9-1a Types of Reports

Based on the four characteristics, a workable definition of a *report* is an orderly, objective message used to convey information from one organizational area to another or from one organization to another to assist in decision making or problem solving. Reports have been classified in numerous ways by management and by report-preparation authorities. The form, direction, functional use, and content of the report are used as bases for classification. However, a single report might fit several classifications. The following brief review of classification illustrates the scope of reporting and establishes a basis for studying reports.

- **Formal or informal reports.** The formal/informal classification is particularly helpful because it applies to all reports. A **formal report** is carefully structured; it is logically organized and objective, contains much detail, and is written in a style that tends to eliminate such elements as personal pronouns. An **informal report** is usually a short message written in natural or personal language. An internal memo

formal report
carefully structured report that is logically organized and objective, contains much detail, and is written in a style that tends to eliminate such elements as personal pronouns

informal report
usually a short message written in natural or personal language

Sergej Khakimullin/Shutterstock

informational report
a report that carries objective information from one area of an organization to another

analytical report
a report that presents suggested solutions to problems

vertical report
a report that can be upward- or downward–directed

lateral report
a report that travels between units on the same organizational level

internal report
a report that travels within an organization, such as a production or sales report

external report
a report prepared for distribution outside an organization

periodic report
a report that is issued on regularly scheduled dates

generally can be described as an informal report. All reports can be placed on a continuum of formality, as shown in Figure 9-1. The distinction among the degrees of formality of various reports is explained more fully in Chapter 11.

- **Short or long reports.** Reports can be classified generally as short or long. A one-page memo is obviously short, and a report of 20 pages is obviously long. What about in-between lengths? One important distinction generally holds true: As it becomes longer, a report takes on more characteristics of formal reports. Thus, the classifications of formal/informal and short/long are closely related.

- **Informational or analytical reports.** An **informational report** carries objective information from one area of an organization to another. An **analytical report** presents suggested solutions to problems. Company annual reports, monthly financial statements, reports of sales volume, and reports of employee or personnel absenteeism and turnover are informational reports. Reports of scientific research, real estate appraisal reports, and feasibility reports by consulting firms are analytical reports.

- **Vertical or lateral reports.** The vertical/lateral classification refers to the directions in which reports travel. Although most reports travel upward in

organizations, many travel downward. Both represent vertical reports and are often referred to as *upward-directed* and *downward-directed* reports. The main function of **vertical reports** is to contribute to management *control*, as shown in Figure 9-2. **Lateral reports**, on the other hand, assist in *coordination* in the organization. A report traveling between units on the same organizational level, as between the production department and the finance department, is lateral.

- **Internal or external reports.** An **internal report**, such as a production or sales report, travels within an organization. An **external report**, such as a company's annual report to stockholders, is prepared for distribution outside an organization.

- **Periodic reports.** **Periodic reports** are issued on regularly scheduled dates. They are generally directed upward and serve management control purposes. Daily, weekly, monthly, quarterly, semiannual, and annual time periods are typical for periodic reports. Preprinted forms and computer-generated data contribute to uniformity of periodic reports.

Figure 9-1   Report Formality Continuum

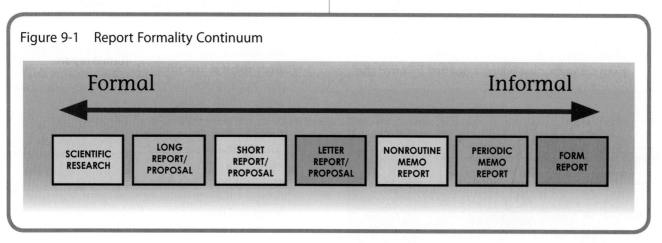

Formal ⟷ Informal

| SCIENTIFIC RESEARCH | LONG REPORT/ PROPOSAL | SHORT REPORT/ PROPOSAL | LETTER REPORT/ PROPOSAL | NONROUTINE MEMO REPORT | PERIODIC MEMO REPORT | FORM REPORT |

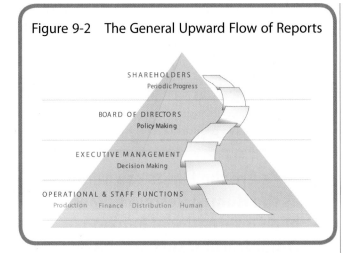

Figure 9-2 The General Upward Flow of Reports

SHAREHOLDERS
Periodic Progress

BOARD OF DIRECTORS
Policy Making

EXECUTIVE MANAGEMENT
Decision Making

OPERATIONAL & STAFF FUNCTIONS
Production   Finance   Distribution   Human

- **Functional reports.** A **functional report** serves a specified purpose within a company. The functional classification includes accounting reports, marketing reports, financial reports, personnel reports, and a variety of other reports that take their functional designation from their ultimate use. For example, a justification of the need for additional personnel or for new equipment is described as a *justification report* in the functional classification.

9-1b Proposals

A **proposal** is a written description of how one organization can meet the needs of another; for example, by providing products or services or solving problems. Businesses issue *calls for bids* that present the specifications for major purchases of goods and certain services. Most governmental and non-profit agencies issue *requests for proposals*, or RFPs. Potential suppliers prepare proposal reports telling how they can meet that need. Those preparing the proposal create a convincing document that will lead to obtaining a contract.

In our information-intensive society, proposal preparation is a major activity for many firms. In fact, some companies hire consultants or designate employees to specialize in proposal writing. Chapter 11 presents proposal preparation in considerable detail.

As you review these report classifications, you will very likely decide—correctly—that almost all reports could be included in these categories. A report may be formal or informal, short or long, informational or analytical, vertically or laterally directed, internal or external, periodic or nonperiodic, functionally labeled, a proposal, or some other combination of these classifications. These report categories are in common use and provide necessary terminology for the study and production of reports.

9-2 Basis for Reports: The Problem-Solving Process

T he upward flow of reports provides management with data that someone might use to make a decision. The purpose is to use the data to solve a problem. Some problems are recurring and call for a steady flow of information; other problems might be unique and call for information on a one-time basis. A problem is the basis for a report. The following steps are used for finding a solution:

1. Recognize and define the problem.
2. Select a method of solution.
3. Collect and organize the data and document the sources.
4. Arrive at an answer.

Only after all four steps have been completed is a report written for presentation. Reports represent an attempt to communicate how a problem was solved. These problem-solving steps are completed *before* the report is written in final form.

9-2a Recognizing and Defining the Problem

Problem-solving research cannot begin until the researchers define the problem. Frequently, those requesting a report will attempt to provide a suitable definition. Nevertheless, researchers should attempt to state the problem clearly and precisely to ensure they are on the right track.

Using Problem Statements, Statements of Purpose, and Hypotheses

The **problem statement**, or statement of the problem, is the particular problem that is to be solved by the research. The **statement of purpose** is the goal of the study and includes the aims or objectives the researcher hopes to accomplish.

functional report
a report that serves a specified purpose within a company

proposal
a written description of how one organization can meet the needs of another

problem statement
the particular problem that is to be solved by the research

statement of purpose
the goal of the study; includes the aims or objectives the researcher hopes to accomplish

Research studies often have both a problem statement and a statement of purpose. For example, a real estate appraiser accepts a client's request to appraise a building to determine its market value. The problem is to arrive at a fair market value for the property. The purpose of the appraisal, however, might be to establish a value for a mortgage loan, to determine the feasibility of adding to the structure, or to assess the financial possibility of demolishing the structure and erecting something else. Thus, the purpose might have much to do with determining what elements to consider in arriving at an answer. In other words, unless you know *why* something is wanted, you might have difficulty knowing *what* is wanted. Once you arrive at the answers to the *what* and *why* questions, you will be on your way to solving the problem.

A **hypothesis** is a statement to be proved or disproved through research. For example, a study of a marketing program might determine whether increased use of social media for marketing purposes would increase sales as compared with current marketing methods. For this problem, the hypothesis could be formulated in this way:

> **Hypothesis:** Sales will increase with the use of social media for marketing purposes as compared with our current marketing methods.

Because the hypothesis tends to be stated in a way that favors one possibility or is prejudiced toward a particular answer, many researchers prefer to state hypotheses in the null form. The *null hypothesis* states that no relationship or difference will be found in the factors being studied, which tends to remove the element of prejudice toward a certain answer. The null hypothesis for the previous example could be written as follows:

> **Null hypothesis:** No significant difference will be found in sales between the use of current marketing methods and the introduction of social media for marketing purposes.

Using the problem/purpose approach, the hypothesis approach, or both, is a choice of the researcher. In many ways, the purpose of a study is determined by the intended use of its results.

Limiting the Scope of the Problem

A major shortcoming that often occurs in research planning is the failure to establish or to recognize desirable limits. The *scope* of the report helps to establish boundaries in which the report will be researched and prepared. Assume, for instance, that you want to study salaries of computer technicians. Imagine the enormity of such a task. Millions of people are employed in computer jobs. Perhaps a thousand or so different types of jobs fall into this classification. Use the *what*, *why*, *when*, *where*, and *who* questions to reduce such a problem to reasonable proportions.

Here Are the Limits You Might Set as the Human Resources Manager of an International Banking Organization, Such as Chase:

What: A study of salaries of computer technicians employed in banking branches

Why: To determine whether salaries in our firm are competitive and consistent

When: Current

Where: United States

Who: Computer technicians employed in banking branches

Now you can phrase the problem this way:

Statement of purpose: *The purpose of this study is to survey salaries of computer technicians employed in banking branches working in the United States to determine whether our salaries are competitive and consistent.*

Note that this process of reducing the problem to a workable size has also established some firm limits to the research. You have limited the problem to current salaries, the particular area, and a certain type of business. Note, too, how important the *why* was in helping to establish the limits. Limiting the problem is "zeroing in on the problem."

In some reports, it is desirable to differentiate between the boundaries that were placed on the project outside the control of the researchers and those that were chosen by the researchers. Boundaries imposed outside the control of the researchers are called *limitations*; they might include the assignment of the topic, allotted budget, and time for completion of the report. These boundaries affect what and how the topic can be researched. Boundaries chosen by the researchers to make the project more manageable are called *delimitations*; they might include the sources and methods chosen for research.

© iStockphoto.com/Mercè Bellera

Plagiarism is the presentation of someone else's ideas or words as your own. To safeguard your reputation against plagiarism charges, be certain to give credit where credit is due. Specifically, provide a citation for each (1) direct quotation and (2) passage from someone else's work that you stated in your own words rather than using the author's words—the words are your own, but the idea is not. To attribute information to another source, develop complete, accurate citations and a reference page according to some recognized referencing method.

9-4b Collecting Data through Surveys

The method of distribution and the makeup of the questionnaire are critical factors in successful survey research.

Selecting a Data Collection Method

Selecting an appropriate data collection method is crucial to effective research. Researchers must consider various factors when selecting an appropriate method for collecting data, as illustrated in Figure 9-5 below.

Developing an Effective Survey Instrument

No matter which survey technique or combination of techniques is used, the way in which the survey instrument is designed and written has much to do with the validity and reliability of results, response rate, and quality of information received.

The construction of the survey instrument—usually a questionnaire or interview guide—is critical to obtaining reliable and valid data. Before developing items for a questionnaire or opinion survey, a researcher should visualize the ways responses will be compiled and included in a final report. Here are some suggestions for developing an effective questionnaire:

- **Provide brief, easy-to-follow directions.** Explain the purpose of the study in a cover letter or in a brief statement at the top of the questionnaire so that the respondents understand your intent. While a screening question might be needed to determine whether the respondent is qualified to answer a set of questions, minimize confusing "skip-and-jump" instructions such as the following:

   If you answered Yes to item 4, skip directly to item 7; if you answered No, explain your reason in items 5 and 6.

Consider using electronic survey systems that advance respondents to the next question based on answers to screening questions.

- **Arrange the items in a logical sequence.** If possible, the sequence should proceed from easy to difficult items; simple, nonthreatening items involve respondents and encourage them to finish. You might group related items such as demographic questions or those that use the same response options (multiple choice, rating scales, open-ended questions).

- **Create an appealing, easy-to-comprehend design.** Use typefaces, bold, underline, and italics to emphasize important ideas. Use text boxes and graphic lines to partition text so that the reader can identify and move through sections quickly.

- **Use short items that ask for a single answer to one idea.** Include only the questions needed to meet the objectives of your study, since long questionnaires affect the return rate negatively.

- **Design questions that are easy to answer and to tabulate.** Participants might not take the time to answer numerous open-ended questions that require essay-style answers. When open-ended questions are included, provide enough space for respondents to answer adequately.

- **Strive to write clear questions that all respondents will interpret in the same way.** Avoid words with imprecise meanings (e.g., several, usually) and specialized terms and difficult words that respondents might not understand. Use accurate translations for each concept presented if other cultures are involved. Provide examples for items that might be difficult to understand.

- **Ask for information that can be recalled readily.** Asking for "old" information might not result in sound data.

> **plagiarism**
> the presentation of someone else's ideas or words as your own

Figure 9-5 Selecting an Appropriate Data Collection Method

METHOD	ADVANTAGES	LIMITATIONS
Mailed surveys	• Are relatively inexpensive to administer • Can reach a wide number of people who complete the survey at their convenience • Allow anonymity, which may produce more honest responses • Remove difference-in-status barriers	• Can be expensive if follow-up mailings are required • Yield a low response rate • Are not useful for obtaining detailed information
Telephone surveys	• Provide inexpensive and rapid data collection • Allow personal contact between interviewer and respondent for clarification or follow-up questions	• Must be relatively short to minimize perceived intrusion and to increase typical small return rate • May exclude respondents with unlisted numbers and those without telephones
Personal interviews	• Are useful to obtain in-depth answers and explore sensitive topics • Allow personal contact between interviewer and respondent for clarification and follow-up questions	• Are time-consuming and resource intensive • Require proper interviewer • Vary in value, depending on quality and consistency of interviewer
Email polling	• Is inexpensive • Provides for easy response • Yields quick results that can be updated electronically as responses are received	• Is limited to respondents with computer access

• **Provide all possible answer choices on multiple-choice items.** Add an "undecided" or "other" category so that respondents are not forced to choose a nonapplicable response.

• **Ask for factual information whenever possible.** Opinions might be needed in certain studies, but

opinions might change daily. As a general rule, the smaller the sample, the less reliable are any conclusions based on opinions.

• **Decide on an optimal number of choices to place on a ranking scale.** Ranking scales, also called Likert scales, allow participants to indicate their opinion on a numbered continuum. When deciding the numbers to place on the scale, consider the tendency of some groups to choose the noncommittal midpoint in a scale with an odd number of response choices (for instance, choosing 3 on a scale from 1 to 5).

- **Avoid questions that might be threatening or awkward to the respondent.** For sensitive issues, such as age and income, allow respondents to select among ranges if possible. Ensure that ranges do not overlap, and provide for all possible selections.

- **Consider the advisability of prompting a forced answer.** A forced answer question can be used to determine which single factor is most critical to a respondent, as shown in the following examples:

Of all the problems listed, which is the single most critical problem for you personally?

Should city taxes be levied to fund a city recreational complex?

❑ *Yes*　　❑ *No*

When using forced choice items, avoid "leading questions" that cause people to answer in a way that is not their true opinion or situation. The following item is an example of such a question:

Have you stopped confronting employees who disagree with your management decisions?

❑ *Yes*　　❑ *No*

- **Include a postage-paid envelope with a mailed questionnaire.** A higher response rate results when this courtesy is provided. Include your return information at the bottom of the questionnaire in the event the envelope is misplaced.

Various types of items can be used in questionnaire design, depending on your purpose and the characteristics of your participants. Figure 9-6 on the next page illustrates the principles of effective questionnaire design.

A final step in questionnaire design is to test the instrument by asking others to complete and critique the questionnaire. For surveys of major importance, researchers typically conduct a pilot study, administering the questionnaire to a small group of the population involved. This process allows them to correct problems in clarity and design, and typically leads to better response and quality of answers. A pilot study might uncover factors affecting your results, which you can

address in the final research design and before conducting the actual survey.

Researchers must select from among the several formats available the one best suited to the situation. Criteria for selecting one alternative over the others might include the following: Which format leaves the least chance for misinterpretation? Which format provides information in the way it can best be used? Can it be tabulated easily? Can it be cross-referenced to other items in the survey instrument?

9-4c Avoiding Data-Gathering Errors

If acceptable data-gathering techniques have been used, data will measure what they are intended to measure (have validity) and will measure it accurately (have reliability). Hopefully, a carefully designed research process will yield useful data for analysis.

> ### Some Common Errors at the Data Gathering Stage:
>
> ☒ Using samples that are too small
> ☒ Using samples that are not representative
> ☒ Using poorly constructed data-gathering instruments
> ☒ Using information from biased sources
> ☒ Failing to gather enough information to cover all important aspects of a problem
> ☒ Gathering too much information

9-4d Documenting Sources of Information

A crucial part of ethical, honest research writing is documenting or referencing sources fairly and accurately. Although time consuming and tedious, careful attention to documentation marks you as a respected, highly professional researcher.

An important first step is to pledge that you will not, for any reason, present someone else's ideas as your own. Then, develop a systematic checklist for avoiding plagiarism. Carelessly forgetting to enclose someone else's words within quotation marks or failing to paraphrase another's words can cause others to question your ethical conduct. When you feel that the tedious work required to document sources fairly and

Figure 9-6   Example of an Effective Questionnaire

1. **Rank the following job factors in order of their importance to you. Add other factors important to you in the space provided.**

		1	2	3	4	5	6	7
a.	Wages	○	○	○	○	○	○	○
b.	Health and retirement benefits	○	○	○	○	○	○	○
c.	Job security	○	○	○	○	○	○	○
d.	Ability to maintain balance between work and family life	○	○	○	○	○	○	○
e.	Creativity and challenge of work assignment	○	○	○	○	○	○	○
f.	Perceived prestige of work	○	○	○	○	○	○	○
g.	[_____]	○	○	○	○	○	○	○
h.	[_____]	○	○	○	○	○	○	○

2. **Which of the following is the single job satisfaction factor that you feel needs more attention in our company? (Please select only one.)**

- ○ Wages
- ○ Health and retirement benefits
- ○ Job security
- ○ Ability to maintain balance between work and family life
- ○ Creativity and challenge of work assignment
- ○ Perceived prestige of work
- ○ Other (specify) [_____ ▼]

3. **How would you rate your overall job satisfaction?**

Very unsatisfied 1	Unsatisfied 2	Somewhat unsatisfied 3	Somewhat satisfied 4	Satisfied 5	Very satisfied 6
○	○	○	○	○	○

4. **How would you rate your overall job satisfaction 12 months ago?**

Very unsatisfied 1	Unsatisfied 2	Somewhat unsatisfied 3	Somewhat satisfied 4	Satisfied 5	Very satisfied 6
○	○	○	○	○	○

5. **Indicate your age group:**

- ○ 20–29
- ○ 30–39
- ○ 40–49
- ○ 50–59
- ○ 60–69
- ○ 70 years and over

6. **Indicate your time with the company:**

- ○ Less than 1 year
- ○ 1–3 years
- ○ 4–6 years
- ○ 7–10 years
- ○ Over 10 years

7. **What could the company do to enhance your satisfaction as a company employee?**

[_____]

Thanks for your participation. Click to submit your questionnaire.

[Submit]

Callout annotations:

- Uses variety of items to elicit different types of responses.
- Uses clear, concise language to minimize confusion.
- Provides clear instructions for answering each item.
- Provides additional lines to allow for individual opinions.
- Provides even number of rating choices to eliminate "fence" responses.
- Asks for easily recalled information.
- Provides nonoverlapping categories of response and open-ended final category.

Format Pointers
Provides adequate space for answering open-ended item.

Keeps length as short as possible while meeting survey objectives.

Includes instructions for submitting completed questionnaire.

4LTR Press solutions are designed for today's learners through the continuous feedback of students like you. Tell us what you think about BCOM5 and help us improve the learning experience for future students.

YOUR FEEDBACK MATTERS.

Complete the Speak Up
survey in CourseMate at
www.cengagebrain.com

Follow us at
www.facebook.com/4ltrpress

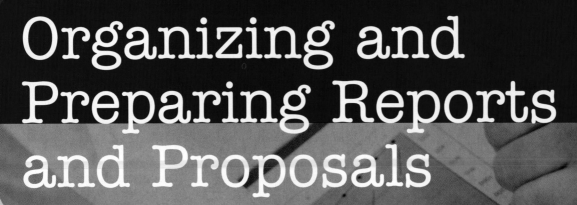

Organizing and Preparing Reports and Proposals

the report itself. The three basic addenda parts are the references, appendices, and index. Addenda parts continue with the same page numbering system used in the body of the report.

References

The references (also called *works cited* or *bibliography*) section is an alphabetical listing of the sources used in preparing the report. Because the writer may be influenced by any information consulted, some reference manuals require all sources consulted to be included in the reference list. When the reference list includes sources not cited in the report, it is referred to as a *bibliography* or a list of *works consulted*. If a report includes endnotes rather than in-text parenthetical citations (author and date within the text), the endnotes precede the references. Using word processing software to create footnotes and endnotes reduces much of the effort of preparing accurate documentation.

Appendix

An appendix contains supplementary information that supports the report but is not appropriate for inclusion in the report itself. This information may include questionnaires and accompanying transmittal letters, summary tabulations, verbatim comments from respondents, complex mathematical computations and formulas, legal documents, and a variety of items the writer presents to support the body of the report and the quality of the research. Placing supplementary material in an appendix helps prevent the report body from becoming excessively-long.

If the report contains more than one appendix, label each with a capital letter and a title. For example, the two appendices (or appendixes) in a report could be identified as follows:

> **Appendix A: Cover Letter Accompanying**
> **Customer Satisfaction Survey**
>
> **Appendix B: Customer Satisfaction Survey**

Each item included in the appendix must be mentioned in the report. A reference within the report to the two appendices mentioned in the previous example might appear as follows:

> **The cover message (Appendix A) and the**
> **customer satisfaction survey (Appendix B)**
> **were distributed by email to 1,156 firms on**
> **February 15, 2013.**

There is a different image for this spec, same credit

Index

The index is an alphabetical guide to the subject matter in a report. The subject and each page number on which the subject appears are listed. Word-processing software can generate the index automatically. Each time a new draft is prepared, a new index with revised terms and correct page numbers can be generated quickly and easily.

11-2 Organization of Formal Reports

The authors of certain types of publications known as tabloids typically have no valid documentation to support their claims, so they make up their own support. Hopefully, absolutely no one believes them. The purpose of such publications is to entertain, not to inform. The writer of a bona fide report, however, must do a much more convincing and thorough job of reporting.

11-2a Writing Convincing and Effective Reports

As discussed in Chapter 9, reports often require you to conduct research to find quotes, statistics, or ideas from others to back up the ideas presented. This support from outside sources serves to bolster the research as well as your credibility. Doing research and taking notes, however, are only parts of the process of putting together a well-documented, acceptable report. Careful organization and formatting ensure that the reader will understand and comprehend the information presented. While many companies have their own style manuals that give examples of acceptable formats for reports, this section presents some general organization guidelines.

Outlining and Sequencing

The content outline serves as a framework on which to build the report. In the development of the outline, the writer identifies the major and minor points that are to be covered and organizes them into a logical sequence. Outlining is an essential prerequisite to writing the report. The outline is a planning document and is thus subject to modification as the writer develops the report.

Developing an outline requires the writer to think about the information to be presented and how it can best be organized for the clear understanding of the reader. Assume, for instance, you must select the type of Internet service for employees to use in a new start-up company. You are deciding between installing Ethernet cabling or a wireless system. You must choose the Internet system that will best serve portable computing needs of a small company and present your reasons and recommendations in a **justification report**.

You gather all available information from suppliers of the two Internet systems, research their use in companies of similar size, and compare the two against a variety of criteria. Your final selection is a wireless system. Why did you select it? What criteria served as decision guides? When you write the report, you will have to tell the reader—the one who will pay for the equipment—how the selection was made so that he or she is "sold" on your conclusion.

If you organize your report so that you tell the reader everything

justification report
a report that outlines comparative information clearly to the reader; used commonly when comparing items for purchase

about the two systems—wireless versus Ethernet—each in a separate section, the reader may have trouble making comparisons. Your content outline might look like this:

I.   **Introduction**
   A.   **The Problem**
   B.   **The Method Used**
II. **Wireless Internet**
III. **Ethernet**
IV. **Conclusion**

Note that this outline devotes two Roman numeral sections to the findings, one to the introduction that presents the problem and the method, and one to the conclusion. This division is appropriate because the most space must be devoted to the findings. However, the reader may have difficulty comparing the Internet service because the information is in two different places. Would discussing the differences in Internet service in the same section of the report be better? Would prices be compared more easily if they were all in the same section? Most reports should be divided into sections that reflect the criteria used rather than into sections devoted to the alternatives compared.

If you selected your service based on cost, service/warranties, expandability, and availability of applications, these criteria (rather than the Internet systems themselves) might serve as divisions of the findings. Then your content outline would appear this way:

I.   **Introduction**
   A.   **The Problem**
   B.   **The Methods Used**
II. **Product Comparison**
   A.   **Wireless Is Least Expensive**
   B.   **Ethernet Is More Reliable**
   C.   **Wireless Is More Convenient**
   D.   **Ethernet Is Costly to Maintain**
III. **Conclusion: Wireless Internet Is the Best Choice**

The outline now has three major sections, with the product comparison consisting of four subsections. When the report is prepared in this way, the features of each Internet system (the evaluation criteria) are compared in the same section, and the reader is led logically to the conclusion.

hfng/Shutterstock.com

Designing and Delivering Business Presentations

OBJECTIVES

12-1 Plan a business presentation that accomplishes the speaker's goals and meets the audience's needs.

12-2 Organize and develop the three parts of an effective presentation.

12-3 Select, design, and use presentation visuals effectively.

12-4 Deliver speeches with increasing confidence.

12-5 Discuss strategies for presenting in alternate delivery situations such as culturally diverse audiences, teams, and distance presentations.

12-1 Planning an Effective Business Presentation

The simplicity of writing email and talking on the phone has deterred many workers from learning to communicate in front of people with authority and authenticity.[1] Being a skilled business communicator requires skill in both writing and speaking. A business presentation is an important means of exchanging information for decision making and policy development, relating the benefits of the services offered, and sharing our goals, values, and vision. Because multiple people receive the message at the same time and are able to provide immediate feedback for clarification, presentations can significantly reduce message distortion and misunderstanding.

Many of the presentations you give will be formal, with sufficient time allowed for planning and developing elaborate visual support. You might present information and recommendations to external audiences such as customers and clients whom you've never met or to an internal audience made up of coworkers and managers you know well. You can also expect to present some less formal presentations, often referred to as **oral briefings**. An oral briefing might entail a short update on a current project requested during a meeting without advance notice or a brief explanation in the hallway when your supervisor walks past. Sales representatives give oral briefings daily as they present short, informal pitches for new products and services.

Regardless of the formality of the presentation, the time given to prepare, the nature of the audience (friends or strangers), or the media used (live, distant, Web, or DVD delivery on demand), your success depends on your ability to think on your feet and speak confidently as you address audience needs. Understanding the purpose you hope to achieve through your presentation and conceptualizing your audience will enable you to organize the content in a way the audience can understand *and* accept.

12-1a Identify Your Purpose

Determining what you want to accomplish during a presentation is a fundamental principle of planning an effective presentation. Some speech coaches recommend completing the following vital sentence to lay the foundation for a successful presentation: "At the end of my presentation, the audience will _____." In his book *Do's and Taboos of Public Speaking*, Axtell provides two excellent mechanisms for condensing your presentation into a brief, achievable purpose that will direct you in identifying and supporting the major points:[2]

- Ask yourself, "What is my message?" Then, develop a phrase, a single thought, or a conclusion you want the audience to take with them from the presentation. This elementary statement will likely be the final sentence in your presentation—the basic message you want the audience to remember.

- Imagine a member of your audience has been asked to summarize your message. Ideally, you want to hear them describe your central purpose.

12-1b Know Your Audience

A common mistake for many presenters is to presume they know the audience without attempting to find out about them. If you expect to get results, you

oral briefings
informal presentations prepared and presented with little time for planning and developing

must commit the time to know your audience and focus your presentation on them—from planning your speech to practicing its delivery.

As a general rule, audiences *do* want to be in tune with a speaker. Yet people listen to speeches about things of interest to them. "What's in it for me?" is the question most listeners ask. A speech about global warming to a farm group should address the farmers' problems, for example, and not focus on theories of global warming. Additionally, different strategies are needed for audiences who think and make decisions differently. For instance, different strategies are needed for making a successful presentation to sell software to a group of lawyers than to a group of doctors. Lawyers typically think quickly and are argumentative and decisive while doctors are often cautious, skeptical, and don't make quick purchasing decisions.[3]

To deliver a presentation that focuses on the wants and expectations of an audience, you must determine who they are, what motivates them, how they think, and how they make decisions. Helpful information you can obtain about most audiences includes ages, genders, occupations, educational levels, attitudes, values, broad and specific interests, and needs. In addition, you should also consider certain things about the occasion and location. Patriotic speeches to a group of military veterans will differ from speeches to a group of new recruits, just as Fourth of July speeches will differ from Veterans Day speeches. Seek answers to the following questions when you discuss your speaking engagement with someone representing the group or audience:

1. *Who* is the audience and *who* requested the presentation? General characteristics of the audience should be considered, as well as the extent of their knowledge and experience with the topic, attitude toward the topic and you as a credible speaker, anticipated response to the use of electronic media, and required or volunteer attendance.

2. *Why* is this topic important to the audience? What will the audience do with the information presented?

3. *What* environmental factors affect the presentation?
   - How many will be in the audience?
   - Will I be the only speaker? If not, where does my presentation fit in the program? What time of day?
   - How much time will I be permitted? Minimum? Maximum?
   - What are the seating arrangements? How far will the audience be from the speaker? Will a microphone or other equipment be available?

Answers to these questions reveal whether the speaking environment will be intimate or remote, whether the audience is likely to be receptive and alert or nonreceptive and tired, and whether you will need to use additional motivational or persuasive techniques.

12-2 Organizing the Content

With an understanding of the purpose of your business presentation—why you are giving it and what you hope to achieve—and a conception of the size, interest, and background of the audience, you are prepared to outline your presentation and identify appropriate content. First introduced by famous speech trainer Dale Carnegie and still recommended by speech experts today, the simple but effective presentation format includes an introduction, a body, and a closing. In the introduction, tell the audience what you are going to tell them; in the body, tell them; and in the closing, tell them what you told them.

Although this design might sound repetitive, it works quite well. The audience processes information verbally and cannot slow the speaker down when information is complex. Thus, repetition aids the listener in processing the information that supports the speaker's purpose.

12-2a Introduction

What you say at the beginning sets the stage for your entire presentation and initiates your rapport with the audience. However, inexperienced speakers often settle for unoriginal and overused introductions, such as "My name is …, and my topic is …" or "It is a pleasure …," or negative statements, such as apologies for lack of preparation, boring delivery, or late arrival, that reduce the audience's desire to listen. An effective introduction accomplishes the following goals:

- **Captures attention and involves the audience.** Choose an attention-getter that is relevant to the subject and appropriate for the situation.

> ## Attention-Getting Techniques Might Include:
>
> - A shocking statement or startling statistic.
> - A quotation by an expert or well-known person.
> - A rhetorical or open-ended question that generates discussion from the audience.
> - An appropriate joke or humor.
> - A demonstration or dramatic presentation aid.
> - An anecdote or timely story from a business periodical.
> - A personal reference, compliment to the audience, or a reference to the occasion of the presentation.

To involve the audience directly, ask for a show of hands in response to a direct question, allow the audience time to think about the answer to a rhetorical question, or explain why the information is important and how it will benefit the listeners. Consider the following examples.

A drug awareness speech to young people might begin with a true story:

> **"I was a medical student with dreams of becoming a surgeon, then I began to use street drugs to stay awake, first, to study for exams and later during my internship. Then I began to use prescription drugs I stole from the hospital where I worked. Eventually, it all came crashing down, ending my dream of becoming a doctor."**

A report presenting a plan for merger could introduce the subject and set the stage for the findings (inductive sequence) or the recommendation (deductive sequence):

Inductive: "While investigating options to put our excess funds to work, a management team recommended that we acquire a firm that would enable us to enter the lucrative energy development field."

Deductive: "By acquiring an alternative energy development company, we can invest stockpiled funds and diversify our product and service offerings by entering the lucrative energy industry."

- **Establishes rapport.** Initiate rapport with the listeners; convince them that you are concerned that they benefit from the presentation and that you are qualified to speak on the topic. You might share a personal story that relates to the topic but reveals something about yourself, or discuss your background or a specific experience with the topic being discussed.

- **Presents the purpose statement and previews the points that will be developed.** To maintain the interest you have captured, present your purpose statement directly so that the audience is certain to hear it. Use original statements and avoid clichés such as "My topic today is …" or "I'd like to talk with you about …"

> **"Communication skills are consistently identified as the key to management and organizational success. Our online certificate program will help you to enhance your professional communication skills better enabling you to vie for management positions in your organization."**

Next, preview the major points you will discuss in the order you will discuss them. For example, you might say, "First, I'll discuss … , then … , and finally … ."

Revealing the presentation plan will help the audience understand how the parts of the body are tied together to support the purpose statement, thus increasing their understanding. For a long, complex presentation, you might display a presentation visual that lists the points in the order they will be covered. As you begin each major point, display a slide that contains that point and perhaps a related image. These section slides partition your presentation just as headings do in a written report, and thus move the listener more easily from one major point to the next.

12-2b Body

In a typical presentation of 20 to 30 minutes, limit your presentation to only a few major points (typically three to five) to combat time constraints and your audience's ability to concentrate and absorb. Making every statement in a presentation into a major point—something to be remembered—is impossible, unless the presentation lasts only two or three minutes.

Once you have selected your major points, locate your supporting material. You can use several techniques to ensure the audience understands your point and to reinforce it:

- **Provide support in a form that is easy to understand.** Three techniques will assist you in accomplishing this goal:

    1. **Use simple vocabulary and short sentences that the listener can understand easily and that sound conversational and interesting.** Spoken communication is more difficult to process than written communication; therefore, complex, varied vocabulary and long sentences often included in written documents are not effective in a presentation.

    2. **Avoid jargon or technical terms that the listeners might not understand.** Instead, use plain English that the audience can easily comprehend. Make your speech more interesting and memorable by using word pictures to make your points. Matt Hughes, a speech consultant, provides this example: "If your message is a warning of difficulties ahead, you might say: 'We're climbing a hill that's getting steeper, and there are rocks and potholes in the road.'"⁴

    3. **Use a familiar frame of reference.** Drawing analogies between new ideas and familiar ones is another technique for generating understanding. For example, noting that the U.S. blog-reading audience is already one-half the size of the newspaper-reading population helps clarify an abstract or complex concept. Saying that "infodumping" is the verbal equivalent of email spam explains well the expected consequences of overloading an audience with too many details.⁵

- **Provide relevant statistics.** Provide statistics or other quantitative measures to lend authority and credibility to your points. A word of warning: Do not overwhelm your audience with excessive statistics. Instead, round off numbers and use broad terms or word pictures that the listener can remember. Instead of "68.2 percent" say "more than two-thirds;" instead of "112 percent rise in production" say "our output more than doubled."

- **Use quotes from prominent people.** Comments made by other authorities are helpful in establishing credibility.

- **Use interesting anecdotes.** Audiences like and remember anecdotes or interesting stories that tie into the presentation and make strong emotional connections. In her book *Whoever Tells the Best Story Wins*, Annette Simmons stresses that when telling stories, the storyteller allows the audience to feel his or her presence and reveals a trace of humanity, which is vital for developing understanding, influence, and strong relationships with the audience. She encourages leaders to craft personal stories into specific, intentional messages that communicate values, vision, and important lessons.⁶ While communicating their values, leaders communicate the values they expect from employees. As with jokes, be sure you can get straight to the point of a story.

- **Use jokes and humor appropriately.** A joke or humor can create a special bond between you and the audience, ease your approach to sensitive subjects, disarm a nonreceptive audience, or make your message easier to understand and remember. Plan your joke carefully so that you can (1) get the point across as quickly as possible, (2) deliver it in a conversational manner with interesting inflections and effective body movements, and (3) deliver the punch line effectively. If you cannot tell a joke well, use humor instead—amusing things that happened to you or someone you know, one-liners, or humorous quotations that relate to your presentation. Refrain from any humor that reflects negatively on race, color, religion, gender, age, culture, or other personal areas of sensitivity.

- **Use presentation visuals.** Presentation visuals, such as handouts, whiteboards, flip charts, transparencies, electronic presentations, and demonstrations, enhance the effectiveness of the presentation. Develop presentation visuals that will enable your audience to see, hear, and even experience your presentation.

- **Encourage audience involvement.** Skilled presenters involve their audiences through techniques such as asking reflective questioning, role playing, directing audience-centered activities, and incorporating current events or periodicals that tie directly to the message. One communications coach's advice for getting an audience "to sit up and listen" is to make

next and time for your audience to absorb your idea. Presenting an idea (sound bite) and then pausing briefly is an effective way to influence your audience positively. The listener will not notice the slight delay, and the absence of meaningless words will make you appear more confident and polished. Also avoid annoying speech habits, such as clearing your throat or coughing, that shift the audience's attention from the speech to the speaker.

The following activities will help you achieve good vocal qualities:

- **Breathe properly and relax.** Nervousness affects normal breathing patterns and is reflected in vocal tone and pitch. The better prepared you are, the better your phonation will be. Although relaxing might seem difficult to practice before a speech, a few deep breaths, just as swimmers take before diving, can help.

- **Listen to yourself.** A recording of your voice reveals much about pitch, intensity, and duration. Most people are amazed to find their voices are not quite what they had expected. "I never dreamed I sounded that bad" is a common reaction. Nasal twangs usually result from a failure to speak from the diaphragm, which involves taking in and letting out air through the larynx, where the vocal cords operate. High pitch can occur from the same cause, or it can be a product of speaking too fast or experiencing stage fright.

- **Develop flexibility.** A good speaking voice is somewhat musical, with words and sounds similar to notes in a musical scale. Read each of the following sentences aloud and emphasize the *italicized* word in each. Even though the sentences are identical, emphasizing different words changes the meaning.

I am happy you are here.	*Maybe I'm the only happy one.*
I am happy you are here.	*I really am.*
I am happy you are here.	*Happy best describes my feeling.*
I am happy you are here.	*Yes, you especially.*
I am happy you are here.	*You may not be happy, but I am.*
I am happy you are here.	*Here and not somewhere else.*

Articulation involves smooth, fluent, and pleasant speech. It results from the way in which a speaker produces and joins sounds. Faulty articulation is often caused by not carefully forming individual sounds. Common examples include:

- dropping word endings—saying workin' for working

- running words together—saying kinda for kind of, gonna for going to

- imprecise enunciation—saying dis for this, wid for with, dem for them, pin for pen, or pitcher for picture

These examples should not be confused with *dialect*, which people informally call an *accent*. A dialect is a variation in pronunciation, usually of vowels, from one part of the country to another. Actually, everyone speaks a dialect; speech experts can often identify, even pinpoint, the section of the country from where a speaker comes. In the United States, common dialects are New England, New York, Southern, Texan, Mid-Western, and so forth. Within each of these, minor dialects often arise regionally or from immigrant influence. The simple fact is that when people interact, they influence each other even down to speech sounds. Many prominent speakers have developed a rather universal dialect, known as Standard American Speech or American Broadcast English, that seems to be effective no matter who the audience is. This model for professional language is widely used by newscasters and announcers and is easily understood by those who speak English as a second language because they likely listened to this speech pattern on television as they learned the language.

You can improve the clarity of your voice, reduce strain and voice distortion, and increase your expressiveness by following these guidelines:

- **Stand up straight with your shoulders back and breathe from your diaphragm rather than your chest.** If you are breathing correctly, you can then use your mouth and teeth to form sounds precisely. For example, vowels are always sounded with the mouth open and the tongue clear of the palate. Consonants are responsible primarily for the distinctness of speech and are formed by an interference with or stoppage of outgoing breath.

- **Focus on completing the endings of all words, not running words together, and enunciating words correctly.** To identify recurring enunciation errors, listen to a recording and seek feedback from others.

- **Obtain formal training to improve your speech.** Pursue a self-study program by purchasing recordings that help you reduce your dialect and move more closely to a universal dialect. You can also enroll in a diction course to improve your speech patterns or arrange for private lessons from a voice coach.

articulation
smooth, fluent, and pleasant speech

pronunciation
using principles of phonetics to create accurate sounds, rhythm, stress, and intonation

Pronunciation involves using principles of phonetics to create accurate sounds, rhythm, stress, and intonation. People might articulate perfectly but still mispronounce words. A dictionary provides the best source to review pronunciation. Two pronunciations are often given for a word, the first one being the desired pronunciation and the second an acceptable variation. An American adopting a pronunciation commonly used in England, such as *shedule* for *schedule* or *a-gane* for *again*, could be seen negatively. In some cases, leeway exists in pronunciation. The first choice for pronouncing *data* is to pronounce the first *a* long, as in *date*; but common usage is fast making pronunciation of the short *a* sound, as in *cat*, acceptable. Likewise, the preferred pronunciation of *often* is with a silent *t*. Good speakers use proper pronunciation and refer to the dictionary frequently in both pronunciation and vocabulary development.

When your voice qualities combine to make your messages pleasingly receptive, your primary concerns revolve around developing an effective delivery style.

12-4c Delivery Style

Speaking effectively is both an art and a skill. Careful planning and practice are essential for increasing speaking effectiveness.

Before the Presentation

Follow these guidelines when preparing for your presentation:

- **Prepare thoroughly.** You can expect a degree of nervousness as you anticipate speaking before a group. This natural tension is constructive because it increases your concentration and your energy and enhances your performance. Even Kara DioGuardi, a fourth judge added to the 2009 *American Idol* season, admitted being nervous as she adjusted to giving short, meaningful advice in front of 30 million people on the most-watched TV show in the nation.[13]

  Being well prepared is the surest way to control speech anxiety. Develop an outline for your presentation that supports your purpose and addresses the needs of your audience, and take advantage of every opportunity to gain speaking experience.

- **Prepare effective presentation support tools.** Follow the guidelines presented in the preceding section to select and design visuals, handouts, and notes pages appropriate for your audience and purpose. Additionally, develop a contingency plan in the event of technical difficulties with computer equipment, such as hard copies of the slides or a backup computer pre-loaded and ready. Arrive early so you can troubleshoot unexpected technological glitches. Despite your degree of planning, however, technical problems might occur during your presentation. Remain calm and correct them as quickly and

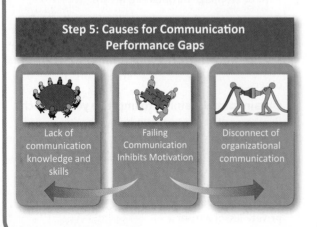

Figure 12-3 Causes for Communication Performance Gaps

- Lack of communication knowledge and skills
- Failing communication inhibits motivation
- Disconnect of organizational communication

Step 5: Causes for Communication Performance Gaps

Lack of communication knowledge and skills

Failing Communication Inhibits Motivation

Disconnect of organizational communication

© Yuri Arcurs/Shutterstock

"Never, never, never give a speech on a subject you don't believe in. You'll fail. On the other hand, if you prepare properly, know your material, and believe in it … your audience will not only hear but feel your message."
—John Davis, a successful speech coach[14]

professionally as you can. Take heart in the fact that Bill Gates' computer once crashed when he introduced a new version of Windows!

- **Practice, but do not rehearse.** Your goal is to become familiar with the key phrases on your note cards so that you can deliver the presentation naturally as if you are talking with the audience—not reciting the presentation or acting out a role. Avoid overpracticing, which can make your presentation sound mechanical and limit your ability to respond to the audience.

- **Practice the entire presentation.** This practice will allow you to identify (1) flaws in organization or unity, (2) long, complex sentences or ineffective expressions, and (3) "verbal potholes." Verbal potholes include word combinations that could cause you to stumble, words you have trouble pronouncing ("irrelevant" or "statistics"), and words that accentuate your dialect ("get" can sound like "git" regardless of the intention of a Southern speaker).

- **Spend additional time practicing the introduction and conclusion.** You will want to deliver these important parts with finesse while making a confident connection with the audience. A good closing leaves the audience in a good mood and can help overcome some possible weaknesses during the speech. Depending on the techniques used, consider memorizing significant brief statements to ensure their accuracy and impact (e.g., direct quotation, exact statistic, etc.).

- **Practice displaying presentation visuals so that your delivery appears effortless and seamless.** Your goal is to make the technology virtually transparent, positioned in the background to support *you* as the primary focus of the presentation. First, be sure you know basic commands for advancing through your presentation without displaying distracting menus. Develop skill in returning to a specific slide in the event of a computer glitch or an audience question.

- **Seek feedback on your performance to help you to polish your delivery and improve organization.** Critique your own performance by practicing in front of a mirror and evaluating a recording of your presentation. If possible, present to a small audience ahead of time for feedback and to minimize anxiety when presenting to the real audience.

- **Request a lectern to hold your notes and to steady a shaky hand, at least until you gain some confidence and experience.** Keep in mind, though, that weaning yourself from the lectern will eliminate a physical barrier between you and the audience. Without the lectern, you will speak more naturally. If you are using a microphone, ask for a portable microphone so that you can move freely.

- **Request a proper introduction if the audience knows little about you.** An effective introduction will establish your credibility as a speaker on the subject and will make the audience eager to hear you. You can prepare your own introduction as professional speakers do, or you can provide concise, targeted information that answers these three questions: (1) Why is the subject relevant? (2) Who is the speaker? and (3) What credentials qualify the speaker to talk about the subject? Talk with the person introducing you to verify any information, especially the pronunciation of your name, and to review the format of the presentation (time limit, question-and-answer period, etc.). Be certain to thank the person who made the introduction as you begin your presentation. "Thank you for your kind introduction, Ms. Garcia" is adequate. Then, follow with your own introduction to your presentation topic.

- **Dress appropriately to create a strong professional image and to bolster your self-confidence.** An audience's initial impression of your personal appearance, your clothing and grooming, affects their ability to accept you as a credible speaker. Because first impressions are difficult to overcome, take time to groom yourself immaculately and to select clothing that is appropriate for the speaking occasion and consistent with the audience's expectations.

- **Arrive early to become familiar with the setup of the room and to check the equipment.** Check the location of your chair, the lectern, the projection screen, light switches, and electrical outlets. Check the microphone and Internet connection and ensure that all equipment is in the appropriate place and working properly. Project your electronic presentation so you can adjust the color scheme to ensure maximum readability. Finally, identify the technician who will be responsible for resolving any technical problems that might occur during the presentation.

During the Presentation

The following are things you can do during your presentation to increase your effectiveness as a speaker:

- **Communicate confidence, warmth, and enthusiasm for the presentation and the time spent with the audience.** "Your listeners won't care how much you know until they know how much you care," is pertinent advice.[15]

- **Exhibit a confident appearance with alert posture.** Stand tall with your shoulders back and your stomach tucked in. Stand in the "ready position"—no slouching, hunching over the lectern, or rocking. Keep weight forward with knees slightly flexed so you are ready to move easily rather than rooted rigidly in one spot, hiding behind the lectern.

- **Smile genuinely throughout the presentation.** Pause as you take your place behind the lectern, and smile before you speak the first word. Smile as you finish your presentation and wait for the applause.

- **Maintain steady eye contact with the audience in random places throughout the room.** Stay with one person approximately three to five seconds—long enough to finish a complete thought or sentence to convince the listener you are communicating individually with him or her. If the audience is large, select a few friendly faces and concentrate on speaking to them rather than to a sea of nondescript faces.

- **Refine gestures to portray a relaxed, approachable appearance.** Vary hand motions to emphasize important points; otherwise, let hands fall naturally to your side. Practice using only one hand to make points unless you specifically need two hands, such as when drawing a figure or showing dimensions or location. Eliminate any nervous gestures that can distract the audience (e.g., clenching your hands in front of or behind your body, steepling your hands, placing your hands in your pockets, jingling keys or change, or playing with a ring or pen).

- **Move from behind the lectern and toward the audience to reduce the barrier created between you and the audience.** You can stand to one side and casually present a relaxed pose beside the lectern. However, avoid methodically walking without a purpose.

- **Exercise strong vocal qualities.** Review the guidelines provided for using your voice to project confidence and credibility.

- **Watch your audience.** They will tell you how you are doing and whether you should shorten your speech. Be attentive to negative feedback in the form of talking, coughing, moving chairs, and other signs of discomfort.

- **Use your visuals effectively.** Many speakers will go to a great deal of effort to prepare good presentation visuals—and then not use them effectively. Inexperienced speakers often ignore the visual altogether or fall into the habit of simply nodding their heads toward the visual. Neither of these techniques is adequate for involving the audience with the visual. In fact, if the material is complex, the speaker is likely to lose the audience completely.

- **Step to one side of the visual so the audience can see it.** Use a pointer if necessary. Direct your remarks to the audience, so that you can maintain eye contact and resist the temptation to look over your shoulder or turn your back to read the information from the screen behind you.

- **Paraphrase the visual rather than reading it line for line.** To increase the quality of your delivery, develop a workable method of recording what you plan to say about each graphic.

- **Handle questions from the audience during the presentation.** Questions often disrupt carefully laid plans. At the same time, questions provide feedback, clarify points, and ensure understanding. When people ask questions that will be answered later in the presentation, say, "I believe the next slide will clarify that point; if not, we will come back to it." If the question can be answered quickly, you should do so while indicating that it will also be covered more later.

  Anticipate and prepare for questions that might be raised. You can generate presentation visuals pertaining to certain anticipated questions and display them only if the question is posed. An audience will appreciate your thorough and complete explanation and your ability to adjust your presentation to their needs—this strategy is much more professional than stumbling through an explanation or delaying the answer until the information is available. Speakers giving electronic presentations have ready access to enormous amounts of information that can be displayed instantly for audience discussion. Hyperlinks created within a presentation file will move a speaker instantaneously to a specific slide, another file, or an embedded music or video file.

- **Keep within the time limit.** Be prepared to complete the presentation within the allotted time. In many organizations, speakers have one or more rehearsals before delivering reports to a group such as a board of directors. These rehearsals, or dry runs, are made before other executives, and are critiqued, timed, revised, and rehearsed again. Presentation software makes rehearsing your timing as simple as clicking a button and advancing through the slides as you practice. By evaluating the total presentation time and the time spent on each slide, you can modify the presentation and rehearse it again until the presentation fits the time slot.

Become proficient in delivering and participating through distance technology.

• improving employees' quality of life by reducing travel time that often cuts into personal time (e.g., Saturday night layovers for a reasonable airfare)

Internet conferencing, or *webcasting*, allows a company to conduct a presentation in real time over the Internet simultaneously with a conference telephone call. Because it runs on each participant's Internet browser, a presentation can reach hundreds of locations at once. While listening to the call, participants can go to a designated Web site and view slides or a PowerPoint presentation that is displayed in sync with the speaker's statements being heard on the phone. Participants key comments and questions in chat boxes or press a keypad system to respond to an audience poll, thus giving valuable feedback without interrupting the speaker.

Companies deliver live Web presentations on issues ranging from internal briefings on new developments and organizational and procedural changes to product strategy and training presentations. Ernst & Young uses Web presentations to announce organizational changes and has found it to be an effective alternative to memos and emails that weren't always remembered or understood. People most affected by an organizational change are able to interact with leaders announcing the change.

Follow these guidelines for adapting your presentation skills to videoconferences and Web presentations:

• **Determine whether a distance delivery method is appropriate for the presentation.** Is the presentation purpose suited to the technology? Can costs in time, money, and human energy be justified? Are key people willing and able to participate? For example, a videoconference for a formal presentation such as an important speech by the CEO to a number of locations justifies the major expense and brings attention to the importance of the message. Distance delivery formats are inappropriate for presentations that cover highly sensitive or confidential issues, for persuasive or problem-solving meetings where no relationship has been established among the participants, and whenever participants are unfamiliar with and perhaps unsupportive of the technology.

• **Establish rapport with the participants prior to the distance presentation.** If possible, meet with or phone participants beforehand to get to know them and gain insights about their attitudes. This rapport will enhance your ability to interpret subtle nonverbal cues and to cultivate the relationship further through the distance format. Emailing or faxing a short questionnaire or posting presentation slides with a request for questions is an excellent way to establish a connection with participants and to ensure that the presentation is tailored to audience needs. Some enterprising distance presenters engage participants in email discussions before the presentation and then use this dialogue to develop positive interaction during the presentation.

• **Become proficient in delivering and participating through distance technology.** Begin by becoming familiar with the equipment and the surroundings. Although technical support staff might be available to manage equipment and transmission tasks, your goal is to concentrate on the contribution you are to make and not your intimidation with the delivery method.

• **Concentrate on projecting positive nonverbal messages.** Keep a natural, friendly expression; relax and smile. Avoid the tendency to stare into the camera. Instead, look naturally at the entire audience as you would in a live presentation. Speak clearly with as much energy as you can. If a lag occurs between the video and audio transmission, adjust your timing to avoid interrupting other speakers. Use gestures to reinforce

Internet conferencing
a method of real-time conferencing that allows a company to conduct a presentation in real time over the Internet simultaneously with a conference telephone call; also called *webcasting*

points, but avoid fast or excessive motion that will appear blurry. Avoid side conversations, coughing, and clearing your throat, which could trigger voice-activated microphones. Pay close attention to other presenters to guard against easy distraction in a distance environment and to capture subtle nonverbal cues. You will need to judge the vocal tone of the person asking a question because you might not see faces.

- **Adjust camera settings to enhance communication.** Generally, adjust the camera so that all participants can be seen, but zoom in more closely on participants when you wish to clearly observe nonverbal language. Project a wide-angle shot of yourself during rapport-building comments at the presentation's beginning and zoom in to signal the start of the agenda or to emphasize an important point during the presentation. Some systems accommodate a split screen, but others allow participants to view either you or your presentation visuals only. You will want to switch the camera between a view of you and your visuals, depending on what is needed at the time.
- **Develop high-quality graphics appropriate for the particular distance format.** Even more than in a live presentation, you will need graphics to engage and maintain participants' attention. Graphics are a welcome variation to the "talking head"—you—displayed on the screen for long periods. Some

companies provide assistance from a webmaster or graphics support staff in preparing slide shows specifically for distance presentations. Also, e-conferencing companies will develop and post presentation slides and host live Web presentations including managing email messages and audience polling. Regardless of the support you receive, you should understand basic guidelines for preparing effective visuals for videoconferencing and Web presentations.

- **Videoconferences.** Readability of text will be a critical issue when displaying visuals during a videoconference because text becomes fuzzy when transmitted through compressed video. Select large, sturdy fonts and choose a color scheme that provides high contrast between the background and the text. Stay with a tested color scheme such as dark blue background, yellow title text, and white bulleted list text to ensure readability. Projecting your visuals ahead of time so you can adjust the color scheme, font selections, and other design elements is an especially good idea.
- **Web presentations.** In addition to considering overall appeal, clarity, and readability, Web presentations must be designed for minimal load time and compatibility with various computers. For your first presentation, consider using a Web template in your electronic presentations software and experiment with the appropriateness of other designs as you gain experience.

Stand-alone presentations designed specifically for Web delivery require unique design strategies to compensate for the absence of a speaker.[21]

- Consider posting text-based explanations in the notes view area or adding vocal narration.
- Develop interactive slide formats that allow viewers to navigate to the most useful information in your presentation. For example, design an agenda slide that includes hyperlinks to the first slide in each section of the presentation.
- Select simple, high-quality graphics that convey ideas effectively.
- Plan limited animation that focuses audience attention on specific ideas on the slide.
- Consider adding video if bandwidth is not an issue.

© AVAVA/Shutterstock

STUDY TOOLS

CHAPTER 12

Located at back of the textbook

❏ Rip out Chapter Review Card

Located at www.cengagebrain.com

❏ Review Key Terms Flashcards (Print or Online)

❏ Download Audio Summaries for on-the-go review

❏ Complete Practice Quizzes to prepare for tests

❏ Play "Beat the Clock" to master concepts

❏ Complete the Crossword Puzzle to review key terms

❏ Watch the video about McDonaldson, a fictitious but all-too-realistic ad agency, whose employees struggle with contemporary business communication issues.

Preparing Résumés and Application Messages

OBJECTIVES

13-1 Prepare for employment by considering relevant information about yourself as it relates to job requirements.

13-2 Identify career opportunities using traditional and electronic methods.

13-3 Prepare an organized, persuasive résumé that is adapted for print and electronic postings.

13-4 Utilize employment tools other than the résumé that can enhance employability.

13-5 Write an application message that effectively introduces an accompanying print (designed) or electronic résumé.

13-1 Preparing for the Job Search

Managing your career begins with recognizing that securing a new job is less important than assessing the impact of that job on your life. Work isn't something that happens from 8 A.M. to 5 P.M., with life happening after 5 P.M. Life and work are interconnected, and true satisfaction comes from being able to fully express yourself in what you do. This means merging who you are—your values, emotions, capabilities, and desires—with the activities you perform on the job.[1]

An ideal job provides satisfaction at all of Maslow's need levels, from basic economic to self-actualizing needs. The right job for you will not be drudgery; the work itself will be satisfying and give you a sense of well-being. Synchronizing your work with your core beliefs and talents leads to enthusiasm and fulfillment. You will probably work 10,000 days of your life, not including time spent commuting and on other related activities. Why spend all this time doing something unfulfilling when you could just as easily spend it doing what you enjoy?

Your **résumé** is a vital communication tool that provides a basis for judgment about your capabilities on the job. In preparing this document, your major tasks will be gathering essential information about yourself and the job using traditional and electronic resources, planning and organizing the résumé to showcase your key qualifications, and adapting the résumé for various types of delivery. You will need to supplement your résumé with examples of your accomplishments and abilities. Finally, you'll prepare persuasive application messages appropriate for the delivery of your résumé.

13-1a Gathering Essential Information

The job search begins with research—collecting, compiling, and analyzing information—in order to assess your marketability. The research phase of the job search involves the steps shown in Figure 13-1 below and are summarized as follows:

1. **Gather relevant information for decision making.** Complete a self-assessment to identify your own job-related qualifications, and an analysis of the career field that interests you and of a specific job in that field. Follow up with an interview of a career person in your field to acquire additional information.

2. **Prepare a company/job profile.** Compile the information you gathered into a format that allows you to compare your qualifications with the company and job requirements. This organized information will help you determine a possible match between you and the potential job.

3. **Identify unique selling points and specific support.** Determine several key qualifications and accomplishments that enhance your marketability. These are the key selling points you'll target in your résumé and later in a job interview.

13-1b Identifying Potential Career Opportunities

Plan to begin your job search for prospective employers months in advance. Waiting too long to begin and then hurrying through the job

résumé
a vital communication tool that provides a basis for judgment about a person's capabilities on the job

Figure 13-1   Process of Applying for a Job

STEP 1	STEP 2	STEP 3	STEP 4	STEP 5
Conduct research and analysis of self, career, and job	Identify a job listing using traditional and electronic sources	Prepare targeted résumé and application message in required formats	Consider supplementing the résumé: Portfolio (print or electronic) or video recording	Interview with companies

RÉSUMÉ PRESENTATION AND DELIVERY OPTIONS

Print (Designed)

- Mail to company accompanied by application letter
- Mail as follow-up to electronic submission

Scannable

- Print résumé formatted for computer scanning

Electronic Postings

- Email to network contacts, career and corporate sites, and career service centers
- Online form
- Electronic portfolio at personal website
- Beamer to PDA or cell phone

search process could affect your ability to land a satisfying job.

Before you begin, take the time to develop an organized strategy for your search efforts. You might download a template such as Microsoft's job search log (**http://office.microsoft.com/en-us/templates/results .aspx?qu=job%20search%20log**) or invest in software such as Winway Résumé and Résumé Maker Deluxe to simplify the task of tracking your contacts. You'll need a record of the name, address, email address, and telephone number of each potential employer. Later, record the date of each job contact you make and receive

(along with what you learned from the contact), the name of the contact person, the date you sent a résumé, and so on.

Your search for potential career opportunities likely will involve traditional and electronic job search sources.

Using Traditional Sources

Traditional means of locating a job include printed sources, networks, career services centers, employers' offices, employment agencies and contractors, and professional organizations.

Printed Sources

Numerous printed sources are useful in identifying firms in need of employees. Responses to advertised positions in the employment sections of newspapers should be made as quickly as possible after the ad is circulated. If your résumé is received early and is impressive, you could get a favorable response before other applications are received. If an ad requests that responses be sent to a box number without giving a name, be cautious. The employer could be legitimate but does not want present employees to know about the ad or does not want applicants to phone or drop by. However, you have a right to be suspicious of someone who wants to remain obscure while learning everything you reveal in your résumé. Print job listings can also be found in company newsletters, industry directories, and trade and professional publications, which often are available on the Internet.

Networks

The majority of job openings are never advertised. Therefore, developing a network of contacts is often the most valuable source of information about jobs. Your network could include current and past employers, guest speakers in your classes or at student organization meetings, business contacts you met while interning or participating in shadowing or over-the-shoulder experiences, and so on. Let these individuals know the type of job you are seeking and ask their advice for finding employment in today's competitive market.

Career Services Centers

You will want to register with your college's career services center at least three semesters before you graduate. Typically, the center has a Web site and a browsing room loaded with career information and job announcement bulletins. Career counseling is available at most career services centers including workshops on résumé writing, interviewing, etiquette, mock interviews, "mocktail" parties for learning to mingle in pre-interview social events, and more. Through the center, you can learn about job fairs at which you can meet prospective employers and schedule on-campus, phone, and video interviews with company recruiters.

Most career services centers use electronic tracking systems. Rather than submitting printed résumés, students input their résumés into a computer file following the specific requirements of the tracking system used by the college or university. A search of the résumé database generates an interview roster of the top applicants for a campus recruiter's needs. Some centers assist students in preparing electronic portfolios to supplement their résumés.

Employers' Offices

Employers who have not advertised their employment needs might respond favorably to a phone or personal inquiry. The receptionist might be able to provide useful information, direct you to someone with whom you can talk, or set up an appointment.

Employment Agencies and Contractors

City, county, state, and federal employment agencies provide free or inexpensive services. Some agencies offer online listings or phone recordings so that applicants can get information about job opportunities and procedures for using their services. The fee charged by private agencies is paid by either the employee or the employer and usually is based on the first month's salary and due within a few months. Some agencies specialize in finding high-level executives or specialists for major firms. Employment contractors specialize in providing temporary employees and might be able to place you in a position on a temporary basis until you find a full-time job.

Professional Organizations

Officers of professional organizations, through their contacts with members, can be good sources of information about job opportunities. Much job information is exchanged at meetings of professional associations. In addition to job listings in journals or organization Web sites, interviews are sometimes conducted at conference locations.

In addition to the professional growth that comes from membership in professional organizations, active participation is a good way to learn about jobs. Guest speakers share valuable information about the industry and its career and job opportunities. Employers are often favorably impressed when membership

almagami/Shutterstock

and experiences gained are included on the résumé and discussed during an interview. They are even more impressed if the applicant has been an officer in the organization, as it indicates leadership, community commitment, and willingness to serve without tangible reward, social acceptance, or high level of aspiration. By joining and actively participating in professional, social, and honorary organizations, you increase your opportunities to develop rapport with peers and professors and gain an edge over less-involved applicants.

Using Electronic Job Searches

An increasing number of companies and job hunters are using the Internet to assist in various stages of the job search process. Convenience, speed, and accessibility are all reasons for the popularity of electronic job searches among human resources managers. The cost of electronic recruiting is lower than traditional methods, and applicants and employers can respond more quickly. Job seekers can use the Internet to complement rather than replace the traditional methods previously discussed.

Locating Career Guidance Information

According to one career consultant, "Most people in the old days could go into an organization [during a job interview] and not really know about it and hope for the best. Now, people can understand the organization before they even apply."[2] The Internet places at your fingertips a wealth of information that will prepare you for the job interview if you use it as a research tool. Suggestions follow for effectively using the career guidance information you can locate on the Internet:

- **Visit career sites for information related to various phases of the job search.** You'll find a wide range of timely discussions at career sites: planning a job search, finding a job you love, researching employers, working a career fair, crafting winning résumés and cover letters, negotiating a salary, and so on.
- **Visit corporate Web sites to learn about companies.** You can locate information online for targeting your résumé appropriately and to prepare for the job interview. Read mission statements or descriptions of services to see how the organization describes itself, and review the annual report and strategic plan to learn about the financial condition and predicted growth rates. Search for "What's New" or "News" sections promoting new developments, as well as career opportunities and job postings. Evaluating the development and professional nature of the Web site will give you an impression of the organization.

Supplement this information with independent sources to confirm the company's stability and status, as negative news likely will not be posted on the Web site.

- **Identify specific skills companies are seeking.** Study the job descriptions provided on corporate home pages and job sites to identify the skills required for the job and the latest industry buzzwords. Use this information to target your résumé to a specific job listing and to generate keywords for an electronic résumé.
- **Network electronically with prospective employers.** It's easy to network online by attending electronic job fairs, chatting with career counselors, participating in news groups and listservs applicable to your field, and corresponding by email with contacts in companies. The value of these electronic networking experiences is to learn about an industry and career, seek valued opinions, and uncover potential job opportunities. By applying effective communication strategies for an online community, you can make a good impression, create rapport with employment contacts online, and polish your interviewing skills.

Identifying Job Listings

You can use the Internet to locate job opportunities in several ways:

- Look in the employment section of companies' corporate Web sites to see if they are advertising job openings.
- Search the electronic databases of job openings of third-party services.
- Access online job classifieds from daily and trade newspapers. CareerBuilder (**www.careerbuilder.com**) offers the classifieds of a number of major newspapers.
- Subscribe to a newsgroup through UseNext (**http://office.microsoft.com/en-us/templates/results.aspx?qu=job%20search%20log**) that gives you access to jobs by geographic location and specific job categories.
- Subscribe to services such as America Online (**http://office.microsoft.com/en-us/templates/results.aspx?qu=job%20search%20log**) that provide job search sites and services by keying "Career."

Online and printed sources will help you learn to search particular databases. The following general suggestions will help you get started:

- Input words and phrases that describe your skills rather than job titles because job titles vary by company.

- Use specific phrases such as "entry-level job" or "job in advertising" rather than "job search."
- Start with a wider job description term, such as "pharmaceutical sales jobs," then narrow down to the specific subject, geographic region, state, and so forth.
- Don't limit yourself to one search engine; try several and bookmark interesting sites.
- Stay focused on your goal and don't get distracted as you go.

Searching for useful career sites among the hundreds available can be quite time consuming. CareerBuilder, JobCentral, and Monster.com are major career sites offering a wide array of information and services.

NAN728 /Shutterstock.com

Another name for "résumé" is "curriculum vitae" or "CV," which is Latin for "course of one's life."

13-2 Planning a Targeted Résumé

In order to match your interests and qualifications with available jobs, you'll need an effective résumé. To win a job interview in today's tight market where job seekers outnumber positions, you need more than a general résumé that documents your education and work history. The powerful wording of a **targeted résumé** reflects the requirements of a specific job listing that you have identified through traditional and electronic job search methods.

An employer typically scans résumés quickly looking for reasons to reject the applicant, schedule an interview, or place in a stack for rereading. This initial scan and a second brief look for those who make the cut give little time to explain why you are the best person for the job. To grab an employer's attention, you must selectively choose *what to say*, *how to say it*, and *how to arrange it* on the page so that it can be read quickly but thoroughly. A concise, informative, easy-to-read summary of your relevant qualifications will demonstrate that you possess the straightforward communication skills demanded in today's information-intensive society.

The goal of the résumé is to get an interview, so ask yourself this question: "Does including this information increase my chances of getting an interview?"

If the answer is "Yes," include the information; if the answer is "No," omit the information and use the space to develop your qualifications. When selecting information to be included, you must also be cautious of the temptation to inflate your résumé to increase your chances of being hired.

13-2a Standard Parts of a Résumé

A winning résumé contains standard parts that are adapted to highlight key qualifications for a specific job. The sample résumés and in-depth explanation of each standard part provided in Figures 13-2 to 13-5 (see pages 242–247) will prepare you for creating a résumé that describes your qualifications best.

Identification

Your objective is to provide information that will allow the interviewer to reach you. Include your name, current address, phone number, and email address. Provide a clear, benign email address that reflects a positive impression (e.g., no "mustangsally"). You should also include your Web site address to provide access to more detailed information.

> **targeted résumé**
> a résumé that reflects the requirements of a specific job listing

To ensure that the interviewer can quickly locate the identification information, center it on the page or use graphic design elements to call attention to your name. You should include a permanent address (parent's or other relative's address) if you are interviewing when classes are not in session. Leave a clear, straightforward greeting on your phone that portrays you as a person serious about securing a job. Eliminate music, clever sayings, or background noise.

Job and/or Career Objective

Following the "Identification" section, state your job/career objective—the job you want. Interviewers can see quickly whether the job you seek matches the one they have to offer. A good job/career objective must be specific enough to be meaningful yet general enough to apply to a variety of jobs. The following example illustrates a general objective that has been revised to describe a specific job:

General Objective	Specific Objective
A challenging position that enables me to contribute to an organization's success.	Position where my customer service skills and experience will enable me to contribute to a company's overall success.
A position with a stable organization that provides an opportunity for development and career advancement.	Position with an innovative marketing team with a special interest in new brand development.

Some experts argue that a statement of your job or career objective can limit your job opportunities; your objective should be obvious from your qualifications. In general, however, making your objective clear at the beginning assures the interviewer that you have a definite career goal.

Career Summary

To survive the interviewer's 40-second scan, you must provide a compelling reason for a more thorough review of your résumé. Craft a persuasive introductory statement that quickly synthesizes your most transferable skills, accomplishments, and attributes and place it in a section labeled "Summary" or "Professional Profile."

In this synopsis of your key qualifications, communicate why you should be hired. Your answer should evolve naturally from the career objective and focus on your ability to meet the needs of the company you have identified from your extensive research.

Combining the career objective with the career statement is an acceptable strategy as noted in the following examples:

Separate Objective and Career Summary

Objective Obtain an entry-level marketing position in an international company with an opportunity to specialize in global marketing strategies.
Career Summary Dual degrees in marketing and international business, including study abroad in Asia; internship experience with three multinational corporations; self-motivated; achievement oriented.

Combined Objective with Career Summary

Professional Profile Position in public relations with advancement potential. Internship experience with two leading public relations firms, creating press materials and Web site content. Strong written and oral communication skills.

Linked Objective and Career Summary

Profile Position as sales representative in which demonstrated commission selling and hard work bring rewards.
Accomplishments:
- Three years' straight commission sales
- Average of $35,000–$55,000 a year in commissioned earnings
- Consistent success in development and growth of territories

A high-impact career summary, once considered optional, has become a standard section of résumés in today's fast-paced information age. Develop your résumé to skillfully target the requirements of a specific position; then compose a career summary sure to interest any interviewer who instantly sees an applicant with exactly the skills needed.

do for the employer—functions that the applicant can perform well. Under each heading, an applicant could draw from educational and/or work-related experience to provide supporting evidence.

A functional résumé requires a complete analysis of self, career, and the job sought. Suppose, for example, that a person seeking a job as an assistant hospital administrator wants to emphasize qualifications by placing them in major headings. From the hospital's advertisement of the job and from accumulated job appraisal information, an applicant sees this job as both an administrative and a public-relations job. The job requires skill in communicating and knowledge of accounting and finance. Thus, headings in the "Qualifications" section of the résumé could be "Administration," "Public Relations," "Communication," and "Budgeting." Under "Public Relations," for example, an applicant could reveal that a public relations course was taken at State University, from which a degree is to be conferred in May, and that a sales job at ABC Store provided abundant opportunity to apply principles learned. With other headings receiving similar treatment, the qualifications portion reveals the significant aspects of education and experience.

Order of importance is the best sequence for functional headings. If you have prepared an accurate self- and job analysis, the selected headings will highlight points of special interest to the employer. Glancing at headings only, an employer can see that you understand the job's requirements and have the qualities needed for success.

Having done the thinking required for preparing a functional résumé, you are well prepared for a question that is commonly asked in interviews: "What can you do for us?" The answer is revealed in your major headings. They emphasize the functions you can perform and the special qualifications you have to offer.

If you consider yourself well qualified, a functional résumé is worth considering. If your education or experience is scant, a functional résumé could be best for you. Using "Education" and "Experience" as headings (as in a chronological résumé) works against your purpose if you have little to report under the headings; the format would emphasize the absence of education or experience.

Chrono-Functional Résumé

The **chrono-functional résumé** combines features of chronological and functional résumés. This format can give quick assurance that educational and experience requirements are met and still use other headings that emphasize qualifications.

13-3 Preparing Résumés for Print and Electronic Delivery

Format requirements for résumés have changed significantly in recent years. Whether presented on paper or electronically, the arrangement of a résumé is just as important as the content. If the arrangement is unattractive, unappealing, or in poor taste, the message might never be read. Errors in keyboarding, spelling, and punctuation could be taken as evidence of a poor academic background, lack of respect for the employer, or carelessness. Recognize that résumés serve as your introduction to employers and indicate the quality of work you'll produce.

As in preparing other difficult documents, prepare a rough draft as quickly as you can and then revise as many times as needed to prepare an effective résumé that sells you. After you are confident with the résumé, ask at least two other people to check it for you. Carefully select people who are knowledgeable about résumé preparation and the job you are seeking and can suggest ways to present your qualifications more effectively. After you have incorporated those changes, ask a skillful proofreader to review the document.

To accommodate employers' preferences for the presentation and delivery of résumés, you'll need three versions of your résumé as shown in Figure 13-1: a designed résumé printed on paper, a scannable résumé to be read by a computer, and a designed résumé accessible through email and Web sites.

13-3a Preparing a Print (Designed) Résumé

Your print (designed) résumé is considered your primary marketing document, and appearance is critical. To win out among hundreds of competing résumés, it must look professional and reflect current formatting and production standards while maintaining a distinctive conservative

chrono-functional résumé
a résumé that combines features of chronological and functional résumés

tone. Follow these guidelines for designing and producing a highly professional résumé:

- **Develop an appealing résumé format that highlights your key qualifications and distinguishes your résumé.** Use the power of your word processing software for style enhancements rather than settle for overused, inflexible templates. Study the example résumés in this chapter and models from other sources for ideas for enhancing the style, readability, and overall impact of the document. Then create a custom design that best highlights your key qualifications.

- **Format information for quick, easy reading.** To format your résumé so that it can be read at a glance, follow these guidelines:

  - Use attention-getting headings to partition major divisions, and add graphic lines and borders to separate sections of text.

  - Use an outline format when possible to list activities and events on separate lines, and include bullets to emphasize multiple points.

  - Use 10-point fonts or larger to avoid reader eye strain.

  - Use type styles and print attributes to emphasize key points. For example, to draw attention to the identification and headings, select a bold sans serif font (e.g., Calibri or Arial) slightly larger than the serif font (e.g., Cambria or Times New Roman) used for the remaining text. Capitalization, indention, and print enhancements (underline, italics, bold), are useful for adding emphasis. Limit the number of type styles and enhancements, however, so the page is clean and simple to read.

  - Include identification on each page of a multiple-page résumé. Place your name and a page number at the top of the second and successive pages with "Continued" at the bottom of the first page. The interviewer is reexposed to your name, and pages can be reassembled if separated.

- **Create an appealing output to produce top professional quality.**

  - Check for consistency throughout the résumé. Consistency in spacing, end punctuation, capitalization, appearance of headings, and sequencing of details within sections will communicate your eye for detail and commitment to high standards.

  - Balance the résumé attractively on the page with approximately equal margins. Allow generous white space so the résumé looks uncluttered and easy to read.

- **Consider adding a statement of your creativity and originality.** Be certain that your creativity will not be construed as gimmicky and distract from the content of the résumé. Demonstrating creativity is particularly useful for fields such as advertising, public relations, graphic design, and those requiring computer proficiency.

- Select paper of a standard size (8 1/2" by 11"), neutral color (white, buff, or gray), and high quality (preferably 24-pound, 100 percent cotton fiber). Consider using a mailing envelope large enough to accommodate the résumé without folding. The unfolded documents on the reader's desk will get favorable attention and will scan correctly if posted to an electronic database.

- Print with a laser printer that produces high-quality output. Position paper so the watermark is read across the sheet in the same direction as the printing.

Some employers insist that the "best" length for a résumé is one page, stating that long résumés are often ignored. However, general rules about length are more flexible. Most students and recent graduates can present all relevant résumé information on one page. However, as you gain experience, you might need two or more pages to format an informative, easy-to-read résumé. A résumé forced on one page will likely have narrow margins and large blocks of run-on text (multiple lines with no space to break them). This dense format is unappealing and complicates the interviewer's task of skimming quickly for key information.

The rule about length is simple: Be certain your résumé contains only relevant information presented as concisely as possible. A one-page résumé that includes irrelevant information is too long. A two-page résumé that omits relevant information is too short.

The résumés illustrated in Figures 13-2 and 13-4 (see pages 242 and 244) demonstrate the organizational principles for the chronological and functional résumés. A references page is illustrated in Figure 13-3 on page 243. Study the various layouts to decide on one that will highlight your key qualifications most effectively.

13-3b Preparing Electronic Résumé Submissions

To this point you have focused on the preparation of a print résumé. However, in the digital age of instant information, you'll use various online methods to apply for a job and present your qualifications to prospective employers.

The easiest and most common method of putting your résumé online is through emailing a résumé to a job bank for posting or to a networking contact who asked you to send a résumé. Many job banks, corporate sites, and career services centers require you to respond to specific openings by completing an online form or pasting your résumé into a designated section of the form. Frequently, you can input information directly on the Web site or download the form to be submitted by email, fax, or mail. You might also choose to post your résumé on your personal Web site as part of an electronic portfolio that showcases evidence of your qualifications. You could also develop a **beamer**, or *beamable résumé*, a quick version of your résumé designed in a format suitable for broadcasting on smartphones. Recruiting professionals predict that millions of these electronic résumés will be exchanged silently at conferences, business meetings, and power lunches, similar to exchanging business cards.[8]

Electronic submissions are quick and easy but present new challenges and many opportunities to jeopardize your employment chances and compromise your privacy. Just consider recent struggles you might have faced in dealing with viruses and unwelcomed emails, attempting to access nonworking links, and more. Before sending your résumé into cyberspace, follow these suggestions to ensure that your electronic submission is both professional and technically effective:

- **Choose postings for your résumé with purpose.** Online résumé postings are not confidential. Once your résumé is online, anyone can read it, including your current employer. You might also begin to receive junk mail and cold calls from companies who see your résumé online; even more seriously, you could become a victim of identity theft. To protect your privacy online, limit personal information disclosed in the résumé and post only to sites with password protection allowing you to approve the release of your résumé to specific employers. Dating your electronic résumé will also prevent embarrassment should your employer find an old version of your résumé, which could occur as result of exchange of résumés between career sites and delays in updating postings.

  Protect your references' privacy by omitting their names when posting online. Withholding this information will prevent unwelcomed calls by recruiters and other inappropriate contacts and threats to privacy. Because technology allows broadcast of your résumé to all available positions on a career site, read postings carefully and apply only to those that match your qualifications. This action improves the efficiency of the job selection process for the company and the applicant and depicts fair, ethical behavior.

- **Don't hurry.** The speed, convenience, and informality of filling in online boxes or composing an email cover letter for an attached résumé can lead to sloppiness that reflects negatively on your abilities and attitude. Make sure every aspect of your electronic submission is top-notch just as you would for a print résumé. Provide all information exactly as requested, write concise, clear statements relevant to the job sought, and proofread carefully for grammatical and spelling errors. If you direct an employer to an electronic portfolio, devote necessary time to make it attractive, informative, and technically sound. Double-check your files to ensure they can be opened and retain an appealing format. Finally, read the posting carefully to learn how long your résumé will remain active, how to update it, and how to delete it from the site.

"The best references are people who work for the organization you are looking to join."
—Bob Daugherty, U.S. Recruiting, PricewaterhouseCoopers

Chris Ryan/Jupiter Images

beamer
a quick version of a résumé designed in a format suitable for broadcasting on smartphones; also called a *beamable résumé*

Figure 13-2 **GOOD :-)** Chronological Résumé

Kenneth Franklin
159 Avenida Aprenda
Sacramento, CA 95009
909-755-4918
kfranklin@gmail.com

OBJECTIVE — Position in forensic accounting that enables me to use my audit team experience and bilingual language skills to effectively serve client needs.

CAREER SUMARY — Technical proficiency in ERP systems, ACL, database, and spreadsheet software; forensic and audit experience through an internship with a regional CPA firm; superior leadership and team orientation developed through student organizations; fluency in Spanish

EDUCATION — Bachelor of Accounting, **Central California University**, expected graduation, May 2013
GPA 3.9 on a 4.0 scale

RELATED EXPERIENCE — Professional Internship, Lewis Associates, CPAs, Sacramento, CA, June–August, 2012
- Involved in audits of companies in the oil and gas and retail sectors
- Developed time management, team building, and communication skills while completing independent projects with diverse work teams
- Demonstrated ability to accept and respond to criticism, learn job tasks quickly, and perform duties with minimal supervision

Teller (part-time), Sacramento Bank and Loan, Sacramento, CA, 2010 to present
- Provide customer service support to small business and individual customers, answering questions about their accounts and banking products and services
- Maintained a balanced cash drawer of $4,000 daily
- Attended quarterly training seminars on banking products and services

LANGUAGES — Native fluency in English
Fluent in Spanish

SKILLS — Proficient in Microsoft Office Suite
Technical proficiency in ERP systems, ACL, database, and spreadsheet software

LEADERSHIP — Beta Alpha Psi, 2009–2012
- Served as local chapter president
- Received commendation from chapter advisor

Includes email address that reflects professional image.

Reveals position sought and powerful summary of qualifications.

Positions education as top qualification for recent graduate. Includes high GPA.

Edges out competition by expanding on related experience and work achievements.

Lists academic recognitions and highlights relevant skills.

Format Pointers
Places name at top center for easy viewing (top right is also acceptable). Uses bold font to distinguish identification section and headings from remaining text.

Uses two-column format for easy location of specific sections.

Creates visual appeal through custom format rather than commonly used template, short readable sections focusing on targeted qualifications, and streamlined bulleted lists.

Diversity Considerations
Follows standard format and rules for résumés for application with U.S. company. Specific formats vary for specific countries and federal government.

Figure 13-5 GOOD :-) Scannable Résumé

SAMANTHA BARRETT
742 Elm Street
Brooklyn, NY 04800
430-324-9044
sbarrett@netdoor.com
www.netdoor/sbarrett

Professional Profile
- Experience in loan department preparing client applications, meeting with clients to review loan products, and communicating with clients about the status of the loan process
- Superior leadership and team orientation developed through student organizations
- Strong written and spoken communication skills
- Experienced user of Word, Excel, Access, and PowerPoint

Keywords
Entry-level loan officer position. Bachelor's degrees in finance. Professional internship. Loan department team player. Strong written and spoken communication skills. Word, Excel, Access, PowerPoint.

Education
B.S., Finance, New York City University, May 2013, GPA 3.6
- Dean's List, 2009-2012
- Beta Gamma Sigma (business honor society, upper 10% of senior class)

Related Employment
Intern, **Commercial Lending Department**, Brooklyn Savings and Loan, Brooklyn, NY summer, 2012
- Prepared application documents for small commercial loans.
- Met with clients to introduce them to loan product options.
- Communicated with clients about the status of the loan process.

Teller (part-time), Brooklyn Savings and Loan, Brooklyn, NY, 2010 to present
- Provide customer service support to small business and individual customers, answering questions about their accounts and banking products and services.
- Maintain a balanced cash drawer of $3,000 daily.

Honor's and Activities
- Dean's List (3.6 GPA or higher)
- Beta Gamma Sigma (business honor society, upper 10% of senior class)
- Student Investment Club

An attractive and fully formatted hard copy version of this document is available upon request.

Last revised 2/15/13

Positions name as first readable item.

Includes position sought and reason to hire in separate section.

Includes "Keyword Summary" section listing qualifications that match job description.

Edges out competition by expanding on related experience and work achievements.

Omits references to use space for additional qualifications; references furnished when requested.

Includes date of last revision to avoid confusion or embarrassment if résumé is accessed after hiring.

Format Pointers
Keeps résumé simple and readable by computer: ample white space especially between sections; easy-to-read font of 10 to 14 points; solid bullets; and no italics, underlining, or graphic lines or borders.

Mails cover letter and print résumé unfolded and unstapled in large envelope.

organized, you can add items that demonstrate you have the characteristics the employer is seeking. Maintain your portfolio even after you are hired because it can demonstrate your eligibility for promotion, salary increase, advanced training, or even justify why you should not be laid off.

For illustration purposes, take a look at Samantha Barrett's electronic portfolio shown in Figure 13-6 on page 248 that was created using a Microsoft Web template and posted to her personal Web site.

13-4b **Employment Videos**

A video recording can be used to extend the impact of the printed résumé visually. A video can capture your stage presence and ability to speak effectively and add a human dimension to the written process. Current technology enables applicants to embed video segments into **multimedia résumés** created with presentation software such as Camtasia Studio and sent to prospective employers on CD or DVD or posted on the applicant's personal Web site.

Figure 13-6   Electronic Portfolio Posted to an Applicant's Personal Web Site

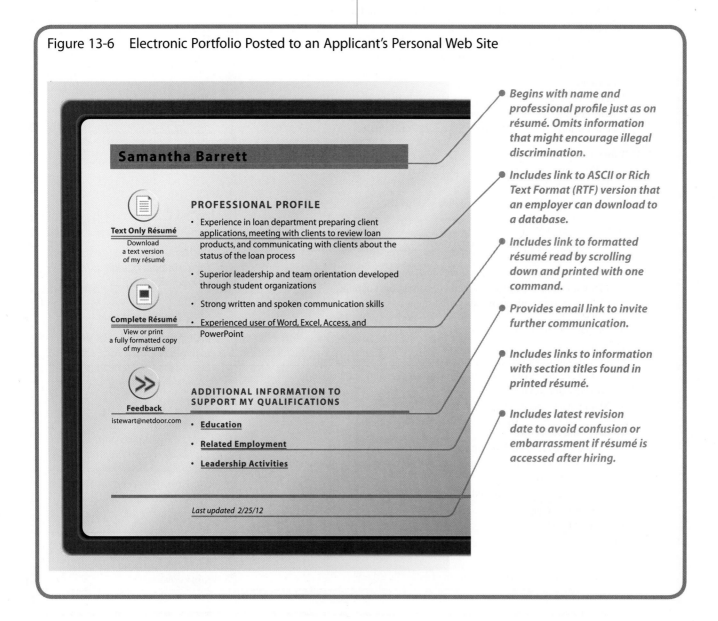

Samantha Barrett

Text Only Résumé
Download
a text version
of my résumé

Complete Résumé
View or print
a fully formatted copy
of my résumé

Feedback
istewart@netdoor.com

PROFESSIONAL PROFILE

- Experience in loan department preparing client applications, meeting with clients to review loan products, and communicating with clients about the status of the loan process

- Superior leadership and team orientation developed through student organizations

- Strong written and spoken communication skills

- Experienced user of Word, Excel, Access, and PowerPoint

ADDITIONAL INFORMATION TO SUPPORT MY QUALIFICATIONS

- **Education**

- **Related Employment**

- **Leadership Activities**

Last updated 2/25/12

- *Begins with name and professional profile just as on résumé. Omits information that might encourage illegal discrimination.*

- *Includes link to ASCII or Rich Text Format (RTF) version that an employer can download to a database.*

- *Includes link to formatted résumé read by scrolling down and printed with one command.*

- *Provides email link to invite further communication.*

- *Includes links to information with section titles found in printed résumé.*

- *Includes latest revision date to avoid confusion or embarrassment if résumé is accessed after hiring.*

Fly Fernandez/Corbis

Video résumés, which job seekers post on sites such as YouTube, are the latest trend in developing creative job qualifications. You can learn some important lessons for your video project by taking a look at the abundance of good and bad examples already posted. If possible, solicit the help of someone with film experience and follow these simple suggestions for creating a visually enhanced résumé that is brief, showcases your key qualifications, and reflects your personality:[10]

- Keep your video simple with one stationary shot using a good camera and tripod. Avoid gimmicky effects and excessive panning that distract from the message.

- Use proper lighting, making sure that the employer can see your face. Avoid light behind you that casts shadows.

- Invest in a good quality microphone and speak clearly and at an appropriate pace for easy listening.

- Choose clothing appropriate for the job you are seeking. Video yourself wearing different clothing and watch the video to select the ideal choice. Avoid

clothing that gaps and bunches when you sit, as well as bright colors and close patterns that tend to vibrate when filmed.

- Edit your video to eliminate dead air and other imperfections that detract from a professional image.

video résumé
a résumé created as a video for posting on the Web, on sites such as YouTube

application message
a message placed on top of the résumé so it can be read first by the employer; also called a *cover message*

Employment videos are more commonly used to obtain employment in career fields for which verbal delivery or visual performance is a key element. These fields include broadcasting and the visual and performing arts. The following guidelines apply when preparing an employment video:

- Be sure the video makes a professional appearance and is complimentary to you. A "home movie" quality recording will be a liability instead of an asset to your application.

- Avoid long "talking head" segments. Include segments that reflect you in a variety of activities; shots that include samples of your work are also desirable.

- Remember that visual media (such as photographs and videos) encourage the potential employer to focus on your physical characteristics and attributes, which might lead to undesired stereotyping and discrimination.

Be sure to advertise the availability of your portfolio and employment video to maximize its exposure. List your URL address in the identification section of your résumé. In your application letter, motivate the prospective employer to view your portfolio or video by describing the types of information included. Talk enthusiastically about the detailed supplementary information available during your job interview and encourage the interviewer to view it when convenient. Note Thomas Kincaid's promotion of his e-portfolio when you read his application letter later in this chapter (see Figure 13-7 below).

13-5 Composing Application Messages

When employers invite you to send either a print or electronic résumé, they expect you to include an **application message** (also known as a *cover message*).

Figure 13-7  **GOOD :-)** Example of an Application Letter

SAMANTHA BARRETT
742 Elm Street
Brooklyn, NY 04800
430-324-9044
sbarrett@netdoor.com

March 18, 2013
Benjamin Withers, Loan Department
Manhattan Bank and Loan
5400 234rd Street
New York, NY 04909

Dear Mr. Withers:

Denise Richard, manager of your consumer loan department, told me of a commercial loan opening in your department. A finance degree, experience working in a bank loan department, and excellent communication skills qualify me for this position.

My finance degree from New York City University prepared me well to work in commercial lending. In addition to foundational finance courses, I was able to complete courses in the bank lending environment, mortgage lending and commercial lending, earning an "A" in each course.

These courses prepared me well for my internship at Brooklyn Savings and Loan. That experience, in addition to my work as a teller, as prepared me for the loan opening in your department by providing:

- The ability to quickly learn bank procedures and policies and rapidly become a productive member of the loan team.
- A proven ability to work effectively with clients to speak knowledgeably about loan products and help them through the loan application process.
- An excellent performance rating from my manager for superior technical proficiency and strong written and spoken communication skills.

Please review the enclosed résumé for additional information about my finance education and related work experience. Work samples and further details are available in my electronic portfolio at www.netdoor/sbarrett. I look forward to talking with you about how my skills and experiences can benefit Manhattan Bank and Loan.

Sincerely,

Samantha Barrett

Samantha Barrett

Enclosure

Addresses letter to specific person using correct name and job title.

Identifies how applicant learned of position, specific position sought, and background.

Discusses how education relates to job requirements.

Uses bulleted list to highlight qualifications corresponding to job requirements.

Introduces résumé and Web site for additional information.

Encourages employer to take action without sounding pushy or apologetic.

Format Pointers
Formats as formal business letter since message is accompanying print résumé.

Abbreviated email message including online résumé in ASCII or RTF format would be appropriate for electronic submission.

Uses same high-quality, standard size paper as for résumé in neutral color; includes writer's address and contact information.

A mailed paper résumé should be accompanied by an application letter. When a résumé is submitted electronically, the application "letter" can take the form of an email message. As you have learned, a résumé summarizes information related to the job's requirements and the applicant's qualifications. An application message complements a résumé by (1) introducing the applicant, (2) attracting interest to the résumé, and (3) interpreting the résumé in terms of employer benefits. When mailed, the application message is placed on top of the résumé so it can be read first by the employer.

Because it creates interest and points out employer benefits, the application message is persuasive and, thus, written inductively. It is designed to convince an employer that qualifications are adequate just as a sales message is designed to convince a buyer that a product will satisfy a need. Like sales messages, application messages can be either solicited or unsolicited. Job advertisements *solicit* applications. Unsolicited application messages have greater need for attention-getters; otherwise, solicited and unsolicited application messages are based on the same principles.

Unsolicited application messages are the same basic message (perhaps with slight modifications) sent to many prospective employers. By sending unsolicited messages, you increase your chances of locating potential openings and possibly alert employers to needs they had not previously identified for someone of your abilities. However, sending unsolicited messages has some disadvantages. Because the employer's specific needs are not known, the opening paragraph will likely be more general (less targeted to a specific position) than the opening paragraph in solicited messages. The process could also be time consuming.

Thomas Kincaid wrote the letter in Figure 13-7 to accompany a chronological résumé he prepared after completing the company/job profile of an entry-level auditor. The time Thomas devoted to analyzing the job, the company, and his qualifications was well spent.

13-5a Persuasive Organization

A persuasive message is designed to convince the reader to take action, which in this case is to read the résumé and invite you to an interview. Because an application message is persuasive, organize it as you would a sales message:

Sales Message	Application Message
Gets attention	Gets attention
Introduces product	Introduces qualifications
Presents evidence	Presents evidence
Encourages action	Encourages action
=	=
(sells a product, service, or idea)	(results in an interview)

Like a well-written sales message, a well-written application message uses a central selling feature as a theme. The central selling feature is introduced in the first or second paragraph and stressed in paragraphs that follow. Two to four paragraphs are normally sufficient for supporting evidence. Consider order of importance as a basis for their sequence, with the most significant aspects of your preparation coming first.

Gain the Receiver's Attention

To gain attention, begin the message by identifying the job sought and describing how your qualifications fit the job requirements. This information will provide instant confirmation that you are a qualified applicant for an open position. An employer who reads hundreds of application letters and résumés will appreciate this direct, concise approach.

For an announced job, you should indicate in the first paragraph how you learned of the position—for example, employee referral, customer referral, executive referral, newspaper advertising, or job fair. Your disclosure will confirm you are seeking an open job as well as facilitate evaluation of the company's recruiting practices. Note that the opening of the letter in Figure 13-7 indicates the applicant learned of the position through a referral from a professor.

An opening for an unsolicited message must be more persuasive: You must convince the interviewer to continue to read your qualifications even though a job might not exist. As in the opening of a solicited message, indicate the type of position sought and your qualifications

unsolicited application message
an unrequested message sent to many prospective employers and containing the same basic message

but be more creative in gaining attention. The following paragraph uses the applicant's knowledge of recent company developments and an intense interest in the company's future to gain receiver attention.

> In the past three years, Johnson Foods has experienced phenomenal growth through various acquisitions, mergers, and market expansion. With this growth comes new opportunities, new customers, and the need for new team players to work in store management. While following the growth of Johnson Foods, I have become determined to join this exciting team and am eager to show you that my educational background, leadership abilities, and internship experience qualify me for the job.

Provide Evidence of Qualifications

For graduates entering the world of full-time work for the first time, educational backgrounds are usually more impressive than work histories. They can benefit from interpreting their educational experiences as meaningful, job-related experiences. An applicant for a human resources position should do more than merely report having taken courses in organizational behavior.

> In my business communication class, I could see specific application of principles encountered in my organizational behavior and marketing classes. Questions about leadership and motivation seemed to recur throughout the course: What really motivates people? Why do people fear change? How can those fears be overcome? What communication practices can be used to motivate people and help them accept change? The importance of the communication was a focus of many courses and my research report, "How to Get the Most from Others."

Your application message will not necessarily refer to information learned in a class. Recognizing that managers must be tactful (a point on which the person reading the message will surely agree), the applicant included some details of a class. That technique is a basic in persuasion: Do not just say a product or idea is good; say what makes it good. Do not just say that an educational or work experience was beneficial; say what made it so.

By making paragraphs long enough to include interpretation of experiences on the present or previous job, you show an employer that you are well prepared for your next job. For example, the following excerpt from an applicant whose only work experience was at a retail outlet is short and general:

> I have been the assistant manager at Fashion Flash for the past year and have helped supervised a team of five associates. I received high performance evaluations for my work as a leader.

Added details and interpretation could make the value of the work experience more convincing:

> As assistant manager at Fashion Flash, I have learned to listen to associates' concerns and make them feel valued by acting on their suggestions. I have trained associates in policies and procedures and learned to reinforce those procedures for existing employees. I am able to preserve a good working relationship with my team even in sometimes difficult conversations.

The applicant has called attention to qualities that managers like to see in employees: willingness to listen, speed, accuracy, concern for clients or customers, a positive attitude, fairness, and tact. As a learning experience, the Fashion Flash job has taught or reinforced principles that the employer sees can be transferred to the job being sought.

In this section, you can discuss qualifications you have developed by participating in student organizations, student government, athletics, or community organizations. Be specific in describing gained skills that can be applied directly on the job—for example, organizational, leadership, spoken and written communication skills, and budgeting and financial management. You can also use your involvement as a channel for discussing important personal traits vital to the success of a business, such as interpersonal skills, motivation, imagination, responsibility, and team orientation.

> For the past year, I have served as treasurer for Alpha Chi Epsilon. In that duty, I have managed a $200,000 annual budget. By coordinating our yearly charitable fund-raising event, I have exercised leadership and organizational and communication skills.

Finally, end this section with an indirect reference to the résumé. If you refer to it in the first or second paragraph, readers might turn from the message at that point and look at the résumé. Avoid the obvious statement "Enclosed please find my résumé" or "A résumé is enclosed." Instead, refer indirectly to the résumé while restating your qualifications. The following sentence emphasizes that references can confirm applicant's qualifications:

> **References listed on the enclosed résumé would be glad to comment on my marketing education and experience.**

Encourage Action

Once you have presented your qualifications and referred to your enclosed résumé, the next move is to encourage the receiver to extend an invitation for an interview. The goal is to introduce the idea of action without apologizing for doing so and without being demanding or "pushy." If the final paragraph (action closing) of your message is preceded by impressive paragraphs, you need not press hard for a response. Just mentioning the idea of a future discussion is probably sufficient. If you have significant related experience that you have developed as a central selling feature, mentioning this experience in the action closing adds unity and stresses your strongest qualification one last time. Forceful statements about *when* and *how* to respond are unnecessary and irritating. Avoid these frequently made errors:

- **Setting a date.** "May I have an appointment with you on January 15?" The date you name could be inconvenient; or even if it is convenient for the employer, your forwardness in setting it could be resented.
- **Expressing doubt.** "If you agree," "I hope you will," and "Should you decide" use subjunctive words that indicate lack of confidence.
- **Sounding apologetic.** "May I take some of your time" or "I know how busy you are" might seem considerate, but an apology is inappropriate when discussing ways you can contribute to a company.
- **Sounding overconfident.** "I will call you next week to set an appointment time that works for both of us." This statement is presumptuous and egotistical.
- **Giving permission to call.** "You may call me at 555-6543." By making the call sound like a

privilege ("may call") you could alienate the reader. Implied meaning: You are very selective about the calls you take, but the employer does qualify.

> I hope you will ...
> I know how busy you are ...
> You may call me at 555-6543 ...
>
> When a date and time can be arranged, I would like to talk with you.

The following sentences are possible closing sentences that refer to an invitation to interview. They are not intended as model sentences that should appear in your message. Because finding the right job is so important, you will be well rewarded for the time and thought you invest in original wording.

- **"When a date and time can be arranged, I would like to talk with you."** The statement does not indicate who will do the arranging, and the meeting place and the subject of the conversation are understood.
- **"I would appreciate an opportunity to discuss the marketing assistant's job with you."** The indirect reference to action is not forceful. However, if the applicant has impressive qualifications, the reader will want an interview and will not need to be pushed.
- **"I look forward to talking with you about how my skills and experiences can benefit Beck Restaurant Group."** The statement asks for the interview and re-emphasizes the applicant's strong qualifications.

13-5b General Writing Guidelines

An excellent application message might be the most difficult message you ever attempt to write. It's natural to feel uncomfortable writing about yourself; however, your confidence will increase as you study the wealth of model documents available through your career services center and other sources. The writing principles you've been introduced to in this chapter should help you to write a thoughtful, original message that impresses the interviewer. Instead of standard verbiage included in dozens of models, your self-marketing connects *your* experiences to your future with a specific company and reflects *your* personality and values. The following writing techniques will help distinguish your application message from the competition:

- **Substitute fresh, original expressions that reflect contemporary language.** Overly casual expressions and overused statements will give your message a dull, unimaginative tone. Obvious ideas such as "This is an application," "I read your ad," and "I am writing to apply for," are sufficiently understood without making direct statements. With the application message *and* résumé in hand, a reader learns nothing from "I am enclosing my résumé for your review." Observe caution in choosing overused words such as *applicant, application, opening, position, vacancy,* and *interview.*

- **Avoid overuse of "I" and writer-focused statements.** Because the message is designed to sell your services, some use of "I" is natural and expected; but restrict the number of times "I" is used, especially as the first word in a paragraph. Focus on providing specific evidence that you can meet the company's needs. The employer is not interested in reading about your need to earn more income, to be closer to your work, to have more pleasant surroundings, or to gain greater advancement opportunities.

- **Avoid unconvincing generalizations that could sound boastful.** Self-confidence is commendable, but overconfidence (or worse still, just plain bragging) is objectionable. Overly strong adjectives, self-judgmental terms, and unsupported generalizations damage your credibility. Instead of labeling your performance as "superior" or "excellent," or describing yourself as "an efficient, technically skilled team player" give supporting facts that show the interviewer you can deliver on what you're selling.

- **Tailor the message to the employer's need.** To impress the interviewer that your message is not a generic one sent to everyone, provide requested information and communicate an understanding of the particular company, job requirements, and field.

- **Provide requested information.** Job listings often request certain information: "Must provide own transportation and be willing to travel. Give educational background, work experience, and salary expected." Discuss these points in your application message. Preferably, the question of salary is left until the interview, allowing you to focus your message on your contributions to the company—not what you want from the company (money). Discussion of salary isn't meaningful until after a mutually successful interview; however, if an ad requests a statement about it, the message should address it. You may give a minimum figure or range, indicate willingness to accept a figure that is customary for work of that type, or indicate a preference for discussing salary at the interview.

- **Communicate knowledge of the company, job requirements, and language of the field.** Your statements about a company's rapid expansion or competitive advantage show you really are interested in the company, read widely, do more than you are required to do, and gather information before making decisions. However, phrase these statements carefully to avoid the perception of insincere flattery. For example, referring to the employer as "*the* leader in the field," "*the* best in the business," or "a great company" could appear as an attempt to get a favorable decision as a reward for making a complimentary statement. To reflect your understanding of the job requirements, use indirect statements that are informative and tactful. Direct statements such as "The requirements of this job are …" presents information the employer presumes you already know; "An auditor should be able to …" and "Sales personnel should avoid …" sound like a lecture and could be perceived as condescending. Discussing experiences related to a specific job requirement or your preference for work that requires this skill reveals your understanding without a direct statement. Including terminology commonly used by the profession allows you to communicate clearly in terms the reader understands; it also saves space and implies your background in the field.

- **Focus on strengths and portray a positive attitude.** Concentrate on the positive aspects of your education or experience that have prepared you for the particular job. Apologizing for a shortcoming or admitting failure only weakens your case and raises questions about your self-esteem. Do not discuss your current employer's shortcomings. Regardless of how negatively you perceive your present employer, that perception has little to do with your prospective employer's needs. Also, if you speak negatively of your present employer, you could be perceived as someone who would do the same to the next employer.

13-5c Finishing Touches

The importance of professional formatting and careful proofreading of a print document is generally understood. However, proofing and formatting a "real" résumé and letter appears more important to some applicants than producing quality email submissions. Employers frequently voice concern with the sloppiness and unprofessional appearance and content of electronic submissions. To survive the skeptical eye of an interviewer scanning for ways to reject an applicant, allow yourself time to produce a professional-looking document regardless of the presentation or delivery option you've chosen. Include these steps in your finishing phase:

- Regardless of your delivery option, address your application letter or email message to the specific individual who is responsible for hiring for the position you are seeking rather than sending the document to the "Human Resources Department" or "To Whom It May Concern." If necessary, consult the company's annual report or Web site, or call the company to locate this information.

- Verify the correct spelling, job title, and address, and send a personalized message to the appropriate individual.

- Keep the message short and easy to read. A one-page letter is sufficient for most applications from students and graduates entering the job market.

- Apply visual enhancements learned previously to enhance the appeal and readability of the message and to draw attention to your strengths.

- Definitely keep the paragraphs short and consider listing your top four or five achievements or other important ideas in a bulleted list.

- Use paper that matches the résumé (color, weight, texture, and size). The watermark should be readable across the sheet in the same direction as the printing. Since you're using plain paper, include your street address and city, state, and zip code above the date or formatted as a letterhead at the top of the page.

- Include "Enclosure" below the signature block to alert the employer that a résumé is enclosed. The proper letter format is shown in the example in Figure 13-7.

- Get opinions from qualified individuals and make revisions where necessary.

When preparing an application message for email submission, career experts recommend formatting it as a business letter with the complete address of the company exactly as presented in a letter sent by mail and a formal closing such as "Sincerely." To help people reach you, include a full signature block with your mailing and email addresses, and phone number(s). The recipient can easily contact you without opening your attachments. While seemingly unnecessary, the email address is useful when a recipient forwards your email to someone else who might want to reply to you but cannot see your email address. Exclude quotes from your signature block that could be misunderstood or offensive. Add an enclosure notation drawing attention to your résumé attachment provided as requested by the employer, such as "Résumé attached as Word document."

To compete with the high volumes of junk mail, daily messages, and fear of computer viruses, you must provide a motive for an interviewer to open an unexpected message from an unknown person. Messages with missing or vague subject lines might be ignored or deleted immediately. To bring attention to your message, include the name of the person referring you to the position directly in the subject line or mention your email is a follow-up to a conversation, for example, "RE: Follow-up: Résumé for ... ." If the message is unsolicited, describe the specific value you can add to the company, for example, "Résumé for Forensics Accountant with Extensive ACL Skills." Stay away from tricks such as marking an email "urgent" or adding "re" to pass your message off as a reply to an earlier message.

Check any instructions provided by the prospective employer and follow them precisely. Typically, however, you will want to send a complete letter and copy of your résumé by regular mail as a follow-up to the email submission. These suggestions are illustrated in Figure 13-8, a sample application letter an applicant sent after talking with a prospective employer at a career fair.

Figure 13-8   Example of Application Message Sent by Email

New Message

To: <dharris@newyorkbank.com>
From: sbarrett@netdoor.com
Subject: Career Fair Follow-up: Résumé for Samantha Barrett

Attachment: samantha_barrett.doc 📎

February 25, 2013

Donald Harris
Recruiter
New York Bank and Trust
1240 27th Avenue
New York, NY 03140-1000

Dear Mr. Harris:

It was a pleasure meeting you at the career fair this morning. The opportunities offered in commercial lending identify your company as a leader in today's financial products marketplace.

My experience and knowledge of banking and commercial lending enable me to be a valuable asset to your company:

• Knowledge of banking and commercial lending practices, necessary documentation, and consumer laws.
• Demonstrated commitment to delivering excellent customer service to customers and clients.
• Hard-working and achievement oriented as demonstrated by part-time employment throughout college, leadership, and maintenance of a 3.6 GPA.

After you have reviewed the attached résumé that you requested for additional information about my education and related work experience, please message me so we can discuss my joining New York Bank and Trust.

Sincerely,

Samantha Barrett
742 Elm Street
Brooklyn, NY 04800
430-324-9044
sbarrett@netdoor.com

Résumé text included in email below and attached as MS Word attachment.

Provides specific subject line that ensures message will be opened.

Email program automatically shows attached file containing resume.

Reveals how applicant learned of position and confirms knowledge of and interest in company.

Condenses persuasive application message to one screen. Avoids tendency to send impersonal message stating résumé is attached.

Introduces résumé and reminds interviewer that submission was requested.

Encourages employer to take action without sounding pushy or apologetic.

Includes email address in .sig file to simplify access to all contact information without opening attached résumé.

Includes enclosure notation pointing out that résumé is sent as required by the company.

Format Pointers
Formats as formal business letter with complete address exactly as done when job credentials are sent by mail. Complete letter and printed copy of résumé will be sent as follow-up to email.

STUDY TOOLS

CHAPTER 13

Located at back of the textbook

❑ **Rip out Chapter Review Card**

Located at www.cengagebrain.com

❑ **Review Key Terms Flashcards (Print or Online)**

❑ **Download Audio Summaries for on-the-go review**

❑ **Complete Practice Quizzes to prepare for tests**

❑ **Play "Beat the Clock" to master concepts**

❑ **Complete the Crossword Puzzle to review key terms**

❑ **Watch the video about McDonaldson, a fictitious but all-too-realistic ad agency, whose employees struggle with contemporary business communication issues.**

Interviewing for a Job and Preparing Employment Messages

OBJECTIVES

14-1 Explain the nature of structured, unstructured, stress, group, and virtual interviews.

14-2 Explain the steps in the interview process.

14-3 Prepare effective answers to questions often asked in job interviews, including illegal interview questions.

14-4 Compose effective messages related to employment (including application, follow-up, thank-you, job-acceptance, job-refusal, resignation, and recommendation request messages).

14-1 Understanding Types of Employment Interviews

Most companies conduct various types of interviews before hiring a new employee. While the number and type of interviews vary among companies, applicants typically begin with a screening interview often completed by phone or videoconferencing, an in-depth interview, an on-site interview with multiple interviewers, and sometimes a stress interview. Depending on the goals of the interviewer, interviews follow a structured or an unstructured approach.

14-1a Structured Interviews

In a **structured interview** the interviewer follows a predetermined agenda, including a checklist of questions and statements designed to elicit necessary information and reactions from the interviewee. Because each applicant answers the same questions, the interviewer has comparable data to evaluate. A particular type of structured interview is the behavior-based interview, in which you are asked to give specific examples of occasions in which you demonstrated particular behaviors or skills. The interviewer already knows what skills, knowledge, and qualities successful candidates must possess. The examples you provide will indicate whether you possess them.[1]

Many companies are finding computer-assisted interviews to be a reliable and effective way to conduct screening interviews. Applicants use a computer to provide answers to a list of carefully selected questions. A computer-generated report provides standard, reliable information about each applicant that enables an interviewer to decide whether to invite the applicant for a second interview. The report flags any contradictory responses (e.g., an applicant indicated he was terminated for absenteeism but later indicated that he thought his former employer would give him an outstanding recommendation), highlights any potential problem areas (e.g., an applicant responded that she would remain on the job less than a year), and generates a list of structured interview questions for the interviewer to ask (e.g., "Todd, you said you feel your former employer would rate you average. Why don't you feel it would be higher?").

Research has shown that applicants prefer computer interviews to human interviews and that they respond more honestly to a computer, feeling less need to give polite, socially acceptable responses. Because expert computer systems can overcome some of the inherent problems with traditional face-to-face interviews, the overall quality of the selection process improves. Typical interviewer errors include talking too much, forgetting to ask important questions, being reluctant to ask sensitive or tough questions, forming unjustified negative first impressions, obtaining unreliable and illegal information that makes an applicant feel judged, and using interview data ineffectively.[2] Regardless of whether the interview is face-to-face or computer assisted, you will need to provide objective, truthful evidence of your qualifications as they relate to specific job requirements.

14-1b Unstructured Interviews

An **unstructured interview** is a freewheeling exchange and can shift from one subject to another, depending on the interests of the

structured interview
interview format generally used in the screening process in which the interviewer follows a predetermined agenda, including a checklist of items or a series of questions and statements designed to elicit the necessary information or interviewee reaction

unstructured interview
a freewheeling exchange that may shift from one subject to another, depending on the interests of the participants

Log onto www.cengagebrain.com for additional resources including flashcards, games, self-quizzing for chapter review, grammar exercises, and more.

Yuri Arcurs/Fotolia

participants. Some experienced interviewers are able to make a structured interview seem unstructured. The goal of many unstructured interviews is to explore unknown areas to determine the applicant's ability to speak comfortably about a wide range of topics.

14-1c Stress Interviews

A **stress interview** is designed to place the interviewee in an anxiety-producing situation so an evaluation can be made of the interviewee's performance under stress. In all cases, interviewees should attempt to assess the nature of the interview quickly and adjust behavior accordingly. Understanding that interviewers some-times deliberately create anxiety to assess your ability to perform under stress should help you handle such interviews more effectively. As the follow-ing discussion of different interviewer styles reveals, you can perform much bet-ter when you understand the interviewer's purpose.

stress interview
interview format designed to place the interviewee in an anxiety-producing situation so an evaluation of the interviewee's performance under stress may be made

virtual interview
interview conducted using videoconferencing technology

14-1d Series Interviews

As organizations have increased emphasis on the team approach to management and problem solving, select-ing employees who best fit their cultures and styles has become especially important. Involving key people in the organization in the candidate selection process has led to new interview styles. In a series interview, the candidate meets individually with a number of differ-ent interviewers. Each interviewer will likely ask ques-tions from a differing perspective; for instance, a line manager might ask questions related to the applicant's knowledge of specific job tasks while the vice president of operations might ask questions related to the appli-cant's career goals. Some questions will likely be asked more than once in the process. A popular trend in orga-nizations that desire a broad range of input in the hir-ing decision but want to avoid the drawn-out nature of series interviews is to conduct group interviews.

14-1e Virtual Interviews

Technology is allowing much business activity, including job interviews, to be con-ducted virtually. Companies such as IBM, Microsoft, Nike, and Hallmark Cards save money and time by screening candidates through video interviews from remote locations. **Virtual interviews** help to widen the applicant pool and decrease the cost of travel (since they can be conducted regardless of ge-ography) and fill the position more quickly. The consen-sus is that the video interview is excellent for screening applicants, but a face-to-face interview is appropriate whenever possible for the important final interview.

Various companies have direct hookups with the career services centers of colleges and universities to interview students. These virtual interviews allow stu-dents to meet large companies whose representatives typically would not visit colleges with small applicant pools and to interview with companies whose represen-tatives could not travel because of financial constraints or other reasons. Students simply sit in front of a cam-era, dial in, and interview with multiple interviewers; in some cases, several applicants are interviewed simul-taneously. As you would imagine, some candidates who interview well in person can fail on camera or in a group conference call. Virtual interviewing is an excellent method for screening out candidates who are unable to communicate their competence, enthusiasm, and conviction in a technology-rich environment.

You should prepare for a virtual interview differ-ently than you would for a traditional interview. First, suggest a preliminary telephone conversation with the interviewer to establish rapport. Arrive early and acquaint yourself with the equipment; know how to adjust the volume and other camera functions for optimal performance after the interview begins. Second, concentrate on projecting strong nonverbal skills: speak clearly but do not slow down; be certain you are centered in the frame; sit straight; look up, not down; and use gestures and an enthusiastic voice to communicate energy and reinforce points while avoiding excessive motion that will appear blurry. Third, realize voices can be out of step with the pictures if there is a lag between the video and audio transmissions. You will need to adjust to the timing (e.g., slow down your voice) to avoid interrupting the interviewer.

14-2 Preparing for an Interview

College students frequently schedule on-campus interviews with representatives from various business organizations. Following the on-campus interviews, successful candidates often are invited for further interviews at the company location. The purpose of the second interview is to give executives and administrators other than the human resources interviewer an opportunity to appraise the candidate. Whether on campus or at the company location, interview methods and practices vary with the situation.

Pre-interview planning involves learning something about the company or organization, studying yourself, and making sure your appearance and mannerisms will not detract from the impression you hope to make.

14-2a Research the Company

Nothing can hurt a job candidate more than knowing little about the organization. No knowledge indicates insincerity, and the interviewer does not want to waste precious interview time providing candidates with information they should have considered long before. Preparation will also arm candidates with information needed to develop pertinent qualifications and point their stories to solve an employer's specific problems.

Companies that have publicly traded stock are required to publish annual reports that are available in school libraries or online. Be sure to read news items and blog posts and sign up to receive news alerts from the prospective company for current company information

up until the day of the interview. Use social networking utilities such as LinkedIn and Hoovers.com to find profiles of company leaders and gain insights on the types of managers this company employs.

Employees of the company or other applicants who have interviewed might be of help to the interviewee. Employee reviews of selected companies, salaries, and sample interview questions are available online, and some universities share taped interviews with various company recruiters. Information about the company and the job sought pertinent in an interview includes the following:

Company Information

Be sure to research the following on the companies with which you interview:

- **Name.** Know, for example, that the publishing company Cengage Learning was so named to reflect the company's mission to be a "center of engagement" for its global customers.[3]
- **Status in the industry.** Know the company's share of the market, its *Fortune* 500 standing (if any), its sales, and its number of employees.
- **Latest stock market quote.** Be familiar with current market deviations and trends.
- **Recent news and developments.** Read current business periodicals, news, and blogs for special feature articles on the company, its new products, and its corporate leadership.
- **Scope of the company.** Is it local, national, or international?
- **Corporate officers.** Know the names of the chairperson, president, and chief executive officer.
- **Products and services.** Study the company's offerings, target markets, and innovative strategies.

Job Information

Be sure to know the following about the job you are seeking:

- **Job title.** Know the job titles of typical entry-level positions.
- **Job qualifications.** Understand the specific knowledge and skills desired.
- **Probable salary range.** Study salaries in comparable firms, as well as regional averages.
- **Career path of the job.** What opportunities for advancement are available?

14-2b Study Yourself

When you know something about the company, you will also know something about the kinds of jobs or training programs the company has to offer. Next, compare your qualifications to the company/job profile. This systematic comparison of your qualifications and job requirements helps you identify pertinent information (strengths or special abilities) to be included in your résumé. If you cannot see a relationship between you and the job or company, you might have difficulty demonstrating the interest or sincerity needed to sell yourself.

14-2c Plan Your Appearance

An employment interviewer once said she would not hire a job applicant who did not meet her *extremities* test: fingernails, shoes, and hair must be clean and well kept. This interviewer felt that if the candidate did not take care of those details, the candidate could not really be serious about, or fit into, her organization. Other important guidelines include avoiding heavy makeup

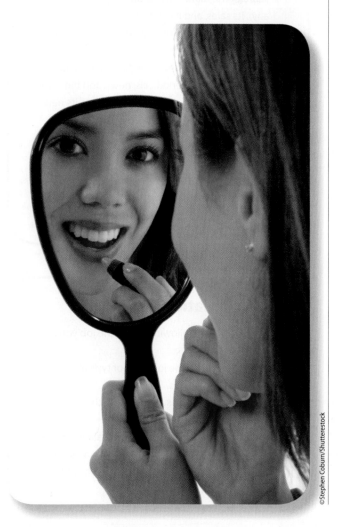

©Stephen Coburn/Shutterstock

and large, excessive jewelry. Select conservative clothes, and be certain clothing is clean, unwrinkled, and properly fitted. Additionally, avoid smoking, drinking, or wearing heavy fragrance

You can locate a wealth of information on appropriate interview dress from numerous electronic and printed sources. Additionally, talk with professors in your field, professors of business etiquette and professional protocol, personnel at your career services center, and graduates who have recently acquired jobs in your field. Research the company dress code—real or implied—ahead of time. If you *look* and *dress* like the people who already work for the company, the interviewer will be able to visualize you working there.

14-2d Plan Your Time and Materials

One of the worst things you can do is be late for an interview. If something should happen to prevent your arriving on time, phone an apology. Another mistake is to miss the interview entirely. Plan your time so that you will arrive early and can unwind and review mentally the things you plan to accomplish. Be sure to bring a professional briefcase or notebook that contains everything you will need during the interview. These items might include copies of your résumé, a list of references and/or recommendations, a professional-looking pen, paper for taking notes, highlights of what you know about the company, a list of questions you plan to ask, and previous correspondence with the company.

14-2e Practice

The job interview could be the most important face-to-face interaction you ever have. You will be selling yourself in competition with others. How you listen and how you talk are characteristics the interviewer will be able to measure. Your actions, your mannerisms, and your appearance will combine to give the total picture of how you are perceived. Added to the marketable skills you have acquired from your education, experience, and activities, your interview performance can give a skilled interviewer an excellent picture of you. Practicing for an interview will prepare you to handle the nervousness that is natural when interviewing. However, do not memorize answers, as it will sound rehearsed and insincere. Instead, think carefully about how your accomplishments match the job requirements and practice communicating these ideas smoothly, confidently, and professionally.

Prepare for standard interview questions and other interview issues following suggestions provided later in this chapter. Once you are satisfied you have identified your key selling points, have a friend ask you interview questions you have developed and surprise you with others. Participate in mock interviews with someone in your career services center or with a friend, alternating roles as interviewer and interviewee. Then follow each practice interview with a constructive critique of your performance.

14-3 Conducting a Successful Interview

The way you handle an interview will vary somewhat depending on your stage in the hiring process. Regardless of whether you are being screened by a campus recruiter in person, by phone or videoconference, or have progressed to an on-site visit, an interview will have three parts: the opening formalities, an information exchange, and the closing.

14-3a The Opening Formalities

According to management consultant Dan Burns, most candidates don't realize that in the first 60 seconds, interviewers typically decide whether the candidate will be moved to the top of the list or dropped from consideration. Burns emphasizes that skills missing during the interview are important because he assumes these same deficiencies will carry over during employment.[4] Clearly, since the impression created during the first few seconds of an interview often determines the outcome, you cannot afford to take time to warm up in an interview. You must enter the door selling yourself!

Common courtesies and confident body language can contribute to a favorable first impression in the early moments when you have not yet had an opportunity to talk about your qualifications:

- **Use the interviewer's name and pronounce it correctly.** Even if the interviewer calls you by your first name, always use the interviewer's surname unless specifically invited to do otherwise.

- **Apply a firm handshake.** Usually, the interviewer will initiate the handshake, although you may do so. In either case, apply a firm handshake. You do not want to leave the impression that you are weak or timid. At the same time, you do not want to overdo the firm grip and leave an impression of being overbearing.

© iStockphoto.com/OlegPrikhodko

Interviewers typically decide about a candidate in the first 60 seconds. You must enter the door selling yourself!

- **Wait for the interviewer to ask you to be seated.** If you aren't invited to sit, choose a chair across from or beside the interviewer's desk.

- **Maintain appropriate eye contact, and use your body language to convey confidence.** Sit erect and lean forward slightly to express interest. For a professional image, avoid slouching, chewing gum, and fidgeting.

- **Be conscious of nonverbal messages.** If the interviewer's eyes are glazing over, end your answer, but expand it if they are bright and the head is nodding vigorously. If the interviewer is from a different culture, be conscious of subtle differences in nonverbal communication that could affect the interviewer's perception of you. For example, a North American interviewer who sees eye contact as a sign of trust might perceive an Asian female who keeps her eyes lowered as a sign of respect to be uninterested or not listening.[5] Women should also be aware of typical "feminine behavior" during the interview. For instance, women nod more often than men when an interviewer speaks. Women are also likely to smile more and have a rising intonation at the end of sentences; such behaviors can convey a subservient attitude.[6]

Following the introductions, many interviewers will begin the conversation with nonbusiness talk to help you relax and to set the stage for the information exchange portion of the interview. Other interviewers bypass these casual remarks and move directly into the interview.

14-3b The Information Exchange

Much of the information about you will appear on your résumé or application form and is already available to the interviewer. Thus, the interviewer most likely will seek to go beyond such facts as your education, work experience, and extracurricular activities. He or she will attempt to assess your general attitude toward work and the probability of your fitting successfully into the organization.

Presenting Your Qualifications

Your preparation pays off during the interview. Like a defense attorney ready to win a case, you are ready to present evidence that you should be hired. According to Joyce Kennedy and Thomas Morrow, leading career consultants, your case will have three major points: You must convince the interviewer that you (1) can do the job, (2) will do the job, and (3) will not stress out everyone else while doing the job.[7] That's an overwhelming task. Where do you begin? You learned during your study of persuasive writing that saying you're the best at what you do is not convincing. To convince an interviewer to allow you to continue to the next interview or to extend you a job offer, you must provide specific, concrete evidence that your qualifications match the job description and equip you to add immediate value to the company. Use the following guidelines to help you relate your skills and knowledge to the job:

- **List five or six key points that you want to emphasize.** You will probably want to present your education as a major asset. You should point out its relationship to the job sought. Even more important, the fact that you have succeeded in academics indicates that you have the ability and self-discipline to learn. Because most companies expect you to learn something on the job, your ability to learn and thus quickly become productive will be your greatest asset. Even lack of work experience can be an asset: You have acquired no bad work habits that you will have to unlearn.

  Additionally, be sure to provide evidence of your interpersonal skills. Communicate that you can get along with others and are sensitive to diversity.

- What did you do in college that helped you get along with others?

- Were you a member, an officer, or president of an organization? What did you accomplish? How did others perceive you? Were you a leader? How did your followers respond to your leadership style? To your commitment to ethical standards?

- Can you organize projects, motivate people to complete important goals, and deal with difficult people?

The extracurricular activities listed on your résumé give an indication of these traits, but how you talk about them in your interview helps to demonstrate them. "I started as public relations vice president and was subsequently elected to higher office for four semesters, eventually becoming president" is a statement that proves your leadership qualities. If you can show your organization moved to greater heights, you will appear successful as well. You can also use questions about your extracurricular activities to show that you have broad, balanced interests rather than a single, time-consuming avocation that could lead to burnout and stress if carried to the job.

What are other skills that graduating students need to succeed in a cross-cultural, interdependent workforce? While academic performance is weighted more heavily for some types of jobs than others, the ability to juggle a complicated schedule is weighed heavily by many employers as an important job-success factor. Additionally, a UNESCO report of employer views revealed certain skills to be essential for workers in today's business climate as shown in Figure 14-1.[8]

Consider these general job-success traits and then use your knowledge of the job requirements and your own strengths to develop your "central selling features." These key points targeted to your audience are the central element of a winning argument: You are able and willing to become a contributing part of a high-performance team that will enhance the company's performance.

- **Be prepared to answer standard interview questions.** These questions are designed to show (a) why you want the job, (b) why you want to work for this organization, and (c) why the company should want you. Practice concise but fully developed answers that reflect your personality and your communication power. While one-word answers aren't adequate, long-winded answers can prevent interviewers from asking you other planned questions critical to making an informed decision.

- **Be prepared to answer behavioral questions.** These questions are designed to challenge you to provide evidence of your skills or the behaviors required

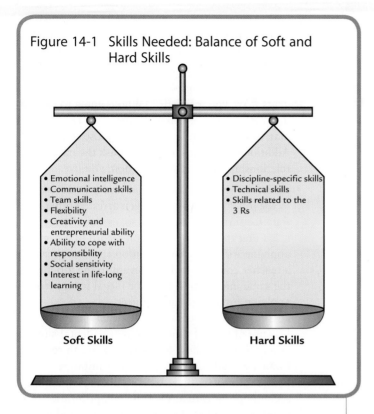

Figure 14-1 Skills Needed: Balance of Soft and Hard Skills

Soft Skills
- Emotional intelligence
- Communication skills
- Team skills
- Flexibility
- Creativity and entrepreneurial ability
- Ability to cope with responsibility
- Social sensitivity
- Interest in life-long learning

Hard Skills
- Discipline-specific skills
- Technical skills
- Skills related to the 3 Rs

to perform the job. Rather than asking applicants how they feel about certain things, interviewers are finding that asking potential employees for specific examples to illustrate their answers is a more objective way to evaluate applicants' skills.

Behavioral questions include the following:

- Describe a time when you worked well under pressure, worked effectively with others, organized a major project, motivated and led others, solved a difficult problem, or used persuasion to convince someone to accept your idea.

- What was the most difficult problem you had to overcome in your last job (or an academic or extracurricular activity)? How did you cope with it? What lesson did you learn from the situation? Share a time you applied the lesson learned.

- Tell me about a time you had difficulty working with a supervisor or coworker (or professor or peer in a team in a class setting). How did you handle the situation?

- Describe something you have done that shows initiative and willingness to work or required you to think on your feet to solve a problem.

- How have your extracurricular activities, part-time work experience, or volunteer work prepared you for work in our company?

- Tell me about a time you hit a wall trying to push forward a great idea.

To prepare for answering behavioral questions, brainstorm to identify stories that illustrate how your qualifications fit the job requirements. These stories should show you applying the skills needed on the job. Career counselors recommend using the STAR method (Situation or Task/Action/Result) as a consistent format to help you present a complete answer to these open-ended questions. You first describe a situation or task you were involved in, the action you took, and finally the result of your effort.[9]

- **Be prepared to demonstrate logical thinking and creativity.** Many interviewers ask applicants to solve brain teasers and riddles, create art out of paper bags, and solve complex business problems. Some are asked to "do the job before we give it to you," for example, write a press release on the spot or field a tech-support call.[10] These techniques are used to gauge an applicant's ability to think quickly and creatively and observe an emotional response to an awkward situation. You cannot anticipate this type of interview question, but you can familiarize yourself with mind teasers that have been used. Most importantly, however, recognize the interviewer's purpose; relax, and do your best to showcase your logical reasoning, creativity, or your courage to even try.

- **Display a professional attitude.** First, communicate your sincere interest in the company; show that you are strongly interested in the company and not just taking an interview for practice. Reveal your knowledge of the company gained through reading published information, and refer to the people you have talked with about the working conditions, company achievements, and career paths.

  Second, focus on the satisfaction gained from contributing to a company rather than the benefits you will receive. What's important in a job goes beyond financial reward. All applicants are interested in a paycheck; any job satisfies that need—some will pay more, some less. Recognize that the paycheck is a part of the job and should not be your primary concern. Intrinsic rewards such as personal job satisfaction, the feeling of accomplishment, and making a contribution to society are ideas to discuss in the interview. You should like what you are doing and find a challenging job that will satisfy these needs.

- **Be prepared to discuss salary and benefits.** For most entry-level positions, the beginning salary is fixed. However, if you have work experience, excellent scholarship records, or added maturity, you might be able to obtain a higher salary. The interviewer should initiate the salary topic. What you should know is the general range for candidates with your qualifications so that your response to a question about how much you would expect is reasonable.

If you have other job offers, you are in a position to compare salaries, jobs, and companies. In this case, you might suggest to the interviewer that you would expect a competitive salary and that you have been offered X dollars by another firm. If salary has not been mentioned, and you really want to know about it, simply ask courteously how much the salary would be for someone with your qualifications. In any case, if you really believe the job offers the non-monetary benefits you seek, do not attempt to make salary a major issue.

Typically, an interviewer will introduce the subject of benefits without your asking about them. In some cases, a discussion of total salary and "perks" is reserved for a follow-up interview. If nothing has been said about certain benefits, you should take the liberty of asking, particularly when an item is especially important to you.

- **Be knowledgeable of interview questions and information on your social networking sites that might lead to discriminatory hiring practices.** The Equal Employment Opportunity Commission (EEOC) and Fair Employment Practices Guidelines make it clear that an employer cannot legally discriminate against a job applicant on the basis of race, color, gender, age, religion, national origin, or disability. Interviewers must restrict questions to an applicant's ability to perform specific job-related functions essential to the job sought. Generally, the following topics should not be introduced:

- *National origin and religion.* "You have an unusual accent; where were you born?" "What religious holidays will require you to miss work?"

- *Age.* "I see you attended Central High School; what year did you graduate?" "Could you provide a copy of your birth certificate?"

- *Disabilities, health conditions, and physical characteristics not reasonably related to the job.* "Do you have a disability that would interfere with your ability to perform the job? "Have you ever been injured on the job?" "Have you ever been treated by a psychiatrist?" "How much alcohol do you consume each week?" "What prescription drugs are you currently taking?"

- *Marital status, spouse's employment, or dependents.* "Are you married?" "Who is going to care for your children if you work for us?" "Do you plan to have children?" "Is your spouse employed?" Additionally, employers may not ask the names or relationships of people with whom you live.

- *Arrests or criminal convictions that are not related to the job.* "Have you ever been arrested other than for traffic violations? If so, explain." Keep in mind that the arrest/conviction record of a person applying for a job as a law enforcement officer or a teacher could be highly relevant to the job, but the same information could be illegal for a person applying for a job as an engineer.

Since interviewers may ask illegal questions because of lack of training or an accidental slip, you must decide how to respond. You can refuse to answer and state the question is improper, though you risk offending the interviewer. A second option is to answer the inappropriate question, knowing it is illegal and unrelated to job requirements. A third approach is to provide a low-key response such as "How does this question relate to how I will do my job?" or to answer the legitimate concern that likely prompted the question. For example, an interviewer who asks, "Do you plan to have children?" is probably concerned about how long you might remain on the job. An answer to this concern would be "I plan to pursue a career regardless of whether I decide to raise a family." If you can see no legitimate concern in a question, such as "Do you own your home, rent, or live with parents?" answer, "I'm not sure how that question relates to the job. Can you explain?"[11]

Asking Questions of the Interviewer

Both the interviewer and interviewee want to know as much as possible about each other before making a commitment to hire. A good way to determine whether the job is right for you is to ask pertinent questions.

Good questions show the interviewer that you have initiative and are interested in making a well-informed decision. Responses can provide insight to job requirements that you can then show you possess. Therefore, be sure not to say, "I don't have any questions." Focus on questions that help you gain information about the company and the job that you could not learn from published sources or persons other than the interviewer. Respect the interviewer's time by avoiding questions that indicate you are unprepared (for example, questions about the company's scope, products/services, job requirements, or new developments). Avoid questions about salary, required overtime, and benefits that imply you are interested more in money and the effort required than in the contribution you can make.

14-3c The Closing

The interviewer will provide cues indicating that the interview is completed by rising or making a comment about the next step to be taken. At that point, do not prolong the interview needlessly. Simply rise, accept the handshake, thank the interviewer for the opportunity to meet, and close by saying you look forward to hearing from the company. The tact with which you close the interview can be almost as important as the first impression you made. Be enthusiastic. If you really want the job, you must ask for it.

Your ability to speak confidently and intelligently about your abilities will help you secure a desirable job. Effective interviewing skills will be just as valuable once you begin work. You will be involved in interviews with

your supervisor for various reasons: to seek advice or information about your work and working conditions, to receive informal feedback about your progress, to receive a deserved promotion, and to discuss other personnel matters. In addition, your supervisor will likely conduct a performance appraisal interview to evaluate your performance. This formal interview typically occurs annually on the anniversary of your start of employment.

14-4 Preparing Other Employment Messages

Preparing a winning résumé and application letter is an important first step in a job search. To expedite your job search, you will need to prepare other employment messages. For example, you might complete an application form, send a follow-up message to a company that does not respond to your résumé, send a thank-you message after an interview, accept a job offer, reject other job offers, and communicate with references. A career change will require a carefully written resignation letter.

14-4a Application Forms

Before beginning a new job, you will almost certainly complete the employer's application and employment forms. Some application forms, especially for applicants who apply for jobs with a high level of responsibility, are very long. They can actually appear to be tests in which applicants give their answers to hypothetical questions and write defenses for their answers. Increasing numbers of companies are designing employment forms as mechanisms for acquiring information about a candidate that often is not included in the résumé. Application forms also ensure consistency in the information received from each candidate and can prevent decisions based on illegal topics which might be presented in a résumé.

14-4b Follow-Up Messages

When an application message and résumé do not elicit a response, a follow-up message might bring results. Sent a few weeks after the original message, it includes a reminder that an application for a certain job is on file, presents additional education or experience accumulated and its relationship to the job, and closes with a reference to desired action. In addition to conveying new information, follow-up messages indicate persistence (a quality that impresses some employers). Figure 14-2 shows a good example of a follow-up letter.

14-4c Thank-You Messages

What purposes are served in sending a thank-you message, even though you expressed thanks in person after the interview or a discussion with a special employer at a career fair? After a job interview, a written message of appreciation is a professional courtesy and enhances your image within the organization. To be effective, it must be sent promptly. For maximum impact, send a thank-you message the day of the interview or the following day. Even if during the interview you decided you do not want the job or you and the interviewer mutually agreed that the job is not for you, a thank-you message is appropriate. As a matter of fact, if you've made a positive impression, interviewers might forward your résumé to others who are seeking qualified applicants.

The medium you choose for sending this message depends on the intended audience. If the company you've interviewed with prefers a traditional style, send a letter in complete business format on high-quality paper that matches your résumé and application letter. If the company has communicated with you extensively by email, follow the pattern and send a professional

---

Figure 14-2 **GOOD :-)** Example of a Follow-Up Letter

Dear Mr. Tucker:

Recently, I applied for a marketing position with Friedman Plastics and now have additional qualifications to report.

The enclosed updated resume shows that I recently completed a social media marketing course sponsored by the American Marketing Association. The online course taught me the principles of using social media as an effective, low-cost marketing tool. It also provided many examples of effective social media campaigns that could be easily implemented to promote the products of Friedman Plastics.

Mr. Tucker, I would welcome the opportunity to visit your office and talk more about the contributions I could make as at Friedman Plastics. Please write or call me at (340)642-5003.

States main idea and clearly identifies position being sought.

Refers to enclosed résumé; summarizes additional qualifications.

Assures employer that applicant is still interested in job.

Format Pointers
Format as formal business letter, but could have sent message electronically if previous communication with employer had been by email.

Print letter and envelope with laser printer on paper that matches résumé and application letter.

STUDY TOOLS

CHAPTER 14

Located at back of the textbook

❑ Rip out Chapter Review Card

Located at www.cengagebrain.com

❑ Review Key Terms Flashcards (Print or Online)

❑ Download Audio Summaries for on-the-go review

❑ Complete Practice Quizzes to prepare for tests

❑ Play "Beat the Clock" to master concepts

❑ Complete the Crossword Puzzle to review key terms

❑ Watch the video about McDonaldson, a fictitious but all-too-realistic ad agency, whose employees struggle with contemporary business communication issues.

Polishing your language skills will aid you in preparing error-free documents that reflect positively on you and your company. This text appendix is an abbreviated review that focuses on common problems frequently encountered by business writers and offers a quick "refreshing" of key skills.

GRAMMAR

Sentence Structure

1. **Rely mainly on sentences that follow the normal subject-verb-complement sequence for clarity and easy reading.**

   <u>Jennifer</u> and <u>I</u> <u>withdrew</u> for two <u>reasons</u>.

     (subject)   (verb)   (complement)

Original	Better
There are two <u>reasons</u> for our withdrawal.	Two <u>reasons</u> for our withdrawal are . . . .
	<u>Jennifer</u> and <u>I</u> withdrew for two reasons.
<u>It</u> is necessary that we withdraw.	<u>We</u> must withdraw.
<u>Here</u> is a copy of my résumé.	The enclosed <u>résumé</u> outlines . . . .

   There, it, and *here* are *expletives*—filler words that have no real meaning in the sentence.

2. **Put pronouns, adverbs, phrases, and clauses near the words they modify.**

Incorrect	Correct
Angie put a new type of gel in her hair, <u>which</u> she had just purchased.	Angie put a new type of <u>gel</u>, <u>which</u> she had just purchased, in her hair.
He works <u>only</u> in the call center during peak periods.	He works in the call center <u>only</u> during peak periods.
The clerk stood near the fax machine <u>wearing a denim skirt</u>.	The clerk <u>wearing a denim skirt</u> stood near the fax machine.

3. **Do not separate subject and predicate unnecessarily.**

Incorrect	Clear
<u>She</u>, hoping to receive a bonus, <u>worked</u> rapidly.	Hoping to receive a bonus, <u>she</u> <u>worked</u> rapidly.

4. **Place an introductory phrase near the subject of the independent clause it modifies.** Otherwise, the phrase dangles. To correct the dangling phrase, change the subject of the independent clause, or make the phrase into a dependent clause by assigning it a subject.

Incorrect	Correct
<u>When</u> a young boy, <u>my</u> <u>mother</u> insisted I learn a second language.	<u>When I was a young boy</u>, my mother insisted I learn a second language.
[Implies that the mother was once a young boy.]	
<u>Working</u> at full speed every morning, <u>fatigue</u> overtakes me in the afternoon.	<u>Working</u> at full speed every morning, <u>I</u> become tired in the afternoon.
[Implies that "fatigue" was working at full speed.]	<u>Because I work</u> at full speed every morning, <u>fatigue</u> overtakes me in the afternoon.
<u>To function</u> properly, <u>you</u> must oil the machine every hour.	<u>If the equipment</u> is to function properly, <u>you</u> must oil it every hour.
[Implies that if "you" are "to function properly," the machine must be oiled hourly.]	<u>To function properly</u>, the <u>equipment</u> must be oiled every hour.

1. Despite the dangers, employees change their computer passwords (infrequent, infrequently).

2. Daniel looked (impatient, impatiently) at the new production assistant.

3. The server moved (quick, quickly) from table to table.

4. Of the several people I met during the recent speed networking event, Olivia made the (better, best) impression.

5. The Chicago plant has a higher safety record than (any, any other) plant.

PUNCTUATION

Commas

1. **Use a comma**

   a. Between coordinate clauses joined by *and, but, for, or,* and *nor.*

      He wanted to pay his bills on time, but he did not have the money.

   b. To separate introductory clauses and certain phrases from independent clauses. Sentences that begin with dependent clauses (often with words such as *if, as, since, because, although,* and *when*) almost always need a comma. Prepositional phrases and verbal phrases with five or more words require commas.

Dependent clause:	**If you can postpone your departure, the research team will be able to finalize its proposal submission.** [The comma separates the introductory dependent clause from the independent clause.]
Infinitive:	**To get the full benefit of our insurance plan, complete and return the enclosed card.** [A verb preceded by "to" ("to get").]
Participial:	**Believing that her earnings would continue to increase, she requested a higher credit card limit.**

   [A verb form used as an adjective: "believing" modifies the dependent clause "she requested."]

Prepositional phrase:	**Within the next few days, you will receive written confirmation of this transaction.** [Comma needed because the phrase contains five words.] **Under the circumstances we think you are justified.** [Comma omitted because the phrase contains fewer than five words and the sentence is clear without the comma.]

   c. To separate three or more words in a series.

      You must choose between gray, green, purple, and white. [Without the comma after "purple," no one can tell for sure whether four choices are available, the last of which is "white," or whether three choices are available, the last of which is "purple and white."]

      You must choose between purple and white, gray, and green. [Choice is restricted to three, the first of which is "purple and white."]

   d. Between two or more independent adjectives that modify the same noun.

      New employees are given a long, difficult examination. [Both "long" and "difficult" modify "examination."]

      We want quick, factual news. [Both "quick" and "factual" modify "news."]

      Do not place a comma between two adjectives when the second adjective modifies the adjective and noun as a unit.

      The supervisor is an excellent team player. ["Excellent" modifies the noun phrase "team player."]

   e. To separate a nonrestrictive clause (a clause that is not essential to the basic meaning of the sentence) from the rest of the sentence.

      Kent Murray, who is head of customer resource management, has selected Century Consulting to oversee the product launch. [The parenthetical remark is not essential to the meaning of the sentence.]

The man <u>who is head of customer resource management</u> has selected Century Consulting to oversee the product launch. [Commas are not needed because "who is head of customer resource management" is essential to the meaning of the sentence.]

f. To set off or separate dates, addresses, geographical names, degrees, and long numbers:

On <u>July 2, 2013,</u> Jason Kennedy made the final payment. [Before and after the year in month-day-year format]

I saw him in <u>Tahoe City, California,</u> on the 12th of October. [Before and after the name of a state when the name of a city precedes it]

<u>Jesse Marler,</u> President [Between the printed name and the title on the same line beneath a signature or in a letter address]

Tristan A. Highfield
President of Academic Affairs [No comma is used if the title is on a separate line.]

g. To separate parenthetical expressions or other elements interrupting the flow from the rest of the sentence.

Ms. Watson, <u>speaking on behalf of the entire department,</u> accepted the proposal. [Set off a parenthetical expression]

<u>Cole,</u> I believe you have earned a vacation. [After a direct address]

<u>Yes,</u> you can count on me. [After the words *No* and *Yes* when they introduce a statement]

Arun Ramage, <u>former president of the Jackson Institute,</u> spoke to the group. [Set off appositives when neutral emphasis is desired]

The job requires experience, <u>not formal education.</u> [Between contrasted elements]

EXERCISE 6
Insert needed commas. Write "correct" if you find no errors.

1. The employee who is featured in our latest television commercial is active in the community theatre.
2. Emoticons which are created by keying combinations of symbols to produce "sideway faces" communicate emotion in electronic messages.
3. Sean Cohen a new member of the board remained silent during the long bitter debate.
4. Top social networking sites include Facebook MySpace and Flickr.
5. The entire population was surveyed but three responses were unusable.
6. If you tag websites in a social bookmarking site you can locate them easily for later use.
7. To qualify for the position applicants must have technology certification.
8. We should be spending less money not more.
9. On May 9 2013 the company's Twitter site was launched.
10. Yes the president approved a team-building event to replace our annual golf outing.

Semicolons and Colons

1. **Use a semicolon**

a. To join the independent clauses in a compound sentence when a conjunction is omitted.

Your voice counts; email us with your ideas and concerns.

b. To join the independent clauses in a compound-complex sentence.

As indicated earlier, we prefer delivery on Saturday morning at four o'clock; but Friday night at ten o'clock will be satisfactory.

We prefer delivery on Saturday morning at four o'clock; but, if the arrangement is more convenient for you, Friday night at ten o'clock will be satisfactory.

c. Before an adverbial conjunction. Use a comma after the adverbial conjunction.

Adverbial conjunction:	The shipment arrived too late for our weekend sale; <u>therefore</u>, we are returning the shipment to you.

Other frequently used adverbial conjunctions are *however, otherwise, consequently,* and *nevertheless.*

d. Before words used to introduce enumerations or explanations that follow an independent clause.

Enumeration with commas:	Many factors affect the direction of the stock market; <u>namely</u>, interest rates, economic growth, and employment rates.

Explanation forming a complete thought:	**We have plans for improvement; for example, we intend. . . . The engine has been "knocking"; that is, the gas in the cylinders explodes before the pistons complete their upward strokes.**

NOTE: The following exceptions require a comma to introduce the enumeration or explanation:

Enumeration without commas:	**Several Web 2.0 tools are available, for example, blogs and wikis.** [A comma, not a semicolon, is used because the enumeration contains no commas.]
Explanation forming an incomplete thought:	**A trend is to replace expensive employee networking events with purposeful recreation, for instance, community service events.** [A comma, not a semicolon, is used because the explanation is not a complete thought.]

e. In a series that contains commas.

Some of our workers have worked overtime this week: Smith, 6 hours; Hardin, 3; Cantrell, 10; and McGowan, 11.

2. **Use a colon**

a. After a complete thought that introduces a list of items. Use a colon following both direct and indirect introductions of lists.

Direct introduction:	**The following three factors influenced our decision: an expanded market, an inexpensive source of raw materials, and a ready source of labor.** [The word "following" clearly introduces a list.]
Indirect introduction:	**The carpet is available in three colors: green, burgundy, and blue.**

Do not use a colon after an introductory statement that ends with a preposition or a verb (*are, is, were, include*). The list that follows the preposition or verb finishes the sentence.

Incomplete sentence:	**We need to (1) expand our market, (2) locate an inexpensive source of materials, and (3) find a ready source of labor.** [A colon does not follow "to" because the words preceding the list are not a complete sentence.]

b. To stress an appositive (a noun that renames the preceding noun) at the end of a sentence.

A majority of white collar criminals report that a single factor led to their crimes: pressure to achieve revenue targets.

Our progress is due to the efforts of one person: Brooke Keating.

EXERCISE 7

Insert semicolons, colons, and commas where needed, and delete them where they are unnecessary. Write "correct" if you find no errors.

1. Some privacy concerns have become less important in recent years, however, most people feel extremely vulnerable to privacy invasion.

2. The following agents received bonuses Barnes, $750, Shelley, $800, and Jackson, $950.

3. Employees were notified today of the plant closing they received two weeks' severance pay.

4. This paint does have some disadvantages for example a lengthy drying time.

5. Soon after the applications are received, a team of judges will evaluate them, but the award recipients will not be announced until January 15.

6. The program has one shortcoming: flexibility.

7. The new bakery will offer: frozen yogurt, candies, and baked goods.

8. We are enthusiastic about the plan because: (1) it is least expensive, (2) its legality is unquestioned, and (3) it can be implemented quickly.

Apostrophes

1. **Use an apostrophe to form possessives.**

   a. Add an apostrophe and *s* (*'s*) to form the posessive case of a singular noun or a plural noun that does not end with a pronounced *s*.

Singular noun:	**Jenna's** position
	firm's assets
	employee's benefits
Plural noun without a pronounced *s*:	**men's** clothing
	children's games
	deer's antlers

   b. Add only an apostrophe to form the possessive of a singular or plural noun that ends with a pronounced *s*.

Singular noun with pronounced *s*:	**Niagara Falls'** site
	Ms. Jenkins' interview
Plural noun with pronounced *s*:	two **managers'** decision
	six **months'** wages

   Exception: An apostrophe and *s* (*'s*) can be added to singular nouns ending in a pronounced *s* if an additional *s* sound is pronounced easily.

Singular noun with additional *s* **sound:**	**boss's** decision
	class's party
	Jones's invitation

   c. Use an apostrophe with the possessives of nouns that refer to time (minutes, hours, days, weeks, months, and years) or distance in a possessive manner.

eight **hours'** pay	two **weeks'** notice
today's global economy	ten **years'** experience
a **stone's** throw	a **yard's** length

   EXERCISE 8

   Correct the possessives.

   1. The new hires confidence was crushed by the managers harsh tone.
   2. This companies mission statement has been revised since it's recent merger.
   3. Employees who are retained may be asked to accept a reduction of one weeks pay.
   4. Vendors' have submitted sealed bids for the construction contract that will be opened in two week's.
   5. Younger workers must appreciate older employees extensive company knowledge.

Hyphens

1. **Use a hyphen**

   a. Between the words in a compound adjective. (A *compound adjective* is a group of adjectives appearing together and used as a single word to describe a noun.)

An **eye-catching** device	A **two-thirds** interest

   Do not hyphenate a compound adjective in the following cases:

   (1) When the compound adjective follows a noun.

   A design that is **eye catching.**

   Today's consumers are **convenience driven.**

   NOTE: Some compound adjectives that are familiar hyphenated words or phrases, remain hyphenated when they follow a noun.

   The news release was **up-to-date.**

   For jobs that are **part-time,** . . . .

   (2) An expression made up of an adverb that ends in *ly* and an adjective is not a compound adjective and does not require a hyphen.

   commonly accepted principle

   widely quoted authority

   (3) A simple fraction and a percentage.

Simple fraction:	**Two thirds** of the respondents
Percentage:	**15 percent** sales increase

   b. To prevent misinterpretation.

   Recover a chair [To obtain possession of a chair once more]

   Re-cover a chair [To cover a chair again]

   Eight inch blades [Eight blades, each of which is an inch long]

   Eight-inch blades [Blades eight inches long]

résumé supplements
employment videos, 248–249
professional portfolio, 246, 247
résumé types
beamer, 241
chrono-functional, 239
chronological, 238, 242
functional, 238–239, 244
inline, 243, 245
multimedia, 248
scannable, 245–246, 247
text, 245
video, 249
revising and proofreading
appropriate language, 66
bias-free language, 66–67
clichés, 60
concise communication, 61–62
condescending words, 65
connotative words, 65–66
demeaning expressions, 65
email messages, 74
euphemisms, 64–65
mechanical correctness, 67–70
outdated expressions, 60
profanity, 60
readability of, 57–60
simple, informal words, 60–61
suggestions for, 56–57
tone, 62–64
Robert's Rules of Order, 34
role perception, 29
roles, 29–30
routine claims, 94–96
routine messages about orders and credit, 101–104
routine requests, 97–100
defined, 97
examples of, 97–98
favorable response to, 98, 99
form messages for, 99
for information, 97
positive response to, 99, 100

S

sales messages, 131–140
action, motivating, 137, 138
action oriented, 133
attention-getting devices, 132
central selling point, 131, 134
cohesive, 133
enclosures in, 136
evidence, 134–135
examples of, 138, 139–140
guarantees in, 136
objectivity in, 135–136
original approach to, 133
price resistance and, 136–137
testimonials in, 136
unsolicited and solicited, 131
sales promotional material, 95
sampling, 156–157
Save Our Slides (Earnest), 213
scannable résumé
example of, 247

formatting, 245
searchable, 245–246
Schweitzer, Albert, 10
search engine, 154–155
secondary research, 153–156
defined, 153
electronic sources, 155–156
objectives, 154
printed sources, 154
security in electronic communication, 79–80
segmented bar chart, 173, 174
sentences
active voice used in, 51–52
ideas emphasized in, 52–53
length of, 55–56
passive voice used in, 51–52
structure of, 52–53
subjunctive, 63–64
topic, 53, 54
transition, 190
sequencing
in formal report, 189–190
of ideas, 48, 49, 74
serials, 154
series interview, 260
short report, 150, 192–199
audit, 194–195
email as, 192
examples of, 193–195, 196–199
form reports, 192, 195
letters as, 192, 196–199
memo as, 192, 193
Shriver, Tim, 65
Simmons, Annette, 210
situational leadership model, 23
size of groups or teams, 29
slander, 46
smartphones, 84, 86, 241
social context, 39
socializer, 30
social media, 81–83
social networking sites, 76, 83
weblog (or blog), writing for, 81–82
wikis, writing, 82–83
social networking sites, 76, 83
solicited proposals, 199–200
solicited sales message, 131
solution to research problem, 164–166
data analysis in, 164, 165
data interpretation in, 165–166
source notes, 163–164
spell-check, computer, 67–68
Spitzer, Eliot, 79
spoken messages, 38
stability, 38
stakeholders, 9
standards of ethical conduct, 11
STAR method (Situation or Task/Action/Result), 265
statement of purpose, 151
status, 27, 29
stereotypes
bad listening habits and, 26
bias-free language and, 66–67
defined, 13–14

storming, 30, 31
stress interview, 260
stroke, 21–22
structured interview, 259
subjunctive sentence, 63–64
successful interviews, 263–267
closing, 267
information exchange, 264–267
opening formalities, 263–264
presenting qualifications, 264–266
questions of interviewer, 266, 267
supportive behavior, 23
surveys, 159, 160–161
synergy, 16, 17

T

table of contents, 184
table of figures, 184, 185
tables, 59, 172, 173
tabulations, 191
tabulation techniques, 164
tact used in bad-news messages, 109
talking headings, 189
targeted résumé, 233–239. *See also* résumé
task force, 30
team members
commitment of, 31
contribution of, 31
cooperation of, 27, 28–29, 31
team orientation, 38
team presentations, 223–224
teams. *See also* groups; work teams
commitment of members, 31
communication in, 31
contribution of members, 31
cooperation of members, 27, 28–29, 31
cross-functional, 30
defined, 16
development, stages of, 30–31
environment, 16–17
vs. group, 30–31
organizing, strategies used, 30
presentations in, 223–224
product development, 30
quality assurance, 30
structures, 30, 31
task force, 30
technology, 15–16
changing, 15–16
in electronic communication, 85–86
ethical conduct and, 15
formality in, levels of, 78
telecommuting (or teleworking), 15
telephone, proper use of, 42
telephone surveys, 160
testimonials in sales messages, 136
text in formal report, 186
text messaging, 77–78, 79
text résumé, 245
text-to-voice technology, 85

thank-you messages, 92, 268, 269–270, 272
Theory X, 22–23
Theory Y, 22–23
35MM slides, 212
three Rs, 17
time, interpretation of, 14
title page, 183, 184
tone
connotative, 65–66
defined, 62
positive and tactful, 62–64
topic sentence, 53, 54
Total Quality Management, 23
transition sentences, 190
translation limitations, 15
Tufte, Edward, 171
Twain, Mark, 61

U

unethical behavior, causes of, 10–11
unsolicited application message, 251
unsolicited proposals, 200
unsolicited sales message, 131
unstructured interview, 259–260
upward communication, 7–8

V

validity, 157
verbal fillers, 216–217
vertical report, 150
videoconferencing
guidelines for, 225–226
proper use of, 42
video résumé, 249
virtual interview, 260–261
viruses, 75–76
visual enhancements to improve readability, 58–60
enumerated or bulleted lists, 58
enumerations, 58
headings, 59
images, relevant, 59
lines and borders, 59
tables and graphs, 59
visual kinesic communication, 24
vocal kinesic communication, 24
vocal qualities, 216–218
articulation, 217
phonation, 216–217
pronunciation, 218
voice mail, 42, 83
voice-to-text technology, 85
volume, 216

W

webcasting, 225–226
weblog (or blog), 81–82
Web page, 80–81
accessible, 80
content, 81
extranet, 80
intranet, 80
proper use of, 42
social media, 81–83
writing, rules for, 80–81

Web presentations, 225–226
Whoever Tells the Best Story Wins (Simmons), 210
wiki, 82–83
wireless communication, 84–85
wireless-free quiet zones, 84
words
  compound adjectives, 62
  condescending, 65
  connotative, 65–66
  in email messages, 74
  in formal reports, 191
  jargon, 61
  labeling, 53
  position of, 53
  redundant, 61–62
  in report, 153
  simple and informal, 60–61
works cited, 164, 187
work teams
  communication differences in, 16–17
  defined, 16
  divided, 16
  effectiveness, maximizing, 17
  synergy in, 16, 17
World Wide Web, 80, 155
written messages, 51–70. *See also* first draft; messages

Y

"you attitude," 45
YouTube, 170

Rough Draft of a Letter (excerpt)

September 8, 2012
Fax Transmission

Francis Fordham, President
Happy Cupcakes
2054 State Street
Boise, ~~Idaho~~ ID 83301

Dear Mr. ~~Nunez~~ Fordham:

Congratulations on the opening of your innovative cupcake bakery and wine bar! We are excited to learn of your interest in the Lexor commercial oven line and believe you will find a model that meets your exact needs.

Available with radiant, direct-fired convection and hybrid radiant/convection heating, Lexor ovens are highly energy efficient owing to both heating system design and their low surface-area-to-volume ratio. Fully automated, they incorporate a user-friendly, touch-screen interface, plus full-length viewing doors for visual inspection of the bake at every level and easy access for cleaning and maintenance. Lexor ovens provide enormous advantages over conventional oven technologies, including:

- Improved product quality and consistency. The ultra-compact design is based on a transport technology, where pans are conveyed horizontally through the oven via a vertical "S" configuration.

- Reduced foot space. Typically one space ~~tenth~~ the footspace on an equivalent tunnel oven, Lexor ovens offer a crucial advantage in environments where production floor space is at a premium.

- Superior flexibility. Lexor ovens provide superior flexibility, allowing product changes by simply changing pans and additional tooling.

Mr. Fordham, we are eager to schedule your visit to our nearby showroom to introduce our product line. At your convenience, please review the enclosed brochures and I will call you next week to schedule an appointment.

© Cengage Learning 2013

Adds mailing notation.

Uses two-letter state abbreviation.

Corrects spelling of name.

Adds smooth transition to next paragraph.

Bullet list for emphasis and conciseness.

Eliminates unnecessary comma.

Replace with simple word for clarity.

Errors Undetectable by Spell-Check

Verify spelling of receiver's name, "Fordham."

Correct proofreading grammatical error.

Check correctness of word substitutions: "to" for "too" and "your" for "you."

Improving Readability Through Cautious Use of a Grammar and Style Checker

Step 1: Evaluate and respond to advice given for grammar and style errors detected.

Step 2: Use counts, averages, and readability indexes as guides for adjusting writing level appropriately.

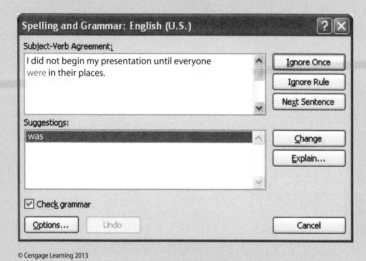

© Cengage Learning 2013

Improving Your Writing with the Computer

Hone your computer skills to spend more time writing and less time formatting.

☑ Draft in a font style and size easily read on-screen; postpone formatting until the revision is done.

☑ Use the *find* and *go to* commands to search and make changes.

☑ Learn time-saving keyboard shortcuts for frequently used commands such as *copy* and *cut*. Customize software so that you can access these commands easily.

☑ Use automatic numbering to arrange numerical or alphabetical lists and to ensure accuracy.

☑ Save time by using built-in styles such as cover pages, headers/footers, list and table formats, text boxes, and graphical effects.

☑ Save frequently used text such as a letterhead or your signature line so you can insert it with a single click.

☑ Use the *citations and bibliography* command to format references and the *document styles* feature to automatically generate a content page and index.

Use formatting features to create an organized and polished appearance.

☑ Add spacing between lines and paragraphs and use crisp, open fonts such as Calibri for a contemporary look that is easy to read on-screen.

☑ Apply color-infused document themes and built-in styles to reflect a consistent brand identity.

Use proofing features to locate errors.

☑ Use spell-check frequently as you draft and revise. Be aware that spell-check will not identify miskeyings (*than* for *then*), commonly misused words, homophones (*principle, principal*), omitted words, missing or out-of-order enumerations, and content errors.

☑ Use grammar check to provide feedback on usage, reading level, comprehension factors, and other errors and weaknesses that cannot be detected electronically.

☑ Use a thesaurus only when you can recognize the precise meaning needed.

Email Format

```
New Message

       To:  All sales staff
       cc:
  Subject:  Addition of Stephen Kerr to Our Staff
  ─────────────────────────────────────────────

  Everyone,

  I'm pleased to announce the appointment of Stephen Kerr as
  communications specialist in the corporate communications department.
  He will fill the position vacated by Kenneth Shaw and will begin work on
  May 6.

  FYI, Steve comes to us from Gynco Industries, where he was in charge of
  mass media relations. His duties with us will include long-range planning
  and acting as liaison with our ad agency. He has degrees in public relations
  and marketing.

  Steve merits your full support. We wish him much success and extend a
  sincere welcome to our organization. :-)

  Thanks,

  Jenny

  Jenny Veitch, Vice President of Operations
  Franklin Corporation
  875 Marshall Freeway, Suite 4500
  Atlanta, GA 30304
  (404) 555-3000, Extension 6139 Fax: (404) 555-9759
```

Includes descriptive subject line.

Includes appropriate salutation for group of coworkers.

Uses emoticon and email abbreviation in informal message to coworkers who understand and approve of this shorthand.

Includes signature file that identifies writer.

Format Pointers

Includes single spaced, unindented paragraphs and short lines for complete screen display.

Uses mixed case for easy reading.

Keeps format simple for quick download and compatibility.

Email Format

While certain email formats are standard, some degree of flexibility exists in formatting email messages. Primarily, be certain your message is easy to read and represents the standards of formality that your company has set. The following guidelines and the model email illustrated above will assist you in formatting professional email messages:

- **Include an appropriate salutation and closing.** You might write "Dear" and the person's name or simply the person's first name when messaging someone for the first time. Casual expressions such as "Hi" and "Later" are appropriate for personal messages but not serious business email. A closing of "Sincerely" is considered quite formal for email messages; instead, a simple closing such as "Best wishes" or "Thank you" provides a courteous end to your message.
- **Include a signature file at the end of the message.** The signature file (known as a .sig file) contains a few lines of text that include your full name and title, mailing address, telephone number, and any other information you want people to know about you. You might include a clever quote that you update frequently.
- **Format for easy readability.** Follow these suggestions:
  - Limit each message to one screen to minimize scrolling. If you need more space, consider a short email message with a lengthier message attached as a word processing file. Be certain the recipient can receive and read the attachment.
  - Limit the line length to 60 characters so that the entire line is displayed on the monitor without scrolling.

- Use short, unindented paragraphs. Separate paragraphs with an extra space.
- Use mixed case for easy reading. Typing in all capital letters is perceived as shouting in email and considered rude online behavior.
- Emphasize a word or phrase by surrounding it with quotation marks or keying in uppercase letters.
- **_Use emoticons or email abbreviations in moderation when you believe the receiver will understand and approve._** **_Emoticons,_** created by keying combinations of symbols to produce "sideways" faces, are a shorthand way of lightening the mood, adding emotion to email messages, and attempting to compensate for nonverbal cues lost in one-way communication:

    | :-) | smiling, indicates humor or sarcasm | %-(| confused |
    | :-(| frowning, indicates sadness or anger | :-0 | surprised |

Alternately, you might put a "g" (for grin) or "smile" in parentheses after something that is obviously meant as tongue-in-cheek to help carry the intended message to the receiver. Abbreviations for commonly used phrases save space and avoid unnecessary keying. Popular ones include BCNU (be seeing you), BTW (by the way), FYI (for your information), FWIW (for what it's worth), HTH (hope this helps), IMHO (in my humble opinion), and LOL (laugh out loud).

Some email users feel strongly that emoticons and abbreviations are childish or inappropriate for serious email and decrease productivity when the receiver must take time for deciphering. Before using them, be certain the receiver will understand them and that the formality of the message and your relationship with the receiver justify this type of informal exchange. Then, use only in moderation to punctuate your message.

GOOD  Good Example of an Email Message

---

New Message

To: Rodney Spurlin, Software Compliance Officer
From: Claire Henderson, Director of Legal Services
Subject: Legal Liability for Downloaded Music

Rodney,

Your immediate attention is needed to address the company's liability for employees' downloading copyrighted music.

The recording industry has announced its intent to prosecute organizations that allow their employees to download and store music files without proper authorization. This threat is real; one company has already agreed to a $1 million settlement.

The Recording Industry Association of America and the Motion Picture Association of America recently sent a six-page brochure to Fortune 1000 corporations. Please review the suggested corporate policies and sample communication to employees and determine whether you believe our corporation is at risk.

Please contact me when you are ready to discuss potential changes to our corporate code of conduct. I'll be online all week if you want to instant message once you've reviewed the brochure.

Later,

Claire

Provides subject line that is meaningful to reader and writer.

Includes salutation and closing to personalize message.

Format Pointer

Composes short, concise message limited to one idea and one screen.

GOOD :-) Good Example of an Apology

New Message

To: Allen Melton <amelton@meltonpr.com>

cc:

Subject: Yesterday's Advertising Presentation

Allen:

Please accept my apology for the inconvenience you experienced yesterday because of the unavailability of computer equipment. Fortunately, you saved the day with your backup transparencies and gave an effective presentation of the new advertising campaign.

The next time you make a presentation at our company, I'll be sure to schedule the LGI room. This room has the latest technology to support multimedia presentations. Just call and let me know the date.

Later,

Thomas Lee Raferty
Administrative Assistant

© Cengage Learning 2013

States the apology briefly without providing an overly specific description of the error.

Reports measures taken to avoid repetition of such incidents, which strengthens the credibility of the apology.

Closes with a positive statement.

Format Pointers

Limits the message to a single idea—the apology.

Composes a short, concise message that fits on one screen.

Includes a salutation and closing to personalize the message.

New Message

To: Ellen Meyer <emeyer@techno.com>
cc: Martha Riggins <mriggins@techno.com>
Subject: Appreciation for Outstanding Contribution

Ellen,

Thank you for spearheading the initiative to improve interpersonal communication within the office and for arranging for the training sessions to achieve that goal. It was a big commitment on your part in addition to your regular duties.

Your efforts are already paying off. I have observed the techniques we learned in the training sessions being used in the department on several occasions already. In times of uncertainty, anxiety can often spill over into people's professional lives, so the seminar was very timely in helping to ensure a collaborative and civil workplace where everyone is treated respectfully.

You have proven yourself a dedicated and insightful employee, a true asset to the continued success of our organization.

Best regards,
Martha

- Extends appreciation for employee's efforts to improve departmental communication.

- Provides specific evidence of worth of experience without exaggerating or using overly strong language or mechanical statements.
- Assures writer of tangible benefits to be gained from the training session.

Format Pointers

Uses short lines, mixed case; omits special formatting such as emoticons and email abbreviations for improved readability.

© Cengage Learning 2013

MODELDOCS DELIVERING BAD-NEWS MESSAGES

Developing the Components of a Bad-News Message

The current subprime mortgage situation and its subsequent effects on the economy have provided an opportunity to better educate loan seekers about the types of financial risk they might safely assume. For this reason, mortgage seekers may be restricted in the number of mortgage loans they might hold.

Begins with statement with which both can agree. Sets stage for reasons for bad news.

As part of the effort to help loan seekers reduce their financial risk, banks now limit the number of mortgages a person might judiciously hold to no more than four. Because of current sluggishness in the housing market, house sellers now have more difficulty selling homes in a timely manner, making such assets much less liquid. If a mortgage holder gets into trouble, he/she will have less ability to resell the property and recover the loan amount. This puts the mortgage holder and the lender at greater financial risk.

Reveals subject of message and transitions into reasons.

Provides rule and clearly applies rule to situation.

In order to secure an additional mortgage, you must first pay off one of your current mortgages. Alternately, our affiliated real estate brokers are available to help you sell one of your properties so that you might secure another. Please call me at 213-555-3400 to discuss these services.

States refusal positively and clearly using complex sentence and positive language.

Includes counterproposal as alternative.

Closes with sales promotion for other services, inferring a continuing business relationship.

© Cengage Learning 2013

Note the closing paragraph is a positive, forward-looking statement that includes sales promotion of other services the mortgage firm and its affiliated real estate brokers can offer.

© iStockphoto.com/Albert Smirnov

Party Time
Unlimited

2937 Fox Cove Lane ❦ **Conway PA 76032-2937 (501) 555-1129   Fax (501) 555-3900**

June 3, 2013

Ms. Dena Marcum
Accounting and Budget
SPL Industries
7821 South Third Street
Conway, AR 72032-7839

Dear Ms. Marcum:

PartyTime Limited was pleased to be part of your staff/alumni banquet and appreciated your staff's compliments on the quality of the food, service, and decorations.

You are correct that the amount of the invoice is more than the price specified by the contract. The contract price was based on the 250-guest estimate provided by your administrative assistant. The estimate considered the amount of food to be served and the number of servers required to serve 250 guests, as well as the cost of decorating the banquet hall.

Your invoice includes an additional $200 for the cost of food served to the 25 unexpected guests of your alumni. Although we typically prepare extra food for large, formal affairs such as yours, we did not anticipate the large number of additional guests that arrived that evening. I was relieved our staff was able to obtain additional food from our warehouse to serve these guests.

Had these 25 guests been included in the original estimate, we would have added $200 to the food cost estimate. We would also have included $80 for the cost of two additional servers. Although we were short-handed, our staff provided your guests with quality service. Your invoice does not include any additional charges for service.

Ms. Marcum, as you begin planning festivities for the upcoming holidays, keep our famous specialty desserts in mind for an extraordinary change from the traditional catered turkey lunch.

Sincerely,

Jared Harrelson

Jared Harrelson
Manager

- *Begins with a statement with which the reader can agree to get the message off to a good start.*

- *Presents a clear explanation for the additional charge.*

- *Continues the explanation.*

- *Uses the subjunctive mood to de-emphasize the refusal.*

- *Shifts emphasis away from the refusal by presenting sales promotion on other services.*

Format Pointer
Illustrates block format—all lines begin at the left margin.

GOOD :-) Good Example of a Persuasive Claim

Palmdale Galleria
3109 Overlook Drive / Palmdale, CA 93550
P: (661) 555-2130 \ F: (661) 555-3129

October 27, 2013

Samantha Reynolds
Senior Architect
Primera Design
3400 Wilshire Boulevard
Los Angeles, CA 90052-3674

Dear Samantha:

When Palmdale Galleria selected your firm to redesign our retail space, we were impressed by the work that you had done in a number of hotels and mall properties in Las Vegas and other upscale developments throughout the country. We were most impressed with the fantasy world that you created for the Insight Hotel's shopping galleria, a space that attended to every aspect of the consumer's shopping experience, including sight, sound, smell, taste, and sensation, through the implementation of the latest technological and design advances.

In our meeting with your creative team, we asked for attention to the visual design, the entertainment elements, and the creation of an ambiance that addressed all aspects of the consumers' sensual experience. After reviewing the initial plan for our redesign, we find the degree of incorporation of entertainment and sensual experiences for consumers to be disappointing. The redesign incorporates the latest trends in architectural design but needs more attention to entertainment features, including spaces for "street" entertainers, mini-concerts, and amusement park rides, including bungee jumping, etc. We also expected a more complete integration of water features, such as fountains, waterfalls, and streams, with the associated opportunities for entertainment, such as a simulated river rafting experience. In the tropical forest region of the mall, we hoped to have a better integration of spaces for zoo animals and an apparatus to create the "smells" and "sounds" of the jungle. Consumers no longer go to malls to simply shop but to want to be transported to a world of leisure, pampering, and entertainment, one that appeals to all of their senses.

With Primera Design's reputation for creative productions, we are confident the redesign plan for the Palmdale Galleria will be revised to incorporate these elements. Please let us know if you would like to meet to discuss and clarify any of the design issues raised here. Because of the importance of this project, I am at your disposal. Please call me at 444-1920 to schedule a meeting.

Sincerely,

Martinique Cole

Martinique Cole
General Manager
Palmdale Galleria

- *Seeks attention by giving sincere compliment that reveals subject of message.*

- *Continues central appeal—commitment to creative redesign—while providing needed details.*

- *Presents reasoning that leads to request and subtle reminder of central appeal.*

- *Connects specific request with firm's commitment to develop a creative redesign.*

Legal and Ethical Consideration
Uses letter rather than less formal email format to emphasize importance of these differences regarding contractual agreement.

GOOD :-) Good Example of a Persuasive Request

Down-Home Restaurants

83 South Pass Road • Chattanooga TN 37426-2723 • (423) 555-5320

March 15, 2013

Mrs. Joyce Smith
976 Thompson Road
Crossville, TN 38555-0976

Dear Mrs. Smith:

Meeting you and touring the building on your property last week was a pleasure. That little building provided me with a fascinating glimpse of the past. You must have found it convenient using the building as a big "attic," storing all your canned goods and old farm implements over the years.

As the manager of the Down-Home Barbeque in Mena, I am constantly looking for items to build and display in our restaurants. Our restaurants are constructed of weathered wood to create a genuine rustic atmosphere, which we think complements our "down-home" menu.

As I toured your building, I couldn't help but notice some of the unique items inside and the old weathered boards hanging outside. The wood from the building and its contents would enable us to build and furnish a new restaurant in Clarksville and refurbish our Jackson location. Marc Lane, owner of Down-Home Restaurants, has asked me to extend you the offer explained in the enclosed proposal.

Naturally, no amount of money can compensate you for a building that holds so many memories for you. However, we would be happy to purchase the entire contents of the building, excluding any special items of sentimental value that you may want to keep.

Although the thought of selling the building may sadden you, think of the "second life" that the old farm equipment, dishes, washboards, seed bags, and weathered boards would have in our restaurants. People who would otherwise never see such Americana will have the opportunity to learn a little about its rich past.

After you have reviewed the proposal, please call me at 555-3253 to discuss our offer to display your treasures in our restaurants.

Sincerely,

Karla Ash

Karla Ash, Manager
Chattanooga Store
Enclosure

Opens with a compliment that introduces an appeal to the owner's pride in the old property.

Introduces the writer's interest in acquiring property and continues the primary appeal (desire to preserve the past).

Offsets reluctance to sell by acknowledging the sentimental value and suggesting options.

Stresses benefits of selling property in terms of the primary appeal.

Connects the specific request for action with the reward for saying "Yes."

Format Pointers

Illustrates modified block format—the date and closing lines (complimentary close and signature block) begin at the horizontal center.

Uses mixed punctuation—a colon follows the salutation, and a comma follows the complimentary close.

Uses an enclosure notation to alert the reader that something is included.

Example of an Effective Questionnaire

- Uses variety of items to elicit different types of responses.
- Uses clear, concise language to minimize confusion.
- Provides clear instructions for answering each item.
- Provides additional lines to allow for individual opinions.
- Provides even number of rating choices to eliminate "fence" responses.
- Asks for easily recalled information.
- Provides non-overlapping categories of response and open-ended final category.

Format Pointers
Provides adequate space for answering open-ended item.

Keeps length as short as possible while meeting survey objectives.

Includes instructions for submitting completed questionnaire.

---

1. Rank the following new vehicle purchase factors in order of their importance to you.

		1	2	3	4	5	6
a.	Price	○	○	○	○	○	○
b.	Overall performance	○	○	○	○	○	○
c.	Reliability	○	○	○	○	○	○
d.	Comfort	○	○	○	○	○	○
e.	Driving enjoyment	○	○	○	○	○	○
f.	Safety record	○	○	○	○	○	○
g.	Fuel economy	○	○	○	○	○	○
h.	Other (specify)	○	○	○	○	○	○

2. Which of the following is the single most important purchase factor that you feel needs more attention by today's car makers? (Please select only one.)

- ○ Price
- ○ Overall performance
- ○ Reliability
- ○ Comfort
- ○ Safety record
- ○ Fuel economy
- ○ Other (specify)

3. Would you purchase this vehicle again?

Definitely not	Probably not	I'm not sure	Only if improved	Probably would	Definitely yes
1	2	3	4	5	6
○	○	○	○	○	○

4. How would you rate your overall purchase satisfaction?

Very unsatisfied	Somewhat dissatisfied	Neutral	Somewhat satisfied	Satisfied	Very satisfied
1	2	3	4	5	6
○	○	○	○	○	○

5. Indicate your age group:

- ○ 20–29
- ○ 30–39
- ○ 40–49
- ○ 50–59
- ○ 60–69
- ○ 70 years and over

6. Indicate how many vehicles you have previously purchased.

- ○ None
- ○ 1–3
- ○ 4–6
- ○ 7–10
- ○ More than 10

7. What could the car maker do to enhance your satisfaction with your new car purchase?

Thanks for your participation. Click to submit your questionnaire.

Submit

SAMPLE REPORT AND REFERENCES PAGES IN APA (6TH EDITION) STYLE

Culturally diverse virtual teams do have a greater potential for conflict than do teams that are homogeneous and are able to meet face to face ("Collaborative Teams," 2008). While variations in beliefs, behaviors, and expectations occur within all cultural groups, certain generalities about one based on his or her cultural group can be useful for others seeking better understanding. "Given little or no other information about an individual's values and behaviours, culture provides a good first impression of that person" (Maznevski & Peterson, 1997, p. 37).

Neyer and Harzing (2008) found that experiences in cross-cultural interactions do serve to improve one's abilities to adapt in such situations. One advantage gained through experience is the overcoming of cultural stereotypes which often stand in the way of effective communication (Williams & O'Reilly, 1998). Cross-cultural experience also leads to the establishment of norms that support interaction among individuals and to the development of mutual consideration for others (Neyer & Harzing, 2008). Studies have established that individuals who learn a foreign language also gain appropriate culturally determined behavior and are thus better able to adapt to specific characteristics of the other culture (Harzing & Feely, 2008).

In addition to possessing strong technical skills, qualities that are important to successful membership on cross-cultural virtual teams include the following (Adler, 1991; Hurn & Jenkins, 2000):

▶ Flexibility and adaptability
▶ Strong interpersonal skills
▶ Ability to think both globally and locally
▶ Linguistic skills

References

Adler, N. J. (1991). *International dimensions of organizational behavior*. Boston: PWS Kent.

Collaborative teams. (2008, June). *Bulletpoint*, 152, 3–5.

Hurn, B. F., & Jenkins, M. (2000). International peer group development. *Industrial and Commercial Training*, 32(4), 128–131. doi: 10.1108/00197850010372205

Maznevski, M. L. & Peterson, M. F. (1997). Societal values, social interpretation, and multinational teams. In C. Granrose (Ed.), *Cross-cultural workgroups* (pp. 27–29). Thousand Oaks, CA: Sage.

Neyer, A., & Harzine, A. (2008). The impact of culture on interactions: Five lessons learned from the European Commission. *European Management Journal*, 26(5), 325–334. doi: 10.1016/j.emj .2008.05.005

Williams, K. Y., & O'Reilly, C. A. (1998). Demography and diversity in organizations. In B. M. Staw & R. M. Sutton (Eds.), *Research in organizational behavior* (pp. 77–140). Stamford, CT: JAI.

Choosing the Appropriate Graphic to Fit Your Objective

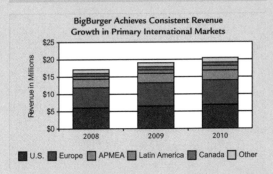

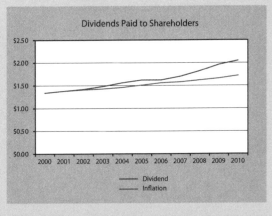

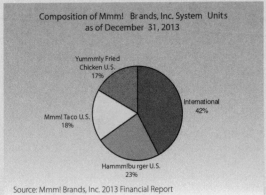

Graphic Type and Objective

Table—To show exact figures

Bar chart—To compare one quantity with another

Line Chart—To illustrate changes in quantities over time

Pie Chart—To show how the parts of a whole are distributed

Graphic Type and Objective

Gantt chart—To track progress toward completing a project

Map—To show geographic relationships

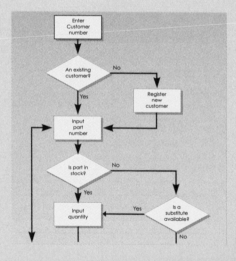

Flowchart—To illustrate a process or procedure

Photograph—To provide a realistic view of a specific item or place

GOOD :-) Short, Periodic Report in Memorandum Format

 **Industries**

233 State Boulvard
Kansas City, MO 64123-7600

TO: Candice Russell, Director, Human Resources
FROM: Tim Johnson, Manager, In-House Exercise Program
DATE: January 1, 2014
SUBJECT: Annual Report on In-House Exercise Program

The in-house exercise center has made significant gains in the past year. Data related to participation in our programs and current staffing follow:

Enrollment: 506 employees, up from 384 at end of 2013
Staff: One full-time trainer/manager and two part-time trainers

Our goal for the coming year is to increase our enrollment in the in-house exercise programs another 10 percent. We also have plans to create a nutrition program that will be rolled out next month. If that program is successful initially, we may need to hire a certified nutritionist. This person might also be used part-time in the company cafeteria to improve the nutritional value of the lunches and snacks provided there.

Employees report overall satisfaction with the quality of the current program. At the end of 2013, we asked program participants to complete a questionnaire. Eighty-eight percent indicated that they were very satisfied or extremely satisfied with our program. The most frequently mentioned suggestion for improvement was the extension of hours until 7 p.m. This change would allow employees to work late and still take advantage of the exercise facility. A copy of the questionnaire is provided for your review.

Call me should you wish to discuss the nutritional program, extended service hours, or any other aspects of this report.

Attachment

Includes header to serve formal report functions of transmittal and title page.

Includes horizontal line to add interest and separate transmittal from body of memo.

Uses deductive approach to present this periodic report requested by management on an annual basis.

Uses headings to highlight standard information; allows for easy update when preparing subsequent report.

Includes primary data from survey completed by program participants.

Attaches material to memorandum, which would be an appendix item in formal report.

Format Pointer
Uses memorandum format for brief periodic report prepared for personnel within company.

GOOD :-) Audit Report in Letter Format

 Paragon Accounting Group

767 RIVER ROAD, SUITE 216
BOSTON, MA 10812-0767
800-555-3000

January 30, 2014

Melinda Forrester, CEO
Randall and Associates
366 State Street
Boston, MA 10810-1796

Dear Ms. Forrester:

We have audited the accompanying balance sheet of Randall and Associates as of December 31, 2013, and the related statement of income, retained earnings, and cash flow for the year ended on that date. These financial statements are the responsibility of the company. Our responsibility is to express an opinion about these statements based on our audit.

PROCEDURES

We conducted our audit using generally accepted auditing standards. Those standards require that we plan and perform the audit to obtain reasonable assurance that the financial statements are free of material mistakes. An audit includes assessing whether generally accepted accounting principles are used and whether the significant estimates made by management and overall financial statement presentation are accurate. We believe that our audit provides a reasonable basis for our opinion on these matters.

FINDINGS

In our opinion, the financial statements referred to above present fairly, in all material aspects, the financial position of Randall and Associates as of December 31, 2013. The results of its operations and its cash flows for the year ended December 31, 2013, are in conformity with generally accepted accounting principles.

Thank you for the opportunity to serve your organization in this manner. Should you wish to discuss any aspects of this report, please call me.

Sincerely,

Karla Schmidt

Karla Schmidt
Senior Auditor

tsr

Letterhead and letter address function as title page and transmittal.

Introduces overall topic and leads into procedures and findings.

Uses side heading to denote beginning of body.

Closes with appreciation for business and offer to answer questions.

Format Pointers
Uses letter format for short report prepared by outside consultant.

Includes reference initials of typist, who did not write message.

Selecting an Appropriate Presentation Visual

VISUAL	ADVANTAGES	LIMITATIONS
HANDOUTS 	• Provide detailed information that audience can examine closely • Extend a presentation by providing resources for later use • Reduce the need for note taking and aid in audience retention	• Can divert audience's attention from the speaker • Can be expensive
BOARDS AND FLIPCHARTS	• Facilitate interaction • Are easy to use • Are inexpensive if traditional units are used	• Require turning speaker's back to audience • Are cumbersome to transport, can be messy and not professional looking • Provide no hard copy and must be developed on-site if traditional units are used
OVERHEAD TRANSPARENCIES 	• Are simple to prepare and use • Allow versatile use; prepare beforehand or while speaking • Are inexpensive and readily available	• Are not easily updated and are awkward to use • Must have special acetate sheets and markers unless using a document camera • Pose potential for equipment failure
ELECTRONIC PRESENTATIONS 	• Meet audience expectations of visual standards • Enhance professionalism and credibility of the speaker • Provide special effects to enhance retention, appeal, flexibility, and reuse	• Can lead to poor delivery if misused • Can be expensive, require highly developed skills, and are time-consuming • Pose technology failure and transportability challenges
35MM SLIDES	• Are highly professional • Depict real people and places	• Require a darkened room • Creates a formal environment not conducive to group interaction • Lacks flexibility in presentation sequence
MODELS OR PHYSICAL OBJECTS 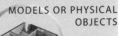	• Are useful to demonstrate an idea	• Can compete with the speaker for attention

Writing Effective Slide Content: Poor (left) and Good (right) Examples

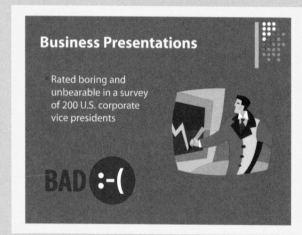

Humor

- Important element in any presentation
- Easy connection with the audience
- Gets attention
- Alleviates boredom
- Reduction of mental tension
- Discourages conflect
- Enhances comprehension
- Shouldn't embarrass people
  - Ethnic jokes are inappropriate
  - Profane language is definitely not recommended

BAD 8-(

**Value of Humor
in a Presentation**

- Establishes a connection with the audience
- Increases audience's willingness to listen
- Makes message more understandable and memorable
- Alleviates negativity associated with sensitive subjects

GOOD 8-)

The revised slide

- Includes a descriptive title that captures major idea of slide, in this case, the value of humor.
- Omits items unrelated to value of humor. Specifically, "important element in any presentation" is a verbal transition and not needed on a slide; "shouldn't embarrass people" and related subpoints will appear on a separate slide focusing on tips for using humor.
- Collapses remaining content into a few memorable points that use parallel structure for clarity and grammatical accuracy (singular action verbs).
- Proofreads carefully to avoid misspellings that damage credibility, such as "conflect" in original slide.

Engaging Conceptual Slide Design: Poor (left) and Good (right) Examples

Business Presentations

Rated boring and unbearable in a survey of 200 U.S. corporate vice presidents

BAD 8-(

How Well Do Business Presentations Measure Up?

Boring.
Unbearable.

Survey of 200 corporate vice presidents, 2005

GOOD 8-)

The revised slide

- Uses descriptive title that captures central idea of dissatisfaction with typical business presentation.
- Selects images that imply intended message—ineffectiveness of business presenters; enlarges images for slide appeal and balance.
- Trims text to emphasize central idea and eliminates bullet, as bulleted list should have at least two items.
- Moves source to less prominent slide position to add credibility to research data while keeping focus on central idea.

GOOD :-) Chronological Résumé

- *Includes email address that reflects professional image.*
- *Reveals type of work sought.*
- *Positions education as top qualification for recent graduate. Includes high GPA (B or better).*
- *Edges out competition reflecting related experience and work achievements.*
- *Uses separate section to emphasize language proficiencies listed in job requirements.*
- *Emphasizes activities that reflect service attitude, high level of responsibility, and people-oriented experiences.*

Format Pointers

Places name at top center, where it can be easily seen when employers place it in file drawer (top right is also acceptable).

Uses bold sans serif font to distinguish identification section and headings from remaining text in serif font.

Creates visual appeal through custom format rather than commonly used template, short readable sections focusing on targeted qualifications, and streamlined bulleted lists.

Cassandra Jensen
783 Ash Street
Palmdale, CA 83307
(204) 555-6789
cjensen@hotmail.com

CAREER OBJECTIVE

Challenging position in finance or investment banking with international promotion opportunities.

EDUCATION

California State University *August 2009–May 2013*
Bachelor of Science in Business Administration
Corporate Finance and International Business
GPA 3.6 on a 4.0 scale

RELATED EXPERIENCE

Intern, **Citicorp,** Los Angeles, CA *June 2012–Present*

- Assisted in the management of guided portfolio management accounts for high net-worth clients
- Interpreted statements and conducted money wire transfers
- Developed an understanding of secured financial transactions

Intern, **Financial Solutions,** *May 2011–October 2011*
Century City, CA

- Conducted research to create stock portfolios, including an organic food portfolio that grew 10% in 8 months.
- Assisted in the management of accounts for high net-worth clients

LANGUAGES

- English: Native fluency
- Spanish: Fluent (speaking, reading, writing, comprehension)

LEADERSHIP & HONORS

Order of Omega Honor Society, *August 20011–Present*
Co-Vice President of Conference
Organized a leadership conference for members of the CSU Greek System

CSU Panhellenic Council, *January 2012–December 2012*
Vice President of Communications

- Developed and produced content for a new Panhellenic website
- Representative at the Western Regional Greek Leadership Conference

Kappa Kappa Gamma, Sorority *August 2012–Present*
Representative at Kappa Kappa Gamma Province Leadership Convention

Matthew and Teresa S. Arnold Endowed Scholarship Recipient *2011/2012 and 2012/2013*

Clarence Foster
715 Armadillo Circle
San Antonio, TX 78710-0715
(512) 555-1396
cfoster@hotmail.com

Position in retail clothing sales with advancement to sales management.   OBJECTIVE

CUSTOMER SERVICE

- Processed customer financial transactions within assigned limits and established guidelines.
- Provided excellent customer service in completing transactions efficiently and in a friendly, professional manner.
- Met sales and referral goals by identifying and selling financial products and services beneficial to the customer needs.
- Identified fraudulent activity to prevent potential losses to the bank.

SALES

- Provided quality customer service to store patrons.
- Handled cash transactions and daily receipt balances.
- Usually surpassed weekly goal of opening new credit accounts.
- Employee of the month.

COMMUNICATION SKILLS AND WORK ETHIC

- Ability to communicate effectively over the phone and in person.
- Ability to work well unsupervised.
- Experience working on team projects both at work and in courses.
- Report consistently and promptly when scheduled for work.

COMPUTER SKILLS

Proficient in spreadsheet and word processing software.

Sales Associate, Claremont Department Store, 2012–Present   EMPLOYMENT HISTORY

Customer Service Associate, Union Bank, 2011–2012

B.S., Marketing, Claremont State College, Expected graduation, May 2013   EDUCATION

Clare Randall, Sales Manager, Claremont Department Store, 435 Main Street, Claremont, TX 78009, (818) 555-2345   REFERENCES

Daniel Shore, Professor, Marketing Department, Claremont State College, 890 Alamo Street, San Antonio, TX 87003, (803) 555-8907

Lisa Cox, Senior Teller, Union Bank, 900 Main Street, Claremont, TX 87303, (818) 555-1234

Includes clear objective statement to grab attention and invite close reading.

Uses headings that show applicant knows what skills are needed to succeed in sales.

Arranges qualifications into sections that emphasize applicant's relevant skills and accomplishments.

Uses employers' names and dates to match skills with work history.

Lists references for employer convenience and to strengthen résumé.

Format Pointers

Creates visual appeal with easy-to-read columnar format and balanced page arrangement.

Places name at top center, where it can be easily seen.

Uses bold font to distinguish identification section and headings from remaining text.

Lists education and work history as quick overview of basic qualifications and to accommodate employers' preference for chronological format.

GOOD :-) Example of a Follow-Up Letter

Dear Mr. Nguyen:

Recently, I applied for an information specialist position at TechPro and now have additional qualifications to report.

The enclosed, updated résumé shows that I have successfully passed the certification exam for Linux operating systems. In addition, I have learned a great deal about troubleshooting corporate computer systems in my recently completed internship with Crandon & Crandon Technology Systems, which I can immediately apply in a position with TechPro.

Mr. Nguyen, I would welcome the opportunity to visit your office and talk more about the contributions I could make as an information specialist at your firm. Please write or call me at (303) 555-8237.

© Cengage Learning 2013

States main idea and clearly identifies position being sought.

Refers to enclosed résumé; summarizes additional qualifications.

Assures employer that applicant is still interested in job.

Format Pointers
Formats as formal business letter but could have sent message electronically if previous communication with employer had been by email.

Prints letter and envelope with laser printer on paper that matches résumé and application letter.

GOOD :-) Example of a Thank-You Message to a Reference

Thank you so much for the letter of recommendation you prepared for my application to law school. I learned today that I have been accepted by Cleveland University for the fall semester.

Because of the rigor of that law program, I believe your comments about my work ethic, dedication to high-quality work, and willingness to seek out feedback for improvement carried a great deal of weight. The dean commented that she was impressed with the detailed evidence and examples you provided to support your statements, unlike the general recommendations she often receives.

Dr. Kenney, I appreciate your helping me secure a seat in a highly competitive academic discipline with such a well-regarded law program. Thanks for the recommendation and your outstanding instruction. I will keep you informed about my law school experience and hope to stop by your office next time I am in town to catch up.

© Cengage Learning 2013

States main idea of appreciation for recommendation. Informs reference of success in acceptance to academic program.

Communicates sincere appreciation for assistance; uses specific examples and avoids exaggeration.

Restates main idea and anticipates continued relationship; is original and sincere.

GOOD :-) Example of a Thank-You Message

New Message

To: wrfann@viking.com
From: mperkins@hotmail.com
Subject: Appreciation for Plant Interview

Dear Mr. Fann:

Thank you for the opportunity to visit Viking Range for a plant interview yesterday. I enjoyed meeting you and appreciated the complete tour of the operation and the opportunity to learn about the exciting research efforts underway at Viking.

Viking's success in developing higher quality products than its competitors after such a short time in the refrigeration market is impressive. Additionally, I was impressed with the many friendly, enthusiastic employees who were willing to share with me their knowledge and commitment to Viking.

After visiting your plant on Thursday, I am confident that my interest and previous experience in research and development at the DIAL labs in Starkville would allow me to contribute to Viking's important research efforts in the refrigeration area. I would also gain valuable real-world experience needed to enhance the mechanical engineering degree I'm pursuing at Mississippi State.

Mr. Fann, I am eager to receive an offer from Viking for the co-op position. If you need additional information in the meantime, please contact me.

Thanks,

Matt Perkins

- States main idea of appreciation for interview and information gained.

- Includes specific points iscussed during interview, increasing sincerity and recall of applicant.

- Assures employer of continued interest in position.

- Politely reminds employer that applicant is awaiting reply.

Format Pointer

Prepared as email message because previous communication with the company has been by email.

© Cengage Learning 2013

GOOD :-) Example of a Job-Refusal Message

I appreciate your spending time with me discussing the sales associate position.

Your feedback regarding my fit for your organization and the opportunities available to me were particularly valuable. Having received offers in both sales and marketing, I feel that a career in the latter field better suits my personality and long-term career goals. Today, I am accepting an entry-level marketing position with Fashion Trends, Inc.

Thank you for your confidence demonstrated by the job offer. When I hear about Marasol's continued success, I will think of the dedicated people who work for the company.

- Begins with neutral but related idea to buffer bad news.

- Presents reasons diplomatically that lead to refusal.

- Ends message on positive note that anticipates future association with company.

© Cengage Learning 2013

BCOM'S READER-FRIENDLY DESIGN AND COMPREHENSIVE COVERAGE ENSURE SUCCESS

As in previous editions, *BCOM 5e* models the concise, coherent writing style demanded in business today. Revisions in *BCOM 5e* apply cognitive theory principles to maximize learning and minimize the mental effort needed to process information.

In response to feedback, the authors have made the following changes to this edition:

Chapter 1

- Updated communication model to transactional model, which recognizes the effect of feedback from both receiver and sender in message perception.
- Corrected the language used to discuss informal and formal communication networks.
- Changed the discussion of strategic forces to contextual forces that affect business communication.
- Revised Figure 1-1 to show transactional communication model process.

Chapter 2

- In discussion of management styles, added a discussion of discursive leadership approaches.
- Updated example in listening section.
- Updated example in group communication section.
- Updated example in virtual team box.

Chapter 3

- Revised objectives list at the beginning of the chapter to include considerations for context, refined language use throughout, and deleted bullet 5.
- Updated Figure 3-1 to include considerations for context.
- Added section, Consider the Applicable Contextual Forces, which includes organizational culture and other contextual considerations.
- Added a section that discusses issues to consider when selecting a communication channel and medium.
- Added Figure 3-2, Use of Communication Media.
- Removed revision sections and moved them to Chapter 4.
- Updated box content, Meeting Diverse Audience's Needs.

Chapter 4

- Updated Figure 4-1 to include consideration of context.
- Revised Figure 4-2.
- Added opening discussion to Revise and Proofread section on cultivating a revision mindset.
- Moved revision discussion from Chapter 3 to this chapter.

Chapter 5

- Revised organization of Instant Messaging section.
- Added discussion of social media and social networking to Web Page Communication section.
- Revised Figures 5-1 and 5-2.

Chapter 6

- Revised Figure 6-2.
- Revised box, "To Express Thanks for a Gift."
- Revised box, "To Extend Thanks for Hospitality."
- Revised example in "Appreciation Messages."
- Revised Figures 6-3 through 6-13.

Chapter 7

- Revised box, "Study the techniques used ...."
- Revised Figures 7-2 through 7-5, and 7-7 through 7-9.

Chapter 8

- Revised Figures 8-2 through 8-9.

Chapter 9

- Revised opening discussion under Objectives.
- Revised hypothesis example.
- Revised box, "Here are the limits ..."
- Revised box, "Keep in mind the differences ..."

Chapter 10

- Updated Figure 10-2.
- Updated Figures 10-4 through 10-8.

Chapter 11

- Revised Project Description and Problem discussion under Problem and/or Purpose heading.
- Revised What the Study Will Cover and Scope discussion under Scope heading.
- Revised Principals discussion under Qualifications heading.
- Revised Figures 11-4 through 11-7.

Chapter 12

- Revised four examples in Introduction section.
- Revised Figure 12-2.

Chapter 13

- Revised box under Job and/or Career Objective heading.
- Revised examples under Provide Evidence of Qualifications heading.
- Revised Figures 13-2 through 13-8.

Chapter 14

- Revised Figures 14-2 through 14-7.

To help you prepare, we've created a Prep Card for each chapter

PREPCARD

CHAPTER 1 ESTABLISHING A FRAMEWORK FOR BUSINESS COMMUNICATION

KEY CONCEPTS

Understanding what communication is and how it occurs is central to successful transactions in the workplace. Business communication does not take place in a vacuum but is impacted by various external forces, including legal and ethical constraints, diversity challenges, changing technology, and team environment.

CONCEPTUAL FIGURES AND TABLES

Figure 1-1 Transactional Process
Figure 1-2 Flow of Information
Figure 1-3 Levels of Commun
Figure 1-4 Factors Influencing Bu
Figure 1-5 Four Dimensions of Bu

This column lists the Figures and Tables in the chapter as well as a number of key Lecture Slides from the PowerPoint slide set.

LEARNING OBJECTIVES

1-1 Define communication and describe the value of communication in business.

1-2 Expl
proc
ulti
com

1-3 Disc
in ar

For quick reference, this column lists the Learning Objectives that will be met in the chapter and presents a chapter outline with page references.

1-4 Explain how legal and ethical constraints, diversity challenges, changing

KEY TERMS

Chronemics 14
Diversity skills 13
Downward communication 6
Ethics 10
Ethnocentrism 13
External messages 8
Formal communication network 5
Horizontal (al) communication 8

Key terms from the chapter are listed here in alphabetical order for quick reference.

Proxemics 14
Stakeholders 9
Stereotypes 13
Synergy 16
Team 16
Telecommuting 15
Upward communication 7

ASSIGNMENTS AND ACTIVITIES

Read

1. Ask students to read the following article about predicted communic
trends: Communication technolog
the future. (2009). *Technology Awa
Available at **www.technology
.org/future_technology/
Communication_Technology_in
the_Future.html.** Have students
break into small groups and discuss the
following:

Write

2. Direct students to take the team player quiz at **www.quintcareers.com/
team_player_quiz.html** and write a brief paper about their team orientation and how being a team player may affect their career success. **(Obj. 4)**

Think

3. Have students research a scandal in the business or popular press using campus resources. Assign students to read the article and respond to questions a–c. **(Obj. 4)**

   a. Who are the stakeholders in the case? What does each stand to gain or lose, depending on your decision?

   b. How does the situation described in the case relate to the four-dimension model shown in Figure 1-4?

   c. What factors might influence your decision as the manager in the case?

To push your students to think critically about the material, or to add an experiential, applied element to your course, each card offers a variety of in-class or homework assignments organized according to essential business communication skills: reading, writing, thinking, speaking, and collaborating.

DIGGING DEEPER

Ask students to respond to the following discussion questions.

1. What aspect of cultural diversity do you feel will impact you most in your career: international, intercultural, intergenerational, or gender? Explain your answer, including how you plan to deal with the challenge.

2. Lack of Internet access is causing some nations to be classified as information "have nots." What international communication problems could result?

3. Considering the four strategic forces discussed, how is business communication today different from that of 30 years ago? In what ways is it easier? In what ways is it more difficult?

KEY CONCEPTS

Understanding what communication is and how it occurs is central to successful transactions in the workplace. Business communication does not take place in a vacuum but is impacted by various external forces, including legal and ethical constraints, diversity challenges, changing technology, and team environment.

CONCEPTUAL FIGURES AND TABLES

Figure 1-1   Transactional Process Model of Communication
Figure 1-2   Flow of Information within an Organization
Figure 1-3   Levels of Communication
Figure 1-4   Factors Influencing Business Communication
Figure 1-5   Four Dimensions of Business Behavior

POWERPOINT HIGHLIGHTS

Lecture Presentation

Slide 5   Communication Channels
Slide 12   Contextual Forces Influencing Business Communication
Slide 15   Four Dimensions of Business Behavior
Slide 17   Diversity Challenges
Slide 20   Impacts of Technology

Resource Presentation

The Instructor Manual contains a menu of resource slides you can integrate into your lecture presentation. Select from a variety of slides with examples, short quizzes, activities, and supplemental information to customize your lecture slide deck to meet the needs of your students and your course.

LEARNING OBJECTIVES

1-1   Define communication and describe the value of communication in business.

1-2   Explain the communication process model and the ultimate objective of the communication process.

1-3   Discuss how information flows in an organization.

1-4   Explain how legal and ethical constraints, diversity challenges, changing technology, and team environment act as contextual forces that influence the process of business communication.

CHAPTER OUTLINE

Value of Communication 3
The Communication Process 3
Communicating within Organizations 4
Communication Flow in Organizations 4
Levels of Communication 8
Contextual Forces Influencing Business Communication 9
Legal and Ethical Constraints 9
Diversity Challenges 12
Changing Technology 15
Team Environment 16

Chronemics 14
Diversity skills 13
Downward communication 6
Ethics 10
Ethnocentrism 13
External messages 8
Formal communication network 5
Horizontal (or lateral) communication 8
Informal communication network 5
Interferences 4
Internal messages 8
Kinesics 14
Organizational communication 4
Proxemics 14
Stakeholders 9
Stereotypes 13
Synergy 16
Team 16
Telecommuting 15
Upward communication 7

ASSIGNMENTS AND ACTIVITIES

Read

1. Ask students to read the following article about predicted communication trends: Communication technology in the future. (2009). *Technology Awards*. Available at **www.technologyawards .org/future_technology/ Communication_Technology_in_ the_Future.html.** Have students break into small groups and discuss the following:

   a. What communication trends are predicted in the workplace? Are any of these surprising? Why?

   b. Which trends are likely to impact your chosen career field most significantly? In what ways?

   c. How do the predicted trends relate to the four strategic forces presented in this chapter?

   d. Select one of the communication means discussed in the article. Share your findings in a short class presentation. **(Obj. 1–4)**

Write

2. Direct students to take the team player quiz at **www.quintcareers.com/ team_player_quiz.html** and write a brief paper about their team orientation and how being a team player may affect their career success. **(Obj. 4)**

Think

3. Have students research a scandal in the business or popular press using campus resources. Assign students to read the article and respond to questions a–c. **(Obj. 4)**

   a. Who are the stakeholders in the case? What does each stand to gain or lose, depending on your decision?

   b. How does the situation described in the case relate to the four-dimension model shown in Figure 1-4?

   c. What factors might influence your decision as the manager in the case?

Speak

4. Have students assemble in groups of three, interview an international student at your institution, and generate a list of English words that have no equivalents in his or her language. Your students should also find out about nonverbal communication that may differ from that used in American culture. Students can share their findings in a short presentation to the class. **(Obj. 4)**

Collaborate

5. Assign students to get into groups and discuss experiences in which "communication failure" was blamed for problems that occurred in their work, academic, or personal interactions. Instruct students to generate three to five additional ways communication can fail and give suggestions for correcting them. Groups can share their results with the case in a short presentation. **(Obj. 1 & 2)**

DIGGING DEEPER

Ask students to respond to the following discussion questions.

1. What aspect of cultural diversity do you feel will impact you most in your career: international, intercultural, intergenerational, or gender? Explain your answer, including how you plan to deal with the challenge.

2. Lack of Internet access is causing some nations to be classified as information "have nots." What international communication problems could result?

3. Considering the four strategic forces discussed, how is business communication today different from that of 30 years ago? In what ways is it easier? In what ways is it more difficult?

KEY CONCEPTS

Behavioral theories form the conceptual basis for business communication. Nonverbal communication, listening, and group communication are essential interpersonal skills for success in today's organizations. A team is a group with a clear identity and a high level of member commitment. Groups and teams communicate via both traditional and electronic meetings, which must be managed successfully to insure that organizational goals are met.

CONCEPTUAL FIGURES AND TABLES

Figure 2-1   The Johari Window
Figure 2-2   Organizational Chart with Hierarchical and Team Structures
Figure 2-3   Sample Formal Generic Agenda for Meetings

POWERPOINT HIGHLIGHTS

Lecture Presentation

Slide 9   Nonverbal Communication Conveys Added Meaning
Slide 13   Understanding Nonverbal Messages
Slide 14   Effective Listeners . . .
Slide 16   Characteristics of Effective Groups
Slide 20   Suggestions for Effective Meetings

Resource Presentation

The Instructor Manual contains a menu of resource slides you can integrate into your lecture presentation. Select from a variety of slides with examples, short quizzes, activities, and supplemental information to customize your lecture slide deck to meet the needs of your students and your course.

LEARNING OBJECTIVES

2-1   Explain how behavioral theories about human needs, trust and disclosure, and motivation relate to business communication.

2-2   Describe the role of nonverbal messages in communication.

2-3   Identify aspects of effective listening.

2-4   Identify factors affecting group and team communication.

2-5   Discuss aspects of effective meeting management.

CHAPTER OUTLINE

Behavioral Theories That Impact Communication 21
Recognizing Human Needs 21
Stroking 21
Exploring the Johari Window 22
Contrasting Management Styles 22
Nonverbal Communication 23
Metacommunication 23
Kinesic Messages 24
Understanding Nonverbal Messages 24
Listening as a Communication Skill 25
Listening for a Specific Purpose 26
Bad Listening Habits 26
Group Communication 27
Increasing Focus on Groups 27
Characteristics of Effective Groups 29
Group Roles 29
From Groups to Teams 30
Meeting Management 32
Face-to-Face Meetings 32
Electronic Meetings 32
Suggestions for Effective Meetings 33

Agenda 33
Brainstorming 34
Casual listening 26
Consensus 34
Cross-functional team 30
Directive behavior 23
Empathetic listening 26
Forming 31
Intensive listening 26
Interpersonal intelligence 21
Listening for information 26
Metacommunication 23
Norm 29
Norming 31
Performing 31
Product development team 31
Quality assurance team 30
Role 27
Status 27
Storming 31
Stroke 21
Supportive behavior 23
Task force 30
Total Quality Management 23
Visual kinesic communication 24
Vocal kinesic communication 24

ASSIGNMENTS AND ACTIVITIES

Read

1. Have students read the following article, which describes the importance of team development activities: Linley, A. (2008, January 29). Our top ten team building exercises. *Ezine*. Available at **http://ezinearticles.com/?Our-Top-Ten-Team-Building-Exercises&id5955336.**

   Ask students to form small groups in which they should discuss the shift in corporate team building over the past two or more years and the value gained from various types of team-building activities. Students should brainstorm ways that they believe these approaches could be used to boost the effectiveness of teams in an academic setting and the projected results. Afterwards, they should share their ideas with the class in a short presentation. **(Obj. 1 & 4)**

2. Have students read the following article, which gives useful suggestions ensuring that nonverbal behavior communicates the intended message: Shephard, L. C. (2007, May 1). Reading body language can offer insight to HR pros. *Employee Benefit News*. Available from Business Source Complete database.

   Instruct students to expand the list of recommended and nonverbal messages and the interpretations mentioned in the article. They should then share their list with the class, complete with demonstrations, in an informal presentation. **(Obj. 2)**

Write

3. Assign students to keep a journal over a period of two to five days that records events involving metacommunication. Describe how each incident influences the understanding of the verbal message involved. **(Obj. 4)**

Think

4. Ask students to consider a distance learning conference or course in which they have participated. How were nonverbal communication, listening, and other factors different from what they have experienced in traditional class settings? How do their experiences relate to the conducting of electronic meetings? **(Obj. 2, 3, & 5)**

Speak

5. Have students locate one or more articles from a database or the Internet that discuss nonverbal communication in various cultures. Assign them to create a list of examples of body language and behaviors that have different meanings among cultures. Then lead the class in a discussion of how ignorance of these differences might affect interpersonal communication. **(Obj. 2)**

Collaborate

6. Assign students to groups of three to five, and have each team visit the website of the Institute for Performance Culture at **http://teaming-up.com.** The groups should take the survey that can be found in the Free Resources menu tab, under "Your team's performance blind spots?" Some of the items may not relate to the short-term project team but will provide students with ideas of issues faced in real-world work teams. After taking the survey, each group should discuss the evaluation report produced from the survey. Have each group send the instructor an email summarizing what the team survey revealed and how they will use the information to improve team performance. **(Obj. 4)**

DIGGING DEEPER

Ask students to respond to the following discussion questions.

1. How can managers use Maslow's need levels, the Johari Window, and the management theories of McGregor and Hersey and Blanchard to improve communication with employees?

2. How do effective conversation and listening impact a business' overall success?

3. Why do some teams never reach the highest stage of team development? What can be done to overcome the obstacles to peak team performance?

KEY CONCEPTS

Effective spoken and written communication involves a process of careful analysis, planning, adaptation, and organization that precedes the actual creation of the message. Chapter 3 focuses on these essential steps of preparation: (1) determining the purpose of the message and an appropriate channel, (2) envisioning the audience, (3) adapting the message to the audience, and (4) organizing the message.

CONCEPTUAL FIGURES AND TABLES

Figure 3-1   Process for Planning and Preparing Spoken and Written Messages
Figure 3-2   Use of Communication Media
Figure 3-3   Process of Selecting an Outline for a Spoken or Written Message

POWERPOINT HIGHLIGHTS

Lecture Presentation

Slide 3   Step 1: Determining the Purpose and Channel
Slide 5   Step 2: Envisioning the Audience
Slide 7   Step 3: Adapting the Message to the Audience
Slide 16   Adapting: Projecting a Positive, Tactful Tone
Slide 18   Step 4: Select an Appropriate Channel and Outline

Resource Presentation

The Instructor Manual contains a menu of resource slides you can integrate into your lecture presentation. Select from a variety of slides with examples, short quizzes, activities, and supplemental information to customize your lecture slide deck to meet the needs of your students and your course.

LEARNING OBJECTIVES

3-1 Consider contextual forces that may affect whether, how, to whom, and when a message is sent.

3-2 Identify the purpose of the message and the appropriate channel and medium.

3-3 Develop clear perceptions of the audience to enhance the impact and persuasiveness of the message, improve goodwill, and establish and maintain the credibility of the communicator.

3-4 Apply tactics for adapting messages to the audience, including those for communicating ethically and responsibly.

3-5 Recognize the importance of organization when planning the first draft.

CHAPTER OUTLINE

Step 1: Consider the Applicable Contextual Forces 37
Organizational Culture 37
Dimensions of Context 39
Step 2: Determine the Purpose and Select an Appropriate Channel and Medium 40
Selecting the Channel and Medium 40
Step 3: Envision the Audience 42
Step 4: Adapt the Message to the Audience's Needs and Concerns 44
Focus on the Audience's Point of View 45
Communicate Ethically and Responsibly 45
Step 5: Organize the Message 47
Outline to Benefit the Sender and the Audience 47
Sequence Ideas to Achieve Desired Goals 47

Deductive 48
Inductive 48
Libel 46
Organizational culture 38
Outlining 47
Slander 46

ASSIGNMENTS AND ACTIVITIES

Read

1. Ask students to conduct an online search to identify strategies companies have adopted to raise their employees' awareness of diversity in the workplace. The students should, in chart form, summarize the indexes they used to locate articles, the companies they read about, and the successful strategies that companies used to promote diversity. **(Obj. 2 & 3)**

Write

2. Assign students to conduct research on social networking sites such as Twitter. They can begin with the following article: Graham, J. (2008, July 21). Twitter took off from simple "tweet" success. *USA Today.* Available from LexisNexis Academic database.

   Once students complete their research, assign the following activities:

   a. Compile a list of advantages and disadvantages of this communication medium, including examples of how two businesses have used this social networking site.

   b. Register at Twitter (or use your existing account) and exchange messages with a small group of students in the class. Prepare an engaging flyer describing efficient use of Twitter that will be distributed to staff as an attachment to an email. **(Obj. 1 & 2)**

Think

3. Ask students to compile a list of the advantages and disadvantages of email, as well as recommended uses and precautions for its use, after reading the following article: Seckler S., & Toomey, R. (2005, December 18). Commentary: E-mail: Career opportunities and pitfalls in workplace communication. *The Daily Record* (Kansas City, MO). Available from LexisNexis Academic database. **(Obj. 1)**

4. Divide the class into a number of small groups in which they should discuss a specific situation in work or educational experience that illustrates the negative effects of an individual who did not consider the impact of his or her message on the receiver.

Speak

5. Have students generate a list of phrases and nonverbal expressions peculiar to their culture that groups from another culture might not understand. Ask them to identify any conflict situations that could arise from the misinterpretation of the collectively understood terms. Have them also consider how group norms play a part in the understanding of collective culture. If time allows, assign each student to select one item from his or her list as the topic for a five-minute presentation to the class. **(Obj. 2)**

Collaborate

6. Explain to students that however experienced businesses are at writing formal business documents, such as press releases, advertising, and financial reports, creating an online brand or authentic voice through an online blog provides a new challenge for many business communicators. To learn more, have students locate the following articles, which are available from Lexis-Nexis database:

   Cardis, P. (2008, October). Blogging for business. *Professional Builder.*

   Get caught in the net. (2007, May 31). *Financial Advisor.*

   How to write a better blog. (July 2007). *Business World* (Weekender).

   After reading the articles, students should work in small teams to prepare an engaging flier describing efficient blog communication that will be distributed to staff as an attachment to an email message. **(Obj. 1 & 2)**

DIGGING DEEPER

Ask students to respond to the following discussion questions.

1. What is empathy and how does it affect business communication? How are empathy and sympathy different?

2. Explain what is meant by writing to *express* and not to *impress*.

3. How can you ensure quality in a collaboratively written document? Perhaps someone on your team makes unnecessary additions or questionable edits such as revising to make the document "sound more professional" while sacrificing clarity. What would you do?

KEY CONCEPTS

Chapter 4 focuses on preparing a first draft and on revising and proofreading for accuracy and desired impact. Such communication is carefully drafted and proofread for correct sentence structure, emphasis on important ideas, coherent paragraphs, and easy readability. After a review of the writing process in Chapters 3 and 4 (and the Grammar and Usage Appendix), students will prepare letters, memos, and a variety of electronic messages (email, instant, and text messages, blogs, and other web communications) and business reports and presentations.

CONCEPTUAL FIGURES AND TABLES

Figure 4-1   Process for Planning and Preparing Spoken and Written Messages
Figure 4-2   Contrast the Readability and Appeal of Bulky (left) versus Broken (right) Text
Figure 4-3   Improving Readability Through Cautious Use of a Grammar and Style Checker
Figure 4-4   Rough Draft of a Letter (excerpt)

POWERPOINT HIGHLIGHTS

Lecture Presentation

Slide 2   Process for Planning and Preparing Spoken and Written Messages
Slide 3   Step 5: Prepare the First Draft
Slide 4   Step 6: Revise and Proofread
Slide 7   Factors Affecting Readability
Slide 10   Visual Enhancements to Improve Connotative tone Readability
Slide 13   Proofreading Procedures

Resource Presentation

The Instructor Manual contains a menu of resource slides you can integrate into your lecture presentation. Select from a variety of slides with examples, short quizzes, activities, and supplemental information to customize your lecture slide deck to meet the needs of your students and your course.

LEARNING OBJECTIVES

4-1   Apply techniques for developing effective sentences and unified and coherent paragraphs.

4-2   Prepare visually appealing documents that grab the audience's attention and increase comprehension.

4-3   Identify factors affecting readability and revise messages to improve readability.

4-4   Revise and proofread a message for content, organization, style, and tone; mechanics; and format and layout.

CHAPTER OUTLINE

Step 6: Prepare the First Draft 51
Craft Powerful Sentences 51
Develop Coherent Paragraphs 53
Revise and Proofread 56
Cultivate a Frame of Mind for Effective Revising and Proofreading 56
Apply Visual Enhancements to Improve Readability 57
Improve Readability 58
Step 7: Revise for Style and Tone 60
Proofreading for Mechanical Correctness 67

Active voice 51

Clichés 60

Coherence 54

Connotative meaning 65

Deductive paragraph 54

Denotative meaning 65

Doublespeak 64

Euphemism 64

Goodwill 65

Inductive paragraph 54

Jargon 61

Passive voice 51

Redundancy 61

Subjunctive sentences 63

Tone 62

Topic sentence 54

ASSIGNMENTS AND ACTIVITIES

Read

1. Have students locate the following article that offers tips on writing powerful business messages: Jolley, D. A. (2009). Clear and compelling messages: The foundation for effective communication. *Public Relations Tactics*. Available from Business Source Complete database. After they've read the article, ask students to respond to the following questions:

    a. What are the "Master P's"?

    b. Explain what the writer means by a "memorable quote." Could you foresee exceptions to the use of this approach for all business messages? Provide examples.

    c. What is the role of rehearsing in assuring clear and compelling messages? **(Obj. 1–4)**

Write

2. Have students conduct an online search related to recent developments in speech (voice-recognition) technology. Students should prepare a brief written report providing information such as (a) current status of speech technology as a viable business application, including challenges that have hampered past developments; (b) examples of leading speech technology applications with related results; and (c) projections for future development of this technology. **(Obj. 1)**

Think

3. Ask students to complete the business usage quiz at **http://businesswriting. com/tests/commonusage.html.** Then have students assess their understanding of 26 common business writing problems. Once they have reviewed the feedback provided for each question, students should compile a list of areas in which they need improvement. Have students email their score to you, along with their plan for improvement. **(Obj. 1–4)**

4. Have students access the Plain Language website at **www.plainlanguage.gov/ examples/index.cfm**, view a variety of documents revised for easy reading following Plain English principles, and then select the "Before and After Comparisons" link. Once students have reviewed the examples posted under the "Using Visual Explanations to Convey Information More Clearly" section, they should complete the following activities:

    a. Have students prepare a brief paper explaining how applying plain English principles improved the readability of these documents. Ask them to suggest revisions to further improve the documents.

    b. Have students develop a new example (from a document they received in the past or one provided by you) that could be added to this site as a "before and after comparison." Ask them to place their two documents on a slide and be prepared to summarize their changes and explain how they improved the impact of the document. **(Obj. 3)**

Speak

5. Jon Warshawsky, coauthor of *Why Business People Speak Like Idiots*, was interviewed by Martha Barnette, who is host of *A Way with Words*, a program that airs on National Public Radio. Ask students to listen to the interview at **www.fightthebull.com/ jwarshawskyinterview1.asp**.

    In the interview, Jon says that many executives might feel "it's dangerous to have an original thought," which often leads to the use of a series of words they think they have to use to be seen as smart. Martha refers to this tendency as *corporate speak*. Assign the following activities:

    a. Ask students to conduct an interview in person, by phone, or online with an executive in the student's chosen career field. Students should ask the executive whether corporate speak is a noticeable problem in the work environment, to identify common examples of corporate speak, and for advice related to communicating effectively in their career field.

    b. Ask students to make a short presentation to the class about how to avoid corporate speak and communicate effectively in their chosen career field. Alternately, students could make a video presentation and post it electronically for class access. **(Obj. 1, 2, & 4)**

DIGGING DEEPER

Ask students to respond to the following discussion questions.

1. What habits hinder your success or enjoyment of writing? Identify ways to overcome them.

2. How does online writing challenge a writer's effort to develop a seamless, coherent document?

3. Why do some writers rush through the proofreading phase of message development?

KEY CONCEPTS

A full chapter is devoted to the preparation of electronic communications—not only because of popular use in organizations but also because of their particular characteristics as informal but powerful forms of communication. Emphasis is given to email, instant and text messaging, Web communications (Web pages, wikis, and weblogs), and voice and wireless communication. Legal and ethical issues related to the use of technology are also discussed.

CONCEPTUAL FIGURES AND TABLES

Figure 5-1   Good Example of an Email Message
Figure 5-2   Good Example of an Instant Message
Figure 5-3   Levels of Formality Required by Various Technologies

POWERPOINT HIGHLIGHTS

Lecture Presentation

Slide 3   Guidelines for Preparing Email Messages
Slide 5   Netiquette Fundamentals
Slide 9   Instant Messaging
Slide 12   Electronic Messages and the Law
Slide 21   Making a Professional Impression with Voice Mail
Slide 24   Cell Phone Communication

Resource Presentation

The Instructor Manual contains a menu of resource slides you can integrate into your lecture presentation. Select from a variety of slides with examples, short quizzes, activities, and supplemental information to customize your lecture slide deck to meet the needs of your students and your course.

LEARNING OBJECTIVES

5-1 Discuss the effective use of email, instant messaging, and text messaging in business communication.

5-2 Explain principles for writing effectively for the Web.

5-3 Discuss the effective use of voice and wireless technologies in business communication.

5-4 Consider legal and ethical implications associated with the use of communication technology.

CHAPTER OUTLINE

Electronic Mail Communication 73
Advantages of Email 73
Guidelines for Preparing Email Messages 73
Effective Use of Email 74
Instant and Text Messaging 76
Text Messaging 77
Electronic Messages and the Law 79
Web Page Communication and Social Media 80
Writing for a Web Site 80
Social Media 81
Voice and Wireless Communication 83
Voice Mail Communication 83
Cell Phone Communication 83
Wireless Communication and the Future 84
Appropriate Use of Technology 85
Determine the Purpose of the Message 85
Determine Whether the Information Is Personal or Confidential 85
Decide Whether Positive Human Relations Are Sacrificed 85

KEY TERMS

Extranet 80
Instant messaging 76
Intranet 80
Netiquette 74
Social networking sites 76
Text messaging 77
Weblog (or blog) 81

ASSIGNMENTS AND ACTIVITIES

Read

1. Have students conduct an electronic search to locate an article that deals with the successful use of electronic communication in a company or organization. They should prepare an abstract of the article that includes the following parts: (1) article citation, (2) name of organization/company, (3) brief description of the communication technique and situation, and (4) outcome(s) of the successful communication. As an alternative to locating an article, propose that students write about a successful communication situation in the organization/company for which they work. **(Obj. 1–4)**

Write

2. For the first part of this activity, have students read the following article, which discusses strategies for making Web information accessible to those who cannot access information in various ways: Tierney J. (2007, April 1). Ignore universal web design at your peril. *Multichannel Merchant*, p. 8. Available at **http://multichannelmerchant.com/ ecommerce/ignore_universal_web/**

   After reading the article, ask students to visit a corporate website of their choice. Assign them to evaluate the accessibility of information on that site to viewers who are physically challenged.

   Students should imagine that they are an employee of that company and send an email to the instructor with recommendations for making the information on the site more accessible. **(Obj. 2)**

Think

3. Ask students to locate a company example of both a well written and a poorly written email message. Students should analyze the strengths and weaknesses of each document and be prepared to discuss their analyses in class. **(Obj. 1)**

Speak

4. In today's world, initial contact with a person is often via the telephone, so those important first impressions are dependent on practicing proper telephone etiquette. Ask students to make a list of ideas for increasing levels of telephone courtesy to build image and trust. Have them prepare a brief presentation providing suggestions for placing calls, answering calls, and taking telephone messages. **(Obj. 3)**

Collaborate

5. Assign students to small groups and ask them to share incidents of inappropriate cell phone behavior they have experienced in a school, work, or public setting. Ask them to explain how each incident affected the individuals involved. They should also discuss etiquette rules they believe are critical for courteous, productive cell phone use. Are some etiquette rules appropriate for business calls but not for personal calls or vice versa? Finally, each group should prepare a brief presentation on the dos and don'ts of cell phone usage. **(Obj. 3)**

DIGGING DEEPER

Ask students to respond to the following discussion questions.

1. Describe three business communication situations in which a technology channel would be inappropriate for exchanging information. Explain your choices.

2. How does a communicator balance the equally important goals of communicating efficiently and building team camaraderie?

3. How is Web communication different from other forms of business communication? How is it similar?

PREPCARD

CHAPTER 6 DELIVERING GOOD- AND NEUTRAL-NEWS MESSAGES

KEY CONCEPTS

Good-news and neutral-news messages are included together in this chapter because the outlines for these communications are both deductive. Strategies and examples are presented for the creation of good-news messages, appreciation messages, routine claims and requests, routine messages about orders and credit, and procedural messages. Strategies for the use of form documents and for adapting messages sent to international audiences are also presented.

CONCEPTUAL FIGURES AND TABLES

Figure 6-1   Direct Outline Used in Good- and Neutral-News Messages Sent in Written, Electronic, or Spoken Form

MODEL DOCUMENT FIGURES

Figure 6-2   Good Example of a Good-News Message
Figure 6-3   Good Example of an Appreciation Message
Figure 6-4   Poor Example of a Routine Claim
Figure 6-5   Good Example of a Routine Claim
Figure 6-6   Poor Example of a Positive Response to a Routine Claim
Figure 6-7   Good Example of a Positive Response to a Routine Claim
Figure 6-8   Poor Example of a Routine Request
Figure 6-9   Good Example of a Routine Request
Figure 6-10   Poor Example of a Positive Response to a Routine Request
Figure 6-11   Good Example of a Positive Response to a Routine Request
Figure 6-12   Good Example of an Online Order Confirmation
Figure 6-13   Good Example of Letter Extending Credit
Figure 6-14   Good Example of a Procedural Email with an Attachment

POWERPOINT HIGHLIGHTS

Lecture Presentation

Slide 3   Advantages of the Deductive Outline
Slide 4   Types of Good-News Messages
Slide 5   Making the Most of Appreciation Messages
Slide 6   Extending Credit: Write Deductively
Slide 7   Guidelines for Procedural Messages

Resource Presentation

The Instructor Manual contains a menu of resource slides you can integrate into your lecture presentation. Select from a variety of slides with examples, short quizzes, activities, and supplemental information to customize your lecture slide deck to meet the needs of your students and your course.

LEARNING OBJECTIVES

6-1 Describe the deductive outline for good and neutral news and its adaptations for specific situations and for international audiences.

6-2 Prepare messages that convey good news, including thank-you and appreciation messages.

6-3 Write messages presenting routine claims and requests and favorable responses to them.

6-4 Write messages acknowledging customer orders, providing credit information, and extending credit.

6-5 Prepare procedural messages that ensure clear and consistent application.

CHAPTER OUTLINE

Deductive Organizational Pattern 89
Good-News Messages 90
   Positive News 90
   Thank-You and Appreciation Messages 90
Routine Claims 94
   Claim Message 94
   Favorable Response to a Claim Message 94
Routine Requests 97
   Requests for Information 97
   Favorable Response to a Routine Request 98
   Positive Response to a Favor Request 99
   Form Messages for Routine Responses 99
Routine Messages about Orders and Credit 101
   Acknowledging Customer Orders 101
   Providing Credit Information 101
   Extending Credit 102
Procedural Messages 104

Acknowledgment message 101
Adjustment messages 94
Claim 94
Deductive (or direct) sequence 89
Good-news messages 89
Neutral-news messages 89
Persuasive claims 94
Persuasive requests 97
Resale 95
Routine claims 94
Routine requests 97
Sales promotional material 95

ASSIGNMENTS AND ACTIVITIES

Read

1. Assign students to conduct an electronic search to locate an article that deals with successful communication in a company or organization. Have them prepare an abstract of the article that includes the following parts: (1) article citation, (2) name of organization/company, (3) brief description of communication technique/situation, and (4) outcome(s) of the successful communication. As an alternative to locating an article, students could also write about a successful communication situation in the organization or company for which they work. **(Obj. 1–5)**

Write

2. Give students the following scenario and have them prepare the exercise listed. As the marketing manager for Pacific Golf Supply Co. (PGS), you have just approved a credit account for Highland Lake Golf Club, a new golf course in northern California. Send Jordan Martin, the golf pro at the club, a letter stating that you have approved a $25,000 initial credit line. PGS offers its customers 2/10, n/30 payment terms and charges interest at an 18 percent annual rate on overdue accounts. Each quarter, PGS reviews its outstanding accounts and offers an increase in its credit line to any customer with a current account. The letter should confirm that the initial order of golf balls, clubs, and accessories has been shipped via UPS ground, with an expected delivery time of 10 days. Encourage Kevin to use his remaining $12,400 credit line to invest in quality display units. Explain

that experience demonstrates that sales increase by 25 percent when the product is displayed using your display units.

Exercise

Write the credit approval/order acknowledgement letter to Jordan at 2500 Country Club Drive, Klamath, CA 95548-1200. **(Obj. 1 & 4)**

Think

3. Have students find an example of both a well written and a poorly written good-news or routine memo, email message, or letter; analyze the strengths and weaknesses of each document; and prepare to discuss them in class. **(Obj. 1–5)**

Speak

4. Assign students to obtain a copy of a business letter written by someone from another culture and to identify the major differences between this letter and a traditional U.S. letter. Their report should include information about cultural differences that might be reflected in the message style. Ask students to create a visual of their letter and share their analysis with the class. **(Obj. 1)**

Collaborate

5. Many companies naively rely on a file of form letters composed to fit almost any conceivable situation in order to protect against potentially poor writing and to get messages out as quickly as possible. While these form letters may form the basis for routine communication, they often miss the mark.

Have students read and discuss the following article about a form letter that Apple sent to would-be iPhone application developers: **www .theregister.co.uk/2008/03/15/apple_ iphone_developer_form_letter/.** After reading the letter, divide the class into groups of three or four. Each group, serving as a company's product development team, will compose a form letter to send to customers who asked for changes in products or services. Using the team's experiences and available consumer research, the group should identify and support an innovative change of their choice (e.g., new features such as unique ring tones, added features, or new phone

design). Ask students to also consider an incentive to try the new product/service. **(Obj. 1–5)**

DIGGING DEEPER

Ask students to respond to the following discussion questions.

1. What criteria should be used in determining whether a good- or neutral-news message would best be communicated on paper, electronically, or verbally?

2. What considerations should be given to a message recipient's culture when planning a good-news or neutral-news message?

3. What role does goodwill play in composing effective deductive messages?

KEY CONCEPTS

Bad-news messages typically require an inductive strategy. Situations covered include sharing bad news, refusing a request, denying a claim, refusing an order, denying credit, delivering constructive criticism, and communicating negative organizational news. The construction of bad-news messages involves more delicate human relations issues than good news and neutral messages.

CONCEPTUAL FIGURES AND TABLES

Figure 7-1   Inductive Outline Used in Bad-News Messages Sent in Written, Electronic, or Spoken Form

MODEL DOCUMENT FIGURES

Figure 7-2   Developing the Components of a Bad-News Message
Figure 7-3   Good Example of a Refusal for a Favor
Figure 7-4   Poor Example of a Refusal to an Employee's Request
Figure 7-5   Good Example of a Refusal to an Employee's Request
Figure 7-6   Poor Example of a Claim Denial
Figure 7-7   Good Example of a Claim Denial
Figure 7-8   Poor Example of a Constructive Criticism
Figure 7-9   Good Example of a Constructive Criticism
Figure 7-10   Poor Example of a Message Announcing Negative Organizational News
Figure 7-11   Good Example of a Message Announcing Negative Organizational News

POWERPOINT HIGHLIGHTS

Lecture Presentation
Slide 6   Advantages of the Inductive Outline
Slide 17   Techniques for Closing Positively
Slide 32   Sharing Negative Organizational News

LEARNING OBJECTIVES

7-1 Explain the steps in the inductive outline, and understand its use for specific situations.

7-2 Discuss strategies for developing the five components of a bad-news message.

7-3 Prepare messages refusing requests and claims.

7-4 Prepare messages handling problems with customers' orders and denying credit.

7-5 Prepare messages providing constructive criticism, communicating negative organizational news, and responding to crises.

CHAPTER OUTLINE

Choosing an Appropriate Channel and Organizational Pattern 109
Channel Choice and Commitment to Tact 109
Use of the Inductive Approach to Build Goodwill 109
Exceptions to the Inductive Approach 111
Developing a Bad-News Message 111
Writing the Introductory Paragraph 111
Presenting the Facts, Analysis, and Reasons 112
Writing the Bad-News Statement 113
Offering a Counterproposal or "Silver Lining" Idea 114
Closing Positively 115
Refusing a Request 115
Denying a Claim 116
Denying Credit 120
Delivering Constructive Criticism 122
Communicating Negative Organizational News 123
Breaking Bad News 124
Responding to Crisis Situations 126

Counterproposal 114
Fair Credit Reporting Act 122

ASSIGNMENTS AND ACTIVITIES

Read

1. Have students conduct an electronic search to locate an article that deals with successful negative communication in a company or organization. Assign them to prepare an abstract of the article that includes the following parts: (1) article citation, (2) name of organization/company, (3) brief description of communication technique/situation, and (4) outcome(s) of the successful communication. Students should present their abstract in a memo and give a short presentation in class. **(Obj. 1–5)**

Think

2. Instruct students to refer to a recent political or business event in which bad news was shared and prepare a written critique that includes (1) an assessment of the effectiveness of the message and the manner in which it was delivered, (2) an analysis of the results, and (3) a summary of what students learned from their analysis. **(Obj. 1, 2, & 5)**

Write

3. Give students the following scenario and have them complete the related exercises. **(Obj. 1, 2, & 4)**

   HGA Electronics is replacing its fleet of 100 automobiles used by its field representatives. As the regional corporate sales representative for the automobile manufacturer, you notice that HGA Electronics has not ordered sound system upgrades to accommodate mp3 players and smartphones that will enhance the employees' driving experience.

Exercises

1. Search the Internet to identify other options that you believe employers should consider for company vehicles.

2. Write an email to Joanny Gayle, the buyer at HGA Electronics, suggesting that she add these options to the automobiles that she's already ordered.

Speak

4. Give students the following scenario and have them complete the related exercise. (Obj. 3)

   Gulf South Communications Corporation has purchased a significant number of season tickets to the Riverside Community Theatre since its inaugural season in 1979. Gulf South distributes the tickets to special customers, vendors, and employees to foster goodwill and promote the company. Because of the financial crisis in the telecommunications industry, Gulf South's management has regrettably been forced to eliminate all noncritical expenditures. As a supervisor in the human resources department, you have been asked by management to inform Steve Cafferty, the business manager of the theatre, that Gulf South will not purchase season tickets this year. Because the loss of your long-time support will be a hard blow to the theatre, you decide to break the news to Steve over lunch at his favorite restaurant.

Exercise

Ask students to develop a script of the conversation they will have with Steve conveying the company's disappointing decision.

Collaborate

5. Despite the benefits of online brainstorming, waves are being generated as companies and individuals become victims of negative postings. The widespread electronic distribution of unflattering and possibly slanderous comments, often posted anonymously, is a major concern to many. Ask students to learn more about the negative effects of being "zapped in cyberspace" by reading the following articles: **(Obj. 1–5)**

   Valiquette, L. (2006). The dangerous myth of online invulnerability, *Ottawa Business Journal*, 11(23), p. 6. Available from Business Source Complete database.

   Sneve, J. (2008, March 12). Professor rating websites entertaining, but not entirely accurate. *The Volante Online*. Available at **http://www .volanteonline.com/2.7416/ professor-rating-web-sites-entertaining-but-not-entirely-accurate-1.783627**

After they've completed the reading, assign students to prepare a presentation that (a) summarizes the advantages and disadvantages of online discussions and (b) provides a checklist for writing an effective reply to an online posting calling for constructive criticism of a company or individual.

After the presentations, have students visit the website that allows students at your college/university to post faculty evaluations and select three to five postings for a professor(s) of their choice. Using their evaluation checklist, students should critique the postings, placing them in rank order of effectiveness. Then, have students make a brief team presentation to the class about their analysis that includes a visual illustrating an example of a poorly written and a well-written posting. Be sure to remind students to omit all identification from the evaluations.

DIGGING DEEPER

Ask students to respond to the following discussion questions.

1. Explain the rationale and significance of this statement: Saying "no" is not difficult; the challenge is to do so while protecting goodwill.

2. Common channels for delivering business messages include written, electronic, and face-to-face means. What criteria would you use in selecting the appropriate channel for delivering bad news?

3. How might standard practices for internal and external communication change when a company is facing uncertain times (e.g., an economic recession, bankruptcy proceedings, and so on)?

KEY CONCEPTS

The persuasive principles presented in Chapter 8 have applications in face-to-face business relationships as well as in written messages. The ability to persuade is useful to a variety of life circumstances in which students will need to motivate action, such as selling a product, a service, or their abilities; gaining acceptance of an idea; or collecting money. Various types of persuasive writing situations are covered.

CONCEPTUAL FIGURES AND TABLES

Figure 8-1   Inductive Outline Used in Persuasive Messages Sent in Written, Electronic, or Spoken Form

MODEL DOCUMENT FIGURES

Figure 8-2   Poor Example of a Sales Message Promoting a Product
Figure 8-3   Good Example of a Sales Message Promoting a Service
Figure 8-4   Good Example of a Sales Message Promoting a Product
Figure 8-5   Poor Example of a Persuasive Claim
Figure 8-6   Good Example of a Persuasive Claim
Figure 8-7   Poor Example of a Persuasive Request (Asking a Favor)
Figure 8-8   Good Example of a Persuasive Request (Asking a Favor)
Figure 8-9   Good Example of a Persuasive Memo

POWERPOINT HIGHLIGHTS

Lecture Presentation

Slide 2   Persuasive Message: Plan Before You Write
Slide 5   Inductive Outline Used in Persuasive Messages
Slide 7   Apply Sound Writing Principles
Slide 12   Ways to Convince Customers
Slide 14   Motivating Action

Resource Presentation

The Instructor Manual contains a menu of resource slides you can integrate into your lecture presentation. Select from a variety of slides with examples, short quizzes, activities, and supplemental information to customize your lecture slide deck to meet the needs of your students and your course.

LEARNING OBJECTIVES

8-1 Develop effective outlines and appeals for messages that persuade.

8-2 Write effective sales messages.

8-3 Write effective persuasive requests (making a claim or asking for a favor or information) and persuasion within an organization.

CHAPTER OUTLINE

Persuasion Strategies 129
  Plan Before You Write 129
  Use the Inductive Approach 130
  Apply Sound Writing Principles 130
Sales Messages 131
  Gain Attention 132
  Focus on a Central Selling Feature 132
  Use an Original Approach 133
  Generate Interest by Introducing the Product, Service, or Idea 133
  Create Desire by Providing Convincing Evidence 134
  Motivate Action 137
Persuasive Requests 140
  Making a Claim 141
  Asking a Favor 141
  Requesting Information 143
  Persuading Within an Organization 143

AIDA 130
Central selling point 131
Persuasion 129

ASSIGNMENTS AND ACTIVITIES

Read

1. Assign students to conduct an electronic search to locate an article that deals with the successful use of persuasive communication in a company or organization. Ask them to prepare an abstract of the article that includes the following: (1) article citation, (2) name of the organization or company, (3) a brief description of the communication technique or situation, and (4) the outcome(s) of the successful communication. As an alternative to locating an article, provide the option of writing about successful communication situations in the organizations or companies in which students work. (Obj. 1–3)

Write

2. Provide students with the scenario below, and assign the accompanying exercise.

   You recently paid $250 to Keller & Jenkins for adding a provision in your will to establish a scholarship endowment at your alma mater. While eating lunch in a crowded restaurant, Abigail Kemp, a clerk at Keller & Jenkins, stopped by your table to commend you on your planned generosity. Although no harm was intended, you were placed in the uncomfortable position of explaining the clerk's comments to your lunch guests. Keller & Jenkins provides its clients with a bill of rights that clearly states that client information will be kept strictly confidential.

Exercise

1. Write a letter to H. Daniel Keller, the lawyer who performed the legal work for you. Inform him of the situation and seek a full refund for the legal services.

Think

3. Wyndham Vacation Resorts is continually expanding the selection of resorts available to its FairShare Plus members. One expansion method is to establish an alliance with an existing, independent resort, enabling FairShare Plus members to use their points to vacation there. Wyndham Vacation Resorts has even extended the "resort" concept by establishing an alliance with Carnival Cruise Lines.

   Ask students to use the Internet or print resources to identify a potential association location. Students should assume that Wyndham Vacation Resorts has just established an alliance with the resort. Ask them to write the script of a voice mail message that Wyndham Vacation Resorts could leave for its FairShare Plus members, which invites them to visit the new location. (Obj. 1 & 2)

Speak

4. Have students form groups of two, then have each group select a tangible item from a collection that you have prepared beforehand (include items such as a cell phone, stapler, pen, backpack, t-shirt, etc). After each group has selected an item, have students complete the following exercises. (Obj. 1 & 2)

Exercises

1. Designate one member of the team as the buyer and one as the seller. The seller will present a compelling sales pitch for the item to the buyer focusing on an appropriate central appeal and convincing evidence. Following the sales pitch, the buyer will give friendly feedback for making the pitch more convincing. Next, have students reverse roles, but this time have the buyer sell himself/herself as a potential employee of the company that makes the item. Again, students should share friendly feedback for improving the presentation and in addition discuss differences they encountered in selling a product versus promoting themselves. Students should be prepared to share their experiences with the class.

2. Ask students to use the experience gained from the previous activity to deliver a one- to two-minute sales pitch on a pet project or idea they genuinely support. Students should choose at least three points that prove their case.

Collaborate

5. Divide the class into groups of three to four students, then give them the following scenario and ask them to complete the related exercise. (Obj. 1 & 3)

   Despite having written what you consider an outstanding business proposal, you have not been successful in persuading any regional banks to finance the new venture. While attending a fund-raising dinner for a local charity, you had the good fortune to meet B. Stephen Richardson, a successful entrepreneur who you believed to be interested in your idea. He gave you his business card stating, "Let me know if I can ever lend a helping hand." More importantly, you interpreted his nonverbal cues as clear interest in financing the project.

Exercises

1. In your groups, identify a retail business you believe would be successful in your community. Assuming you have written a business proposal, write a cover letter to B. Stephen Richardson seeking his financial support of the project. The letter should include a brief summary of the proposed business and your justification for its potential success.

2. Assuming you receive financing for the project, design a company logo that will serve as the centerpiece for advertising campaigns and developing consumer recognition. Be certain that your logo has a contemporary look and portrays the essence of your brand. Be prepared to present your recommended logo to the class in a brief presentation.

DIGGING DEEPER

Ask students to respond to the following discussion questions.

1. Where does one cross the line between being persuasive and being coercive or overbearing?

2. How might a persuasive approach need to be modified when dealing with persons of other cultures?

PREPCARD

CHAPTER 9 UNDERSTANDING THE REPORT PROCESS AND RESEARCH METHODS

KEY CONCEPTS

After having studied informal communications including letters, memos, and electronic communication, students seem to understand the objective and formal nature of reports simply because of the contrast. Chapter 9 follows a sequence that begins with report characteristics and then covers the four steps in problem solving. Methods of research are presented, with considerable attention given to sampling and designing survey instruments used in normative surveys. Information is included for locating both printed and electronic sources of information.

CONCEPTUAL FIGURES AND TABLES

Figure 9-1   Report Formality Continuum
Figure 9-2   The General Upward Flow of Reports
Figure 9-3   Useful Reference Sources
Figure 9-4   A Sample Computer Data Search Using an Online Database
Figure 9-5   Selecting an Appropriate Data Collection Method
Figure 9-7   The Report Process

MODEL DOCUMENT FIGURE

Figure 9-6   Example of an Effective Questionnaire

POWERPOINT HIGHLIGHTS

Lecture Presentation

Slide 4   Formal–Informal Report Continuum
Slide 12   Types of Sources
Slide 13   Objectives of Secondary Research
Slide 16   Reasons for Accurate, Complete Documentation
Slide 18   Common Errors in Data Collection

Resource Presentation

The Instructor Manual contains a menu of resource slides you can integrate into your lecture presentation. Select from a variety of slides with examples, short quizzes, activities, and supplemental information to customize your lecture slide deck to meet the needs of your students and your course.

LEARNING OBJECTIVES

9-1 Identify the characteristics of a report and the various classifications of business reports.

9-2 Apply steps in the problem-solving process and methods for solving a problem.

9-3 Use appropriate printed, electronic, and primary sources of information.

9-4 Demonstrate appropriate methods of collecting, organizing, and referencing information.

9-5 Explain techniques for the logical analysis and interpretation of data.

CHAPTER OUTLINE

Characteristics of Reports 149
  Types of Reports 149
  Proposals 151
Basis for Reports: The Problem-Solving Process 151
  Recognizing and Defining the Problem 151
Selecting a Method of Gathering Information 153
  Secondary Research 153
  Primary Research 156
Collecting and Organizing the Data 157
  Collecting Secondary Data 157
  Collecting Data through Surveys 159
  Avoiding Data-Gathering Errors 161
  Documenting Sources of Information 161
Arriving at an Answer 164
  Analyzing the Data 164
  Interpreting the Data 165

Analytical report 150
Experimental research 156
External report 150
Formal report 150
Functional report 151
Hypothesis 152
Informal report 150
Informational report 150
Internal report 150
Lateral report 150
Longitudinal studies 153
Normative survey research 156
Observational studies 156
Periodic report 150
Plagiarism 159
Primary research 156
Problem statement 151
Procedures (or methodology) 153
Proposal 151
Reliability 157
Sampling 156
Secondary research 153
Statement of purpose 151
Validity 157
Vertical report 150

ASSIGNMENTS AND ACTIVITIES

Read

1. Have students use an online database to locate and read an article related to challenges associated with experimental research. What legal and ethical challenges do researchers face when conducting experimental research with human subjects? How can they be managed? **(Obj. 4)**

Write

2. A focus group is a form of qualitative research in which a group of people are asked about their attitudes toward a product, service, concept, advertisement, idea, or packaging. Questions are asked in an interactive group setting where participants are free to talk with other group members. For marketers, focus groups are an important tool for acquiring feedback regarding product development, such as product name, features, and packaging. Information from the focus group can provide invaluable insight about the potential market acceptance of a product.

Ask students to select an existing product that could be improved and to write five questions that could be asked of a focus group to elicit needed responses for the improvement of the product. Next, students should ask several people to serve as a focus group, selecting participants who are knowledgeable about the product you have selected. After conducting the focus group with the questions they have prepared, students are to prepare reports of their findings and present them to the class. **(Obj. 1–5)**

Think

3. Have students prepare a one-page description of their plans to solve the problem for one of the following research studies. Use the following headings for the problem: (1) Statement of the Problem, (2) Research Method and Sources of Information, (3) Nature of Data to Be Gathered and Analyzed, (4) Hypothesis or Hypotheses to Be Proved or Disproved (if feasible). Here are some ideas to get students started:

- Investigate a problem occurring on your campus (e.g., declining enrollment in some majors, increasing tuition, delayed financial aid payments, high cost of textbooks, or closed classes) or in a job or student organization position you hold.

- Superior Foods, Inc., is considering adding organic versions of its frozen vegetables in an effort to establish itself as a leader in this fast-growing market. To increase its available supply of organic produce, management recognizes the need to assist local growers in adopting organic farming methods. The first step in this process is to recruit experts in organic farming to design and implement training.

- Rainbow Pool and Spas initiated a website to provide answers to frequently asked questions and product-update information. Customer response has been outstanding, freeing up the company's toll-free telephone lines for calls about more technical, nonrecurring problems—a primary goal of the service. As marketing manager, you are considering the possibility of starting a corporate blog and a microblogging site on Twitter to strengthen your relationship and communication with customers.

- As branch manager of a bank, you are faced with the task in a sagging economy of reassuring customers of the solvency of your institution. Your current strategies for casting a positive light on negative performance indicators don't seem to be effective.

- For the first time, Greenwood Consulting Group held an all-company retreat that included customer service training, team-building sessions, and numerous social activities. Eight months following the conference, neither customer service nor employee morale seem to have had any noticeable improvement, and you must decide whether to schedule the retreat for the coming year. **(Obj. 1–5)**

Speak

4. Have students locate an article using either printed or electronic sources that addresses a problem that has occurred for some organization when it failed to realize that research findings that were true for one country or culture were not accurate for another. Ask each student to make a brief presentation to the class about his or her findings. **(Obj. 4 & 5)**

Collaborate

5. Organize students into groups of three or four and have each group design a survey instrument for one of the scenarios in the Think section above. **(Obj. 4)**

DIGGING DEEPER

Ask students to respond to the following discussion questions.

1. How has the process of research changed in recent years? How have the changes been both beneficial and detrimental?

2. What communication skills should an effective researcher possess?

KEY CONCEPTS

To ensure that communication is effective, the elements of quantitative data must be classified, summarized, and condensed into a manageable size, then interpreted and written in common language. Readers remember information they gain from pictures or graphs longer than they remember the text they read. In this chapter, you will find tips for creating effective and ethical charts, descriptions of acceptable types of graphics, and methods for integrating graphics into text.

CONCEPTUAL FIGURES AND TABLES

Figure 10-1 Choosing the Appropriate Graphic to Fit Your Objective

MODEL DOCUMENT FIGURES

Figure 10-2 Effective Table Layout, Identifying Information, Labels, and Source
Figure 10-3 Variety of Bar Chart Formats
Figure 10-4 Line Chart
Figure 10-5 Area Chart
Figure 10-6 Pie Chart
Figure 10-7 Map Conveying Statistical Data
Figure 10-8 Flowchart Simplifying Understanding of Tasks

POWERPOINT HIGHLIGHTS

Lecture Presentation

Slide 2   Communicating Quantitative Information
Slide 3   Using Graphics Effectively and Ethically
Slide 4   Types of Graphic Aids
Slide 5   Preparing Effective Tables
Slide 13   Using Graphics in Text

Resource Presentation

The Instructor Manual contains a menu of resource slides you can integrate into your lecture presentation. Select from a variety of slides with examples, short quizzes, activities, and supplemental information to customize your lecture slide deck to meet the needs of your students and your course.

LEARNING OBJECTIVES

10-1 Communicate quantitative information effectively.

10-2 Apply principles of effectiveness and ethical responsibilities in the construction of graphic aids.

10-3 Select and design appropriate and meaningful graphics.

10-4 Integrate graphics within documents.

CHAPTER OUTLINE

Communicating Quantitative Information 169
Using Graphics 170
   Effective and Ethical Use of Graphics 170
Types of Graphic Aids 171
   Tables 172
   Bar Charts 172
   Line Charts 175
   Pie Charts 175
   Maps 177
   Flowcharts 177
   Other Graphics 178
Including Graphics in Text 179
   Positioning Graphics in Text 179

Area chart 175
Bar chart 173
Common language 169
Flowchart 177
Gantt chart 175
Graphics 170
Grouped bar chart 173
Line chart 175
Map 177
Pictogram 173
Pie chart 175
Segmented bar chart 173
Table 172

ASSIGNMENTS AND ACTIVITIES

Read

1. Business professionals are responsible for communicating quantitative information, but many are unfamiliar with the design practices that make them effective. Have students read the following articles that discuss design strategies for effective charts and graphs:

    Royston, R. A. (2007, November/December). Book review: Show me the numbers: Designing tables and graphs to enlighten. *The Value Examiner*, 11–14. Available from Business Source Complete database.

    Jorge Cameos' Charts. (2008, October). 14 Misconceptions about charts and graphs. Available from **http://www .excelcharts.com/blog/ misconceptions-charts-graphs/**

    After reading the articles, ask students to select three design techniques from these readings that were not covered in this chapter. Students should be prepared to share their insights with the class. **(Obj. 1–3)**

Write

2. Have each student prepare a table that shows the total revenue Scottsdale Fitness earned from membership fees for a fiscal period. Fees were collected by type of membership: single, $25; double, $40; family, $50; corporate, $22.50; senior $20. Scottsdale Fitness has 1,439 single memberships, 642 double, 543 family, 3,465 corporate, and 786 senior memberships. **(Obj. 2–4)**

3. Ask each student to prepare a pie chart that shows the percentage of operating income the Walt Disney Company generated in the following categories during 2010: media networks (56.2%), parks and resorts (22.4%), studio entertainment (12.9%), and consumer products (8.5%). Each student should write a descriptive or talking title that interprets the data depicted in the chart and then write a sentence to introduce the graphic and emphasize its most important idea(s). **(Obj. 2–4)**

Think

4. Have students clip a pictogram from *USA Today* and share it with groups in class. Ask them to discuss the effectiveness of the symbols used and the ethical presentation of the data. **(Obj. 1–3)**

5. Assign students to create graphics that would most effectively aid a human resources manager in identifying potential areas for employees' personal enrichment. Each student should write a descriptive or a talking title that interprets the data depicted in the table below, and each should also write a sentence that introduces the table and emphasizes its most important ideas. **(Obj. 2–4)**

Speak

6. Ask each student to locate a recent annual report of a company of his or her choice. They should prepare short summaries of effective graphic elements they observe; these could include photos, charts, and graphs, as well as the use of color, fonts, positioning, and spacing. In their summaries, students should describe how the graphic elements reflect the message each company wishes to convey. In addition, have each student identify a graphic that violates design principles and revise the graphic incorporating his or her suggestion. In their summaries, have students include the revised graphics and a list of their suggestions for improving it. **(Obj. 2–4)**

Interest by Age Group
January 2013

Age Group	Identity Security	Wireless Networking	Digital Photography	Online Investing
21–35	87	35	45	23
36–50	74	55	54	56
51–65	22	18	67	88

Collaborate

7. A movie theater must determine the genre of the films to show on each screen during its 7:00, 9:00, and midnight show times. A G-rated animated film historically sells 60 percent of the available seats at 7:00 and only 25 percent of the available seats at 9:00. Theaters usually consider 80 percent capacity to be sold out.

    Ask students to play the role of a work group at a software company developing a management information system targeted specifically to movie theaters. Using hypothetical data, they should create the reports the system should generate to enable theaters to manage their screens efficiently. For example, given a limited number of screens, a theater may elect to show an animated film on two screens at 7:00 but switch one of the screens to an action film at 9:00. **(Obj. 1–3)**

DIGGING DEEPER

Ask students to respond to the following discussion questions.

1. A poorly designed electronic slideshow can detract from the effectiveness of your presentation. Compose a list of blunders to avoid in designing effective slideshows.

2. How much is "too much" when considering the use of graphics in a business document?

KEY CONCEPTS

The structure and the preparation of various types of reports are presented including formal reports, letter reports, memorandum reports, and proposals. The problem-solving, research-based orientation of reports is emphasized for each of the various types.

CONCEPTUAL FIGURES AND TABLES

Figure 11-1   Parts of a Formal Report: Preliminary Parts, Report Text, and Addenda
Figure 11-2   The Number of Assisting Parts Increases as the Length of a Report Increases
Figure 11-3   The Basic Outline Expands into a Contents Page

MODEL DOCUMENT FIGURES

Figure 11-4   Short, Periodic Report in Memorandum Format
Figure 11-5   Audit Report in Short Report Format
Figure 11-6   Short Report in Expanded Letter Format, Pages 1–4
Figure 11-7   Short Proposal, Pages 1 and 2

POWERPOINT HIGHLIGHTS

Lecture Presentation

Slide 3   Parts of a Formal Report
Slide 6   Developing a Report Outline
Slide 13   Choosing an Effective Writing Style
Slide 19   Structure of a Proposal
Slide 20   Process for Preparing Proposals

Resource Presentation

The Instructor Manual contains a menu of resource slides you can integrate into your lecture presentation. Select from a variety of slides with examples, short quizzes, activities, and supplemental information to customize your lecture slide deck to meet the needs of your students and your course.

LEARNING OBJECTIVES

11-1   Identify the parts of a formal report and the contribution each part makes to the report's overall effectiveness.

11-2   Organize report findings.

11-3   Prepare effective formal reports using an acceptable format and writing style.

11-4   Prepare effective short reports in memorandum, email, and letter formats.

11-5   Prepare effective proposals for a variety of purposes.

CHAPTER OUTLINE

Parts of a Formal Report 183
Preliminary Parts of a Report 183
Report Text 186
Report Addenda 186

Organization of Formal Reports 187
Writing Convincing and Effective Reports 187

Choosing a Writing Style for Formal Reports 190
Enhancing Credibility 191

Short Reports 192
Memorandum, Email, and Letter Reports 192
Form Reports 192

Proposals 199
Proposal Structure 200
Proposal Preparation 202

Addenda 186
Analytical report 186
Executive summary 185
External proposal 199
Form reports 192
Internal proposals 199
Justification report 188
Preliminary parts 183
Short reports 192
Solicited proposals 200
Unsolicited proposal 200

ASSIGNMENTS AND ACTIVITIES

Read

1. Have students use the selection of databases to which the campus library subscribes to find three articles on firewalls as a means to secure a company's intranet. Students should mark the main points of each article and create a bibliographic citation for each. **(Obj. 2 & 4)**

Write

2. Instruct students to visit a computer lab on your campus. Through observation and interviews, each student should prepare an audit report of the lab's offerings. They should include the following items in their reports: (1) the types of equipment available (e.g., PCs, Macs, mainframe terminals), (2) the quantity of each type, and (3) the operating systems and applications software available (products, versions). Require students to attach a table that summarizes their analyses and submit their work as letter reports. **(Obj. 4)**

Think

3. Assign students to attend a professional meeting of a campus or community organization and take notes on the program presented, the issues discussed, and so on. Students should submit a short report summarizing the events of the meeting and include a section that describes the benefits that might be derived from membership in that organization. **(Obj. 2 & 4)**

Speak

4. Ask each student to obtain a copy of a report prepared by an organization and analyze each of the following elements of the report:

a. Purpose

b. Intended audience

c. Degree of formality

d. Use of graphic support

e. Parts included (see Figure 11-1)

f. Referencing method

Extend the research by having each student make a brief presentation to the class about his or her findings. **(Obj. 1 & 2)**

Collaborate

5. Divide the class into small groups of three or four students each. Present the scenario below and then give them the related exercise. **(Obj. 4 & 6)**

Your team plans to open a business establishment in your city. Do you obtain a franchise or start your own independent restaurant? Select a franchise opportunity and research it. Include in your findings the initial investment cost, start-up expenses, franchise requirements and fees, and success and failure rate.

Exercise

Using the information on team writing, prepare a report that compares the options of franchising versus independent ownership. Make a recommendation as to the more desirable action to take.

6. Provide students with detailed instructions for completing a long or short report or proposal in teams.

a. Ask students to send you weekly progress reports via email. The reports should contain the following information about each meeting held during the week: date, place, and duration of the meeting, members present; report of work accomplished since last meeting; brief description of work accomplished during the current meeting; and work allocated to be completed before the next meeting.

b. About midway through the preparation of their reports, ask each student to send you an email message containing an evaluation of each member of his or her group. Students should assign a percentage indicating the contribution each member has made to the group. The total percentages awarded should equal 100 percent. Each student should also write a brief statement justifying the rating assigned to each member, along with specific, verifiable evidence.

c. Once the reports are completed, have each student email you a debriefing memo that describes his or her perceptions about the team's performance.

DIGGING DEEPER

Ask students to respond to the following discussion questions.

1. How do diversity considerations impact the choices made in report style and format?

2. Considering general trends in society toward more informality in many situations, how might the style of reports be impacted?

KEY CONCEPTS

In today's environment, delivering a successful business report involves not only making an effective spoken presentation but incorporating appropriate visuals as well. The chapter emphasizes timeless techniques of spoken delivery as well as visual and graphic design principles. Because the ability to give presentations using alternate delivery situations is important in today's workplace, the chapter covers strategies for responding to a culturally diverse audience and effective team and distance presentations.

CONCEPTUAL FIGURES AND TABLES

Figure 12-1   Selecting an Appropriate Presentation Visual
Figure 12-2   Designing Compelling Slides

POWERPOINT HIGHLIGHTS

Lecture Presentation

Slide 2   Preparing an Effective Presentation
Slide 6   Organizing Your Presentation
Slide 8   An Effective Introduction
Slide 9   Crafting an Effective Body
Slide 11   Crafting an Effective Closing
Slide 22   Speaking to Culturally Diverse Audiences

Resource Presentation

The Instructor Manual contains a menu of resource slides you can integrate into your lecture presentation. Select from a variety of slides with examples, short quizzes, activities, and supplemental information to customize your lecture slide deck to meet the needs of your students and your course.

LEARNING OBJECTIVES

12-1   Plan a business presentation that accomplishes the speaker's goals and meets the audience's needs.

12-2   Organize and develop the three parts of an effective presentation.

12-3   Select, design, and use presentation visuals effectively.

12-4   Deliver speeches with increasing confidence.

12-5   Discuss strategies for presenting in alternate delivery situations such as culturally diverse audiences, teams, and distance presentations.

CHAPTER OUTLINE

Planning an Effective Business Presentation 207
Identify Your Purpose 207
Know Your Audience 207
Organizing the Content 208
Introduction 208
Body 210
Closing 211
Designing Compelling Presentation Visuals 211
Types of Presentation Visuals 211
Design of Presentation Visuals 211
Design Tips for Audience Handouts and Notes Pages 214
Refining Your Delivery 214
Delivery Method 214
Vocal Qualities 216
Delivery Style 218
Adapting to Alternate Delivery Situations 221
Culturally Diverse Audiences 221
Team Presentations 223
Distance Presentations 224

Articulation 217
Extemporaneous presentation 216
Impromptu presentation 215
Internet conferencing 225
Manuscript presentation 215
Memorized presentation 214
Oral briefings 207
Phonation 216
Pronunciation 218

ASSIGNMENTS AND ACTIVITIES

Read

1. Assign students to read the following article, which offers suggestions for developing business presentations for an international audience: St. Amant K. R. (2005, May). Presentations for international audiences, *Intercom*, 13–15. Available from Business Source Complete Database.

   After they've read the article, have students prepare a grid that compares presentation practices appropriate for audiences of the same culture as compared to international audiences. They should research further as necessary to complete the informational comparison. **(Obj. 1–5)**

Write

2. Have students read the presentation code of ethics for professional communicators and a related article: International Association of Business Communicators (IABC): IABC code of ethics for professional communicators. Available at **www.iabc.com/about/code.htm;** Zielinski, D. (2002, August 10). The presenter's pledge: Do presenters need a code of conduct? *Presentations, 16* (8), 24+. Available at **www.allbusiness.com/services/business-services-advertising/4246997-1.html.**

   After they've read the articles, ask students to consider the ethical challenges presenters face and the behavioral guideposts presented in these readings. Have them write their own presenter's pledge to ensure honesty and integrity in their professional presentations. Students should also be prepared to explain to the rest of the class their rationale for the actions included. **(Obj. 1–5)**

Think

3. Assign students to evaluate the speaking skill of a well-known television newscaster, political figure, or a recognized speaker on your campus. Propose students locate a Webcast or podcast of their most admired CEO or company spokesperson at the company website or at the *Wall Street Journal Online* or *BusinessWeek Online*. What are the strengths and weaknesses? Students can use the "Check Your Communication" checklist on their Review Cards to direct their attention to the various components of effective speaking. Ask each student to draft a proposal offering suggestions for improving the person's spoken communication skills, including paying special attention to vocal qualities, audience eye contact, audience rapport, and organization. **(Obj. 1–5)**

Speak

4. Provide students with specific instructions for presenting a proposal to management. Each student should select a topic from the following list of suggested proposals topics or use them as a springboard for other in-house presentations. **(Obj. 1–5)**

   a. Proposal to develop a policy that provides up to five paid days annually for volunteer work.

   b. Proposal to implement an in-house recycling program.

   c. Proposal to a local business to enhance the customer experience without increasing costs.

   d. Proposal to the board of directors to forge a strategic alliance with another company. Choose two likely companies and present the concept and the benefits that could be derived for each company.

   e. Proposal to extend your company's domestic retail market into an international market of your choice.

   f. Proposal to management for creating a joint venture with another company to offer a business-to-business (B2B) exchange for online commerce and supply-chain services.

   Choose two feasible companies that could take advantage of the benefits of supply-chain management (e.g., HomebuildersXchange links suppliers, distributors, and trade contractors and builders to bring efficiencies to every participant in the construction process).

Collaborate

5. Divide the class into small groups and ask each student to present a one- to two-minute presentation to his or her group explaining a key concept or new development in his or her career field. You should offer a brief period of time for preparation; however, the purpose of the activity is to prepare for impromptu spoken presentations. After all presentations are given, ask each group to briefly discuss the strengths and weaknesses of each presentation and provide each member with a few specific suggestions for improvement in delivering an impromptu presentation. **(Obj. 1, 2, 4, & 5)**

DIGGING DEEPER

Ask students to respond to the following discussion questions.

1. What is the single most important piece of advice you would give for making an effective business presentation?

2. With current advancements in technology, how has the business presenter's role been simplified? How has it become more difficult?

3. How does the advice "communicate a lot, using as little as possible" relate to the design of presentation visuals? Provide an example to support your point.

KEY CONCEPTS

Chapter 13 aids students in seeing the need for career planning, gathering information for inclusion on a résumé, and arranging the information on paper or for electronic distribution. Additionally, students learn to use traditional and electronic means to identify career opportunities and prospective employers to whom the résumé might be sent. The chapter discusses principles for writing a persuasive résumé using appropriate organizational patterns, and it explores alternate delivery options for résumés, including text formats, scannable versions, electronic postings, and YouTube video résumés. The chapter also presents techniques for writing effective application messages.

CONCEPTUAL FIGURES AND TABLES

Figure 13-1   Process of Applying for a Job

MODEL DOCUMENT FIGURES

Figure 13-2   Chronological Résumé
Figure 13-3   References Page
Figure 13-4   Functional Résumé
Figure 13-5   Scannable Résumé
Figure 13-6   Electronic Portfolio Posted to an Applicant's Personal Web site
Figure 13-7   Example of an Application Letter
Figure 13-8   Example of Application Message Sent by Email

POWERPOINT HIGHLIGHTS

Lecture Presentation

Slide 2   Process of Applying for a Job
Slide 6   Standard Résumé Parts
Slide 7   Preparing a Print (Designed) Résumé
Slide 11   Preparing a Scannable Résumé
Slide 12   Making a Résumé Search Friendly
Slide 16   Preparing Effective Application Messages

Resource Presentation

The Instructor Manual contains a menu of resource slides you can integrate into your lecture presentation. Select from a variety of slides with examples, short quizzes, activities, and supplemental information to customize your lecture slide deck to meet the needs of your students and your course.

LEARNING OBJECTIVES

13-1   Prepare for employment by considering relevant information about yourself as it relates to job requirements.

13-2   Identify career opportunities using traditional and electronic methods.

13-3   Prepare an organized, persuasive résumé that is adapted for print and electronic postings.

13-4   Utilize employment tools other than the résumé that can enhance employability.

13-5   Write an application message that effectively introduces an accompanying print (designed) or electronic résumé.

CHAPTER OUTLINE

Preparing for the Job Search 229
Gathering Essential Information 229
Identifying Potential Career Opportunities 229
Planning a Targeted Résumé 233
Standard Parts of a Résumé 233
Types of Résumés 238
Preparing Résumés for Print and Electronic Delivery 239
Preparing a Print (Designed) Résumé 239
Preparing Electronic Résumé Submissions 240
Supplementing a Résumé 246
Professional Portfolios 246
Employment Videos 248
Composing Application Messages 249
Persuasive Organization 251
General Writing Guidelines 253
Finishing Touches 254

Application message 249

Beamer 241

Chrono-functional résumé 239

Chronological résumé 238

Electronic applicant-tracking systems 245

Functional résumé 238

Inline résumé 243

Multimedia résumé 248

Professional portfolio 246

Résumé 229

Scannable résumé 245

Targeted résumé 233

Text résumé 245

Unsolicited application message 251

Video résumé 249

ASSIGNMENTS AND ACTIVITIES

Read

1. Have students read the following article that provides tips for preparing a résumé to post online and shows videos of pitfalls to avoid: YouTube résumé tips: You can learn from others' mistakes. (2007, August 1–7). *Time Out New York*. Available at **http://newyork.timeout.com/articles/features/9523/youtube-resume-tipsa**

   Afterwards, ask students to prepare their own résumés for a job posting in their preferred career field. **(Obj. 3 & 4)**

Write

2. Tell students to imagine a networking contact asked them to email their résumés for a potential opening in his firm. Each student should prepare an abbreviated version of an application letter and email to you the application message with an inline résumé positioned below the letter. Remind students to use a subject line that stands out in an overloaded mailbox as an expected message from a known person. **(Obj. 5)**

Think

3. Ask students to exchange résumés with another class member. Each should critique the document's effectiveness using the guidelines and examples provided in the chapter. Ask students to send their critiques to their partners via email. The emails should contain their overall impressions of the résumés and specific suggestions for improving them. **(Obj. 3)**

Speak

4. Have each student prepare a class presentation that will showcase his or her employment strengths. They may need to assemble a series of materials in a career portfolio. Suggest they emphasize preparation, experiences, and skills that have prepared them for their ideal career positions. **(Obj. 3–5)**

Collaborate

5. Divide the class into small groups, and ask each one to assume the role of a student organization that is initiating an online monthly recruiting newsletter for the organization's website. The vision is to create a fresh, personalized approach to career information specifically related to the needs of the members of the organization and the current competitive market. Each newsletter will include at least one article addressing specific job search skills, highlights of special recruiting events and previews of upcoming events, and an interview providing insights from an employer, returning co-op students, campus recruiters, etc. Students should prepare a one-page issue of the newsletter, after which they should email a copy to you and distribute it to the rest of the class. **(Obj. 1–5)**

DIGGING DEEPER

Ask students to respond to the following discussion questions.

1. Explain the rise in popularity of the "Career Summary" section on résumés. How else have résumés changed in recent years?

2. Is it possible for a candidate to "try too hard" when preparing a résumé? Explain your answer.

KEY CONCEPTS

Because it is probably the type of interview most familiar and of most concern to students, the employment interview receives primary emphasis in Chapter 14. Additionally, employment interviews are a logical continuation of the résumé and application-message topics in Chapter 13. Students are exposed to traditional interviews, as well as more contemporary techniques including computer-assisted, stress, series, and virtual interviews. The chapter gives special attention to preparation for interviews, interview behavior and feedback techniques (paraphrasing and questioning), and dress and grooming.

CONCEPTUAL FIGURES AND TABLES

Figure 14-1 Skills Needed: Balance of Soft and Hard Skills

MODEL DOCUMENT FIGURES

Figure 14-2 Example of a Follow-Up Letter
Figure 14-3 Example of a Thank-You Message
Figure 14-4 Example of a Job-Acceptance Message
Figure 14-5 Example of a Job-Refusal Message
Figure 14-6 Example of a Resignation Message
Figure 14-7 Example of a Thank-You Message to a Reference

POWERPOINT HIGHLIGHTS

Lecture Presentation

Slide 4   Preparing for an Interview
Slide 9   Exchanging Information
Slide 10   Standard Interview Questions
Slide 13   Sample Interviewee Questions
Slide 16   Other Employment Messages

Resource Presentation

The Instructor Manual contains a menu of resource slides you can integrate into your lecture presentation. Select from a variety of slides with examples, short quizzes, activities, and supplemental information to customize your lecture slide deck to meet the needs of your students and your course.

LEARNING OBJECTIVES

14-1   Explain the nature of structured, unstructured, stress, group, and virtual interviews.

14-2   Explain the steps in the interview process.

14-3   Prepare effective answers to questions often asked in job interviews, including illegal interview questions.

14-4   Compose effective messages related to employment (including application, follow-up, thank-you, job-acceptance, job-refusal, resignation, and recommendation request messages).

CHAPTER OUTLINE

Understanding Types of Employment Interviews 259
Structured Interviews 259
Unstructured Interviews 259
Stress Interviews 260
Series Interviews 260
Virtual Interviews 260

Preparing for an Interview 261
Research the Company 261
Study Yourself 262
Plan Your Appearance 262
Plan Your Time and Materials 262
Practice 262

Conducting a Successful Interview 263
The Opening Formalities 263
The Information Exchange 264
The Closing 267

Preparing Other Employment Messages 267
Application Forms 267
Follow-Up Messages 268
Thank-You Messages 268
Job-Acceptance Messages 270
Job-Refusal Messages 270
Resignation Messages 270
Recommendation Requests 272

Stress interview 260
Structured interview 259
Unstructured interview 259
Virtual interview 260

ASSIGNMENTS AND ACTIVITIES

Read

1. Each year, many workers from every career field find themselves out of work. The process of becoming reemployed can be stressful, to say the least. Have students locate the following article that presents strategies for surviving a job termination and successfully becoming re-employed: Lim, F. (2007, March 28). What to do after job termination. Ezine Articles. Available at **http://ezinearticles.com/?What-to-Do-After-Job-Termination&id=506760.**

   Using the information in the article, ask students to develop checklists of strategies for locating and landing a desirable job. They should also add additional strategies of their own and submit the checklists to you. **(Obj. 1–4)**

Write

2. Ask students to assume that they have each applied for a position earlier in the class term. They should assume one of the following about the position: (a) it is an immediate part-time job, (b) it is a full-time job for next summer, (c) it is a cooperative education assignment or internship, or (d) it is a full-time job that begins immediately after graduation. Students should write follow-up letters to their applications, with special mention of the courses they have completed this term. **(Obj. 4)**

Think

3. Ask students, either in small groups or individually, to research a company of their choice. As a guide for their research, they should use the chapter information in the "Study the Company" section and the following article: Daniel, L., & Brandon, C. (2006). Finding the right job fit: Asking the right questions—of yourself and a potential employer—can help ensure that you end up in the right place. *HRMagazine, 51*(3), 62–67. Available at **http://findarticles.com/p/articles/mi_m3495/is_3_51/ai_n26804405/**

   After completing research, each student or group should generate a list of 10 questions to ask an interviewer from the company. The questions should communicate initiative, intelligence, and genuine interest in the company and the job. Have each student or group submit a memo to you that summarizes important facts about the organization and shows the rationale for the selection of the questions. **(Obj. 2 & 3)**

Speak

4. Assign each student to interview a manager, preferably in his or her field, who conducts job interviews regularly. Instruct students to discuss techniques that will improve their interviewing techniques. Students can prepare short presentations to share their findings with the class. Alternatively, you can require them to contribute to a blog related to job interview strategies. **(Obj. 2 & 3)**

Collaborate

5. Divide students into small groups and ask each group to organize an employer panel for a class session on successful interviewing. The following elements should be included in the panel activity:

   a. Contact employers who would be willing to serve on the panel and share their views about successful job interviewing.

   b. In advance of the panel presentation, prepare a list of questions to be asked of the panel.

   c. Select a team member to serve as moderator for the panel discussion.

   d. As part of the panel discussion, solicit questions from the class for response by the guest employers. **(Obj. 1–4)**

DIGGING DEEPER

Ask students to respond to the following discussion questions.

1. How can a job applicant maximize the likelihood of accepting the "right" job?

2. Explain why communication skills are the universal job requirement.

3. How relevant are references when information about an applicant can be easily located through an online search of blogs, social networking sites, and news sources?

Decisions about page format impact the effectiveness of the message. Many companies have policies that dictate the page layout, letter and punctuation style, and other formatting issues. In the absence of company policy, make your format choices from among standard acceptable options illustrated on this style card.

PAGE LAYOUT, PUNCTUATION, AND LETTER STYLE

The default margins set by word processing software typically reflect the standard line length to increase the efficiency of producing business correspondence. Letters are balanced on the page with approximately equal margins on all sides of the letter, a placement often referred to as fitting the letter into a picture frame. Short letters (one or two paragraphs) are centered on the page; all other letters begin 2 inches from the top of the page. Side margins may be adjusted to improve the appearance of extremely short letters.

Current word processing software has increased the default line spacing and space between paragraphs for easier on-screen reading. If you prefer the tighter, traditional spacing, simply adjust the line spacing to 1.0. Also, to conserve space but keep the fresh, open look, try reducing the line spacing in the letter address but retaining the wider line and paragraph spacing in the body of the letter. Another new default is a crisp, open font such as Calibri (replacing the common Times New Roman) designed for easy reading on monitors.

New Document Look

July 24, 2013   **Tap Enter 2 times**

Mr. Bert A. Pittman

1938 South Welch Avenue

Northwood, NE 65432-1938   **Tap Enter 1 time**

Dear Mr. Pittman   **Tap Enter 1 time**

Your recent article, "Are Appraisers Talking to Themselves?" has drawn many favorable comments from local real estate appraisers.
          Tap Enter 1 time

The Southeast Chapter of the Society of Real Estate Appraisers . . .

Traditional Spacing

July 24, 2013   **Tap Enter 4 times (QS)**

Mr. Bert A. Pittman

1938 South Welch Avenue

Northwood, NE 65432-1938   **Tap Enter 2 times (DS)**

Dear Mr. Pittman   **Tap Enter 2 times (DS)**

Your recent article, "Are Appraisers Talking to Themselves?" has drawn many favorable comments from local real estate appraisers.
          Tap Enter 2 times (DS)

The Southeast Chapter of the Society of Real Estate Appraisers . . .

Punctuation Styles. Two punctuation styles are customarily used in business letters: mixed and open. Letters using mixed punctuation style have a colon after the salutation and a comma after the complimentary close. Letters using open punctuation style omit a colon after the salutation and a comma after the complimentary close. Mixed punctuation is the traditional style; however, efficiency-conscious companies are increasingly adopting the open style (and other similar format changes), which is easier to remember.

Letter Styles. Business letters are typically formatted in either block or modified block letter styles. The Sample Letters card has examples of these two styles:

- **Block.** Companies striving to reduce the cost of producing business documents adopt the easy-to-learn, efficient block format. All lines (including paragraphs) begin at the left margin.
- **Modified Block.** Modified block is the traditional letter format still used in many companies. The dateline, complimentary close, and signature block begin at the horizontal center of the page. Paragraphs may be indented one-half inch if the writer prefers or the company policy requires it. However, the indention creates unnecessary keystrokes that increase the production cost. All other lines begin at the left margin.

STANDARD LETTER PARTS

Professional business letters include seven standard parts. Other parts are optional and may be included when necessary.

1

Dateline. When the letterhead shows the company name, address, telephone and/or fax number, and logo, the letter begins with the *dateline.* Use the month-day-year format (September 2, 2013) for most documents prepared for U.S. audiences. When preparing government documents or writing to an international audience, use the day-month-year format (2 September 2013). Company policy may require another format.

2

Letter Address. The *letter address* includes a personal or professional title (e.g., Mr., Ms., or Dr.), the name of the person and company receiving the letter, and the complete address.

3

Salutation. The *salutation* is the greeting that opens a letter. To show courtesy for the receiver, include a personal or professional title (for example, Mr., Ms., Dr., Senator). Refer to the first line of the letter address to determine an appropriate salutation. "Dear Ms. Henson" is an appropriate salutation for a letter addressed to Ms. Donna Henson (first line of letter address). "Ladies and Gentlemen" is an appropriate salutation for a letter addressed to "Wyatt Enterprises," where the company name is keyed as the first line of the letter address.

4

Body. The *body* contains the message of the letter. Because extra space separates the paragraphs, paragraph indention, which requires extra setup time, is not necessary. However, for organizations that require paragraph indention as company policy, the modified block format with indented paragraphs is the appropriate choice.

5

Complimentary Close. The *complimentary close* is a phrase used to close a letter in the same way that you say good-bye at the end of a conversation. To create goodwill, choose a complimentary close that reflects the formality of your relationship with the receiver. Typical examples are "Sincerely," "Cordially," and "Respectfully." Using "yours" in the close has fallen out of popularity (as in "Sincerely yours" and "Very truly yours"). "Sincerely" is considered neutral and is thus appropriate in a majority of business situations. "Cordially" can be used for friendly messages, and "Respectfully" is appropriate when you are submitting information for the approval of another.

6

Signature Block. The *signature block* consists of the writer's name keyed below the complimentary close, allowing space for the writer to sign legibly. A woman may include a courtesy title to indicate her preference (e.g., Miss, Ms., Mrs.), and a woman or man may use a title to distinguish a name used by both men and women (e.g., Shane, Leslie, or Stacy) or initials (E. M. Goodman). A business or professional title may be placed on the same line with the writer's name or directly below it as appropriate to achieve balance.

Title on the Same Line	Title on the Next Line
Ms. Leslie Tatum, President	Ms. E. M. Goodman
Perry Watson, Manager	Assistant Manager
Quality Control Division Head	Richard S. Templeton
	Human Resources Director

7

Reference Initials. The *reference initials* consist of the keyboard operator's initials keyed in lowercase below the signature block. The reference initials and the signature block identify the persons involved in preparing a letter in the event of later questions. Reference initials are frequently omitted when a letter is keyed by the writer. However, company policy may require that the initials of all people involved in preparing a letter be placed in the reference initials line to identify accountability in the case of litigation. For example, the following reference initials show the indicated level of responsibility. The reference line might also include department identification or other information as required by the organization.

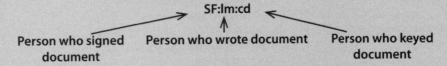

SF:lm:cd

Person who signed document | Person who wrote document | Person who keyed document

OPTIONAL LETTER PARTS

Delivery and Addressee Notations. A *delivery notation* provides a record of how a letter was sent. Examples include Air Mail, Certified Mail, Federal Express, Registered Mail, and Fax Transmission. Addressee notations such as Confidential or Personal give instructions on how a letter should be handled.

Attention Line. An *attention line* is used for directing correspondence to an individual or department within an organization while still officially addressing the letter to the organization. The attention line directs a letter to a specific person (Attention Ms. Laura Ritter), position within a company (Attention Human Resources Director), or department (Attention Purchasing Department). Current practice is to place the attention line in the letter address on the line directly below the company name and use the same format for the envelope address. The appropriate salutation in a letter with an attention line is "Ladies and Gentlemen."

Reference Line. A *reference line* (Re: Contract No. 983–9873) directs the receiver to source documents or to files.

Subject Line. A *subject line* tells the receiver what a letter is about and sets the stage for the receiver to understand the message. For added emphasis, use initial capitals or all capitals, or center the subject line if modified block style is used. Omit the word subject because its position above the body clearly identifies its function.

Second-Page Heading. The second and succeeding pages of multiple-page letters and memorandums are keyed on plain paper of the same quality as the letterhead. Identify the second and succeeding pages with a *second-page heading* including the name of the addressee, page number, and the date. Place the heading one inch from the top edge of the paper using either a vertical or horizontal format as illustrated. The horizontal format is more time-consuming to format but looks attractive with the modified block format and may prevent the document from requiring additional pages.

Vertical Format

Communication Systems, Inc.

Page 2

January 19, 2013

Horizontal Format

Communication Systems, Inc.   2   January 19, 2013

Company Name in Signature Block. Some companies prefer to include the ***company name*** in the signature block, but often it is excluded because it appears in the letterhead. The company name is beneficial when the letter is prepared on plain paper or is more than one page (the second page of the letter is printed on plain paper). Including the company name also may be useful to the writer wishing to emphasize that the document is written on behalf of the company (e.g., a letter establishing an initial customer contact).

Enclosure Notation. An ***enclosure notation*** indicates that additional items (brochure, price list, résumé) are included in the same envelope. Key the plural form (Enclosures) if more than one item is enclosed. You may identify the number of enclosures (Enclosures: 3) or the specific item enclosed (Enclosure: Bid Proposal). Avoid abbreviations (Enc.) that may give the impression that your work is hurried and careless and may show disrespect for the recipient. Some companies use the word Attachment on memorandums when the accompanying items may be stapled or clipped and not placed in an envelope.

Copy Notation. A ***copy notation*** indicates that a courtesy copy of the document was sent to the person(s) listed. Include the person's personal or professional title and full name after keying "c" for copy or "cc" for courtesy copy. Key the copy notation below the enclosure notation, reference initials, or signature block (depending on the optional letter parts used).

Postscript. A ***postscript***, appearing as the last item in a letter, is commonly used to emphasize information. A postscript in a sales letter, for example, is often used to restate the central selling point; for added emphasis, it may be handwritten or printed in a different color. Often handwritten postscripts of a personal nature are added to personalize the printed document. Postscripts should not be used to add information inadvertently omitted from the letter. Because its position clearly labels this paragraph as a postscript, do not begin with "PS."

Computer File Notation. A ***computer file notation*** provides the path and file name of the letter. Some companies require this documentation on the file copy to facilitate revision. Place the computer file notation a single space below the last keyed line of the letter.

Block Letter Style with Open Punctuation

763 Collins Avenue ■ Lansing, MI 48909-0763 ■ (517) 555-9073 ■ Fax (517) 555-9108

Begin 2" from top or 1/2" below letterhead

July 24, 2013   **Tap Enter 2 times**

Mr. Bert A. Pittman

1938 South Welch Avenue

Northwood, NE 65432–1938

Dear Mr. Pittman   **Tap Enter 1 time**

Your recent article, "Are Appraisers Talking to Themselves?" has drawn many favorable comments from local real estate appraisers.

Tap Enter 1 time

The Southeast Chapter of the Society of Real Estate Appraisers has felt a strong need for more information about appraisal report writing. About 200 members will attend our annual seminar. They would be glad to meet you and are interested in hearing you discuss "Appraisal Report Writing." The meeting will be at the Tilton Hotel on Thursday, August 23, at 7 p.m. We promise you a pleasant evening and an attentive audience.

Tap Enter 1 time

Along with your acceptance, we would appreciate a photograph by August 7 so that we can include your picture in the program.

Tap Enter 1 time

Sincerely

Jennifer Malley   **Tap Enter 2 times leaving space for signature**

Jennifer Malley

Program Chair

JM:tw

© Cengage Learning 2013

The document illustrates contemporary spacing with 1.15 spaces between lines. If using traditional single spacing (1.0), tap Enter 2 times to double-space between paragraphs and 4 times to quadruple space after the dateline and the complimentary close.

Modified Block Letter Style with Mixed Punctuation

Begin 2" from top or 1/2" below letterhead

- **Dateline**

October 15, 2013   **Tap Enter 2 times**

- **Letter address**

Mr. Saunders Greyson, Manager

Tropical Importers, Inc.

1240 Coastal Lane

Miami, FL 33140-1000   **Tap Enter 1 time**

- **Salutation**

Dear Mr. Greyson: **Tap Enter 1 time**

- **Body**

It was a pleasure meeting you at the career fair this morning. The opportunities offered in logistics management identifies your company as being a leader in today's international marketplace.   **Tap Enter 1 time**

My experience and knowledge of logistics management enable me to be a valuable asset to your company:

- Realistic international experience with a delivery company.

- Demonstrated commitment to developing an appreciation for international cultures and business practices.

- Excellent performance evaluations, including special recognition for troubleshooting transportation problems to remote locations.

    Tap Enter 1 time

Please message me so we can discuss my joining Tropical Importers.

    Tap Enter 1 time

Sincerely,   **Tap Enter 2 times**
leaving space for signature

- **Complimentary close**

Brandon Shaw

- **Signature block**

Brandon Shaw

© Cengage Learning 2013

Begins dateline, complimentary close, and signature block at horizontal center.

Includes colon after salutation in mixed punctuation style.

Uses single-spaced, unindented paragraphs, but indentions are acceptable with modified block style.

Includes comma after complimentary close in mixed punctuation style.

Signs legibly in available space and identifies writer.

Omits reference initials since writer keyed document

Document illustrates contemporary spacing. If using traditional spacing (1.0) between lines, tap Enter 2 times to double space between paragraphs and 4 times to quadruple space after the dateline and the complimentary close.

ENVELOPES

An envelope should be printed on the same quality and color of paper as the letter and generated using the convenient envelope feature of your word processing program. Adjust defaults as needed to adhere to the recommendations of the United States Postal Service (USPS). To increase the efficiency of mail handling, use the two-letter abbreviations for states, territories, and Canadian provinces. USPS official state abbreviations are available at **www.USPS.gov**.

Most companies today do not follow the traditional USPS recommendation to key the letter address in all capital letters with no punctuation. The mixed case format matches the format used in the letter address, looks more professional, and allows the writer to generate the envelope automatically without rekeying text. No mail handling efficiency is lost as today's optical character readers that sort mail can read both upper- and lowercase letters easily. Proper placement of the address on a large and a small envelope generated using an envelope template available with word processing software is shown here:

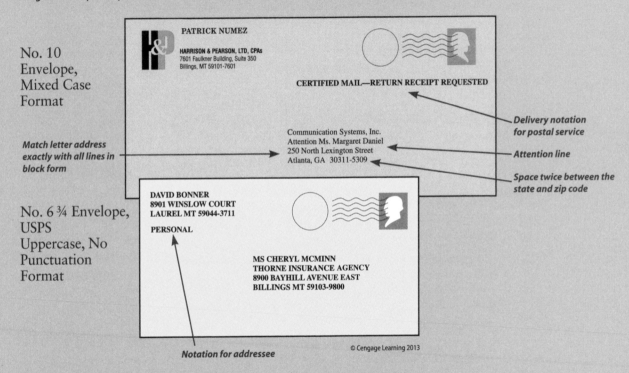

Additionally, to create a highly professional image, business communicators should fold letters to produce the fewest number of creases. Here are the proper procedures for folding letters for large (No. 10) and small (6¾) envelopes:

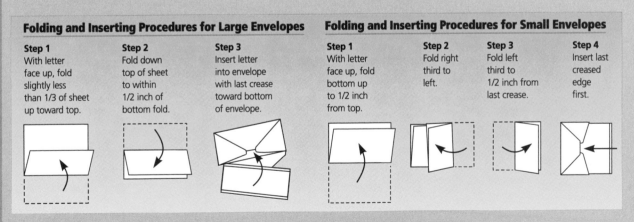

MEMORANDUM FORMATS

To increase productivity of memorandums (memos), which are internal messages, companies use formats that are easy to input and that save time. Most companies use customized or standard memo templates found in most word processing software that include the basic headings (TO, FROM, DATE, SUBJECT) to guide the writer in providing the needed transmittal information. Memos may be printed on memo forms, plain paper, or letterhead depending on the preference of the company. Follow the guidelines for formatting a memo illustrated here.

Memo Format

Litton Best Foods, Inc.
6285 Northwest Blvd.　Laurel, MS 37450
(800)555-5291　Fax: (713)555-9214

Begin 2" from top of page or 1/2" below letterhead

● *Heading*

TO:	Erin W. Lutzel, Vice President
FROM:	Isako Kimura, Marketing Director *IK*
DATE:	July 15, 2013
SUBJECT:	Marketing Activity Report, June 2013

Tap Enter 1 time

The marketing division reports the following activities for June.

Tap Enter 1 time

Advertising

● *Body*

Three meetings were held with representatives at the Bart and Dome agency to complete plans for the fall campaign for Fluffy Buns. The campaign will concentrate on the use of discount coupons published in the Thursday food section of sixty daily newspapers in the Pacific states. Coupons will be released on the second and fourth Thursdays in June and July.

Estimated cost of the program is $645,000. That amount includes 2.2 million redeemed coupons at 20 cents each ($440,000).

A point-of-sale advertising display, shown on the attached sheet, was developed for retail grocery outlets. Sales reps are pushing these in their regular and new calls. The display may be used to feature a different product from our line on a weekly basis.

Sales Staff

We have dropped one sales rep from the northern California section and divided the area between the southern Oregon and Sacramento reps.

Call me should you wish to discuss the information presented.

Attachment

● *Enclosure notation*

● *Omits courtesy titles in informal document.*

● *Includes writer's written initials.*

● *Keys subject line in mixed case or all capitals for added emphasis.*

● *Uses headings to divide message into easy-to-read sections.*

● *Uses single spaced, unindented paragraphs and left-justified margins for easy reading.*

FORMAL REPORT FORMAT

Page arrangement for reports varies somewhat, depending on the documentation style guide followed or individual company preferences. Take advantage of your software's automatic formatting features for efficient formatting and generating report parts. Portions of a sample report are shown below.

Margins. For formal reports, use one-inch side margins. If the report is to be bound, increase the left margin by one-half inch. Use a two-inch top margin for the first page of each report part (table of contents, executive summary) and a one-inch top margin for all other pages. Leave at least a one-inch bottom margin on all pages.

Spacing. While documentation style guides typically specify double spacing of text, company practice is often to single-space reports. Double spacing accommodates editorial comments and changes but results in a higher page count. Even if you choose to double-space the body of a report, you may opt to single-space some elements, such as the entries in your references page and information in tables or other graphic components.

Headings. Several levels of headings can be used throughout the report and are typed in different ways to indicate level of importance. Suggested formatting guidelines for a report divided into three levels are illustrated in the document on the next page. Develop fourth- and fifth-level headings simply by using boldface, underline, and varying fonts.

Formal Report Parts

Title page

Transmittal document

Table of contents

Executive summary

First page of report

Page with graphic

References in APA style

Appendix

Report Format Using Preset Styles

- Capitalizes all letters in report title.

- Places first- and second-level headings at left margin and capitalizes initial letters. Larger font size makes the first level stand out.

- Includes intervening text between first- and second level headings.

- Uses default indentation and decreased spacing between enumerated and bulleted items.

- Places third-level subheadings at left margin and capitalizes first letter.

Format Pointers

This report document illustrates Word 2007 Style Set with style formats applied for the report title, the three heading levels, and the enumerated list. Creating a custom style set allows businesses to create a report style that is consistent with their company image and brand.

The increased spacing after each paragraph eliminates the need for indented paragraphs.

2" top margin

REPORT TITLE Title style(26-point Cambria font)

Tap Enter 1 time

xxx xxxxxx xxxxxxx xxxxx xxxxxxxxx xxxx xxxxx xxxxx xxxxxx xxxxx xx xxxxxx xxxx x xxxxx xxxxx xxxxxxxxxx xxx xxxx xxxxx xxxxx.

Tap Enter 1 time

First-Level Heading Heading 1 (14-point Cambria font)

Tap Enter 1 time

xxx xxxxxx xxxxxxx xxxxx xxxxxxxxx xxxx xxxxx xxxxx xxxxxx xxxxx xx xxxxxx xxxx x xxxxx xxxxx xxxxxxxxxx xxx xxxx xxxxx xxxxx.

Tap Enter 1 time

Second-Level Subheading Heading 2 (13-point Cambria font)

Tap Enter 1 time

xxx xxxxxx xxxxxxx xxxxx xxxxxxxxx xxxx xxxxx xxxxx xxxxxx xxxxx xx xxxxxx xxxx x xxxxx xxxxx xxxxxxxxxx xxx xxxx xxxxx xxxxx.

Tap Enter 1 time

1. xxxx x xxxxxx xx xxxxxx xxxx xxx xxxxxxxxx xx xxxxx xxxxx xx. xx xxxx xxx. Space automatically reduced between enumerated items.

2. xxxx x xxxxxx xx xxxxxx xxxx xxx xxxxxxxxx xx xxxxx xxxxx xx. xx xxxx xxx xxxxx xxxx xx x xxxxxxxxxx.

Tap Enter 1 time

Second-Level Subheading

Tap Enter 1 time

xxx xxxxxx xxxxxxx xxxxx xxxxxxxxx xxxx xxxxx xxxxx xxxxxx xxxxx xx xxxxxx xxxx x xxxxx xxxxx xxxxxxxxxx xxx xxxx xxxxx xxxxx.

Tap Enter 1 time

Heading 3 (11-point Cambria font)

Third-Level Subheading. xxx xxxxxx xxxxxxx xxxxx xxxxxxxxx xxxx xxxxxx xxxxx xxxxxxx xxxxx xx xxxxxx xxxx x xxxxx xxxxx xxxxxxxxxx xxx xxxx xxxxx xxxxx.

Tap Enter 1 time

Third-Level Subheading. xxx xxxxxx xxxxxxx xxxxx xxxxxxxxx xxxx xxxxxx xxxxx xxxxxxx xxxxx xx xxxxxx xxxx x xxxxx xxxxx xxxxxxxxxx xxx xxxx xxxxx xxxxx.

A number of widely used reference styles are available for documenting the sources of information used in report writing. Two of the more popular style manuals for business writing are as follows:

Publication Manual of the American Psychological Association, 5th ed., Washington, DC: American Psychological Association, 2001.

Joseph Gibaldi, *MLA Handbook for Writers of Research Papers*, 6th ed., New York: Modern Languages Association of America, 2003. The *MLA Handbook* is designed for high school and undergraduate college students; the *MLA Style Manual and Guide to Scholarly Publishing*, 2nd ed. (1998) is designed for graduate students, scholars, and professional writers.

These sources, commonly referred to as the APA and MLA styles, provide general rules for referencing and give examples of the citation formats for various types of source materials. This style card reflects the rules along with examples for the MLA style. Whenever you are not required to use a particular documentation style, choose a recognized one and follow it consistently. Occasionally, you may need to reference something for which no general example applies. Choose the example that is most like your source and follow that format. When in doubt, provide more information, not less. Remember that a major purpose for listing references is to enable readers to retrieve and use the sources. This style card illustrates citation formats for some common types of information sources and refers you to various electronic sites that provide further detailed guidelines for preparing electronic citations.

IN-TEXT PARENTHETICAL CITATIONS

The *MLA Handbook* supports the use of ***in-text citations***. Abbreviated information within parentheses in the text directs the reader to a list of sources at the end of a report. The list of sources at the end contains all bibliographic information on each source cited in a report. This list is arranged alphabetically by the author's last name or, if no author is provided, by the first word of the title.

The in-text citations contain minimal information needed to locate the source in the complete list. The *MLA* style includes the author's last name and the page number for both quotes and paraphrases, but not the date of publication. Note the format of the in-text parenthetical citations shown below.

One author not named in the text, direct quotation

"A recent survey . . . shows that more and more companies plan to publish their annual reports on the Internet" (Prinn 13).

Direct quotation, no page number on source

According to James, "traditional college students have a perspective that is quite different from adult consumers" (par. 2).

Use par. 2 in place of missing page number only if paragraphs are numbered in original text.

Multiple authors for sources not named in the text wording

Globalization is becoming a continuous challenge for managers . . . (Tang and Crofford 29).

"For all its difficulty, teamwork is still essential . . . " (Nunamaker et al. 163).

For sources by more than three authors, use et al. after the last name of the first author or include all last names. Do not underline or italicize et al.

More than one source documenting the same idea

. . . companies are turning to micromarketing (Heath 48; Roach 54).

More than one source by the same author documenting the same idea

Past research (Taylor, "Performance Appraisal" 6, "Frequent Absenteeism" 89) shows . . .

Reference to author(s) or date in the text wording

Kent Spalding and Brian Price documented the results . . .

In 2006, West concluded . . . (E2).

Omit a page number when citing a one-page article or nonprint source.

No author provided

. . . virtues of teamwork look obvious ("Teams Triumph in Creative Solutions" 61).

Include full title or shortened version of it.

WORKS CITED

The **works cited** page located at the end of your document contains an alphabetized list of the sources used in preparing a report, with each entry containing publication information necessary for locating the source. A researcher often uses sources that provide information but do not result in citations. If you want to acknowledge that you have consulted these works and provide the reader with a comprehensive reading list, include these sources in the list of works cited and refer to list as Works Consulted. Your company guidelines may specify whether to list works cited only or works consulted. If you receive no definitive guidelines, use your own judgment. If in doubt, include all literature cited and read, and label the page with the appropriate title so that the reader clearly understands the nature of the list.

To aid the reader in locating sources in lengthy bibliographies, you may include several subheadings denoting the types of publications documented, for example, books, articles, unpublished documents and papers, government publications, and nonprint media. Check your reference manual to determine if subheadings are allowed.

FORMATS FOR PRINT AND RECORDED REFERENCES

Reference styles for a variety of print and recorded sources prepared using the MLA style are shown in Figure 3. Note that the following rules apply for MLA works cited.

Indention and spacing	Begin first line of each entry at at left margin and indent subsequent lines one-half inch. While the MLA style manual specifies double spacing within and between entries, common practice in preparing reports is to single space each entry and double space between entries.
Author names	List last name first for first author only. Use "and" before final author's name.
Date	Place date at end of citation for books and after periodical title and volume **for articles. Months are abbreviated.**
Capitalization	In titles of books, periodicals, and article titles, capitalize all main words.
Italicizing and quotation marks	Italicize titles of books, journals, and periodicals (or underline if directed). Place titles of articles within quotation marks.
Page notations	Omit the use of p. or pp. on all citations.

Figure 3 MLA (6th Edition Style)

Works Cited

"Best Business Attire." Executive Communications Group. 2003. 30 May 2006 <http://ecglink.com>.

Brody, Mary. "Dress codes: 'Business Conservative' is Making a Comeback." *HR Briefing* 1 Mar. 2003: 7.

Egodigwe, Laura, and Sonya Alleyne. "Here Come the Suits." *Black Enterprise Mar.* 2003: 59–60.

Hudson, Repps. "'Business Casual' on the Wane." *St. Louis Post Dispatch* 15 Apr. 2002. 30 May 2006 <http://seattlepi.nwsource.com>.

Jones, Clark. "Experts Discuss Ways to Dress in Business Attire for Summer." *Las Vegas Review* 8 June 2003.

Business and Company Resource Center. University of Houston Lib. 29 July 2006 <http:bcrc.college.com/>.

Koestner, Maury. "What Exactly is Business Casual?" *The News-Herald 7* May 2005.

General Businessfile. Texas A & M lib. 31 May 2006 <http://www.epnet.com/>.

Molloy, John T. "Executives Find as Dress Gets Sloppier, Attitudes Slip." *The Houston Chronicle* 9 December 2005: D2.

White, Ronald. D. "Clashing Dress Styles." *Careerbuilder* 26 Aug. 2001. 12 June 2006 <http://www.latimes.com>.